# INTERNATIONAL CRIMINAL JUSTICE AND THE POLITICS OF COMPLIANCE

*For Korana and Tyler*

# International Criminal Justice and the Politics of Compliance

CHRISTOPHER K. LAMONT
*University of Ulster, UK*

ASHGATE

Published by
Ashgate Publishing Limited
Wey Court East
Union Road
Farnham
Surrey, GU9 7PT
England

Ashgate Publishing Company
Suite 420
101 Cherry Street
Burlington
VT 05401-4405
USA

www.ashgate.com

**British Library Cataloguing in Publication Data**
Lamont, Christopher K.
International criminal justice and the politics of compliance.
1. International Tribunal for the Prosecution of Persons Responsible for Serious Violations of International Humanitarian Law Committed in the Territory of the Former Yugoslavia since 1991. 2. Criminal justice, Administration of. 3. International obligations. 4. War crime trials--Former Yugoslav republics. 5. Jurisdiction (International law)
I. Title
341.6'9-dc22

**Library of Congress Cataloging-in-Publication Data**
Lamont, Christopher K.
International criminal justice and the politics of compliance / by Christopher K. Lamont.
p. cm.
Includes bibliographical references and index.
ISBN 978-0-7546-7965-3 (hardback) -- ISBN 978-0-7546-9921-7 (ebook)
1. International criminal courts--Former Yugoslav republics. 2. Criminal justice, Administration of--International cooperation. 3. International offenses--Former Yugoslav republics. I. Title.
KZ6304.L36 2009
341.6'909497--dc22

2009038694

ISBN 9780754679653 (hbk)
ISBN 9780754699217 (ebk)

Mixed Sources
Product group from well-managed forests and other controlled sources
www.fsc.org Cert no. SGS-COC-2482
© 1996 Forest Stewardship Council

Printed and bound in Great Britain by
TJ International Ltd, Padstow, Cornwall

# Contents

# List of Figures and Tables

**Figures**



**Tables**

# List of Abbreviations

| | |
|---|---|
| BiH | Bosnia-Herzegovina |
| DPA | Dayton Peace Agreement |
| DS | Democratic Party (Demokratska stranka) |
| DSS | Democratic Party of Serbia (Demokratska stranka Srbije) |
| EU | European Union |
| EUSR | European Union Special Representative |
| FBiH | Federation of Bosnia and Herzegovina |
| HDZ | Croatian Democratic Union (Hrvatska demokratska zajednica) |
| ICC | International Criminal Court |
| ICTR | International Criminal Tribunal for Rwanda |
| ICTY | International Criminal Tribunal for the former Yugoslavia |
| IEBL | Inter-entity Boundary Line |
| IFOR | Implementation Force |
| IHL | International Humanitarian Law |
| IL | International Law |
| ILC | International Law Commission |
| IPTF | International Police Task Force |
| IR | International Relations |
| JIAS | Joint Interim Administrative Structures |
| KFOR | Kosovo Force |
| KTC | Kosovo Transitional Council |
| LDK | Democratic League of Kosovo (Lidhja Demokratike e Kosovës) |
| NATO | North Atlantic Treaty Organization |
| NLA | National Liberation Army |
| OFA | Ohrid Framework Agreement |
| OHR | Office of the High Representative |
| OSCE | Organization for Security and Cooperation in Europe |
| OTP | Office of the Prosecutor within the International Criminal Tribunal for the former Yugoslavia |
| PDK | Democratic Party of Kosovo (Partia Demokratike e Kosovës) |
| RS | Republika Srpska (Bosnian Serb Republic) |
| SAA | Stability and Association Agreement |
| SDP | Social Democratic Party |
| SFOR | Stabilization Force |
| SiCG | State Union of Serbia and Montenegro (Državna zajednica Srbija i Crna Gora) |

| | |
|---|---|
| SKH | League of Communists of Croatia (Savez komunista Hrvatske) |
| SKS | League of Communists of Serbia (Savez komunista Srbije) |
| SPS | Socialist Party of Serbia (Socijalistička partija Srbije) |
| SRJ | Federal Republic of Yugoslavia (Savezna republika Jugoslavije) |
| SRSG | Special Representative of the Secretary General |
| SSM | Social Democratic Union of Macedonia (Socijaldemokratski Sojuz na Makedonija) |
| UÇK | Kosovo Liberation Army (Ushtria Çlimatare e Kosovës) |
| UNMIK | United Nations Mission in Kosovo |
| UNPREDEP | United Nations Preventative Deployment to Macedonia |
| UNSC | United Nations Security Council |
| UNTAES | United Nations Transitional Administration Eastern Slavonia |
| VMRO-DPMNE | Internal Macedonian Revolutionary Organization – Democratic Party for Macedonian National Unity (Vnatrešno Makedonska Revoluciona Organizacija – Demokratska Partija za Makedonsko Nacionalno Edinstvo) |

# Preface

*We are in Your Hands*

In December 1998 the president of the International Criminal Tribunal for the former Yugoslavia (ICTY), Gabriella Kirk McDonald, reported the Federal Republic of Yugoslavia to the United Nations Security Council for "unabashedly" breaching its obligations to the Tribunal under Security Council Resolutions 827, 1160, 1199, 1203, and 1207. After detailing Belgrade's litany of non-compliance acts, which included the denial of visas to ICTY personnel, Kirk McDonald urged the Council to take enforcement action. She pleaded, "not only does the Tribunal depend upon you, all member States look to you for the exercise of your Chapter VII authority which they ceded to you with the adoption of the UN Charter. We are in your hands." Despite Kirk McDonald's testimony, the Security Council failed to confront Belgrade's non-compliance with Tribunal orders. Instead Belgrade's recalcitrance persisted throughout 1999 and hardened during the course of NATO's Operation Allied Force. Then, in the midst of NATO's 78 day air campaign for Kosovo and six months after Kirk McDonald appeared before the UNSC, ICTY Chief Prosecutor Louise Arbour secured the certification of an indictment against Yugoslav President Slobodan Milošević. The indictment of a sitting head of state by an international criminal tribunal was an ambitious act given that recalcitrant local governments across the former Yugoslavia proved reluctant to transfer lowly members of municipal police forces or low ranking military officers. Needless to say the prospect of a sitting head of state taking up residence at the Tribunal's Scheveningen detention facility on the outskirts of The Hague seemed a remote prospect in 1999, even for those working within the Tribunal's Office of the Prosecutor.

Despite the difficulties encountered in securing cooperation from states and international organizations with a presence in the former Yugoslavia during the 1990s, as of January 1, 2009 only two individuals under ICTY indictment remained at-large: Goran Hadžić and Ratko Mladić. In fact, between January 1, 2000 and January 1, 2009, 85 individuals were transferred to Scheveningen, including Slobodan Milošević himself who arrived in The Hague on June 28, 2001. Among others transferred included former government ministers and senior officers from the armed forces of Croatia, the Federation of Bosnia and Herzegovina, the Bosnian Serb republic, and the Federal Republic of Yugoslavia. The rapid pace of transfers left the Tribunal unable to cope with the growing number of accused awaiting trial in the Tribunal's detention facility and brought about an ever increasing pace of trial processes within the ICTY's facilities on Churchillplein square. In a sense the Tribunal was overwhelmed with its own success in securing the transfers of accused.

The dramatic shift in the ICTY's ability to secure custody of persons under Tribunal indictment has been the subject of much anecdotal debate amongst legal professionals and scholars of International Law and International Relations. Goldsmith and Posner concluded that state compliance with Tribunal orders was a response to the projection of "American power" (2005: 116), while former ICTY Chief Prosecutor Carla Del Ponte suggested that 90 percent of the accused in Tribunal custody were transferred due to European Union conditionality, which linked cooperation with the Tribunal to the EU accession processes of states in the former Yugoslavia (2007a). On the other hand, Payam Akhavan, a former legal officer with the ICTY Office of the Prosecutor, argued that the Tribunal's indictments exercised a normative compliance pull over the states of the former Yugoslavia (2001). Goldsmith and Posner, Del Ponte, and Akhavan present three competing causal pathways to compliance, which focus on power, interests, and norms respectively. Despite these competing explanations for compliance, to date there are no comprehensive studies of compliance with ICTY orders. Questions such as why do the subjects of ICTY legal obligations, in some cases states and in others international organizations, comply or not comply with Tribunal orders remain under explored. This book will attempt to fill this gap in international criminal justice literature through a comprehensive exploration of compliance with ICTY orders across the diverse spectrum of states and non-state governing entities within the former Yugoslavia. Was the ICTY in the hands of the UNSC as Kirk-McDonald suggested? Or was compliance the outcome of enforcement action by third party states acting outside the UNSC? Perhaps compliance and non-compliance outcomes did not correspond to material incentives and disincentives but rather reflected international criminal justice norm internalization?

In order to begin to respond to the above questions, this book will explore compliance with ICTY orders on the part of states and territories under international administration that emerged from the former Socialist Federal Republic of Yugoslavia. Field research and interviews were carried out in Croatia, Bosnia-Herzegovina, Serbia, and The Hague in March 2006, January 2007, and December 2007. Documentary sources including public ICTY documents and reports, NGO reports and public statements by local government representatives were also utilized to assess levels of compliance and non-compliance. Interviews were carried out with members of staff of the ICTY Outreach Offices, Registry, and with ICTY Legal Officers. Also interviewed were present and former representatives of regional NGOs, the Croatian and Serbian foreign ministries, UNMIK, EUFOR, and the OSCE. The anonymity of interview subjects who requested that their identities not be revealed in this book has been protected. Those who did not request anonymity are referenced by name and institutional affiliation.

Before returning to the question of compliance, I would like to take this opportunity to thank the many individuals who assisted in making this project possible. First, I would like to thank my family for their support over the course of my research. Second, Dr. Kurt Mills' support played an important part in advancing my research in the former Yugoslavia and integrating my findings into debates within the discipline of IR. In addition, those who took time out of their busy schedules to participate in interviews or otherwise provided assistance during my field work carried out in the former Yugoslavia and The Hague are especially deserving of gratitude. While those who requested anonymity will remain unnamed, I would like to specifically thank those who contributed in a variety of ways to this project: Alexandra Milenov of the ICTY Field Office in Belgrade, Matias Hellman of the ICTY Field Office in Sarajevo, Klara Dokmanović of the ICTY's Outreach Office in Zagreb, Philip Dygeus of the ICTY in The Hague, EUFOR's Nick Foster in Bosnia-Herzegovina, Alexandar Ivanko of the United Nations Mission in Kosovo, and Andrej Nosov of the Youth Initiative for Human Rights in Belgrade. Also, worthy of mention are Dr. Alasdair Young, Dr. Vjeran Pavlaković, Dr. Joel Westra, Dr. Anthony Lang Jr., Dr. Cian O'Driscoll, Dr. Timothy Wittig, Dr. Thomas Johnson, Ariel Ko, Daniel Hammond, Jack Gallagher, and others who commented on my work during my time at Glasgow University's Department of Politics. Financial support from the Department of Politics supported field work carried out in support of this book in Bosnia-Herzegovina and Serbia. Previous field work was carried out in Croatia during my time there as a Fulbright Fellow. Finally, I would like to express my sincere gratitude to the Croft Institute for International Studies at the University of Mississippi and Dr. Donald Dyer. Both played a major part in furthering my interest in the former Yugoslavia.

Chris Lamont
Derry, Northern Ireland
September 2009

# Chapter 1
# International Criminal Justice and the Politics of State Compliance

## Introduction

The United Nations Security Council's (UNSC) establishment of the International Criminal Tribunal for the former Yugoslavia (ICTY) marked the first time since the Nuremburg and Tokyo military tribunals, held in the immediate aftermath of the Second World War, individuals responsible for serious violations of International Humanitarian Law (IHL) were brought to trial before an international court. The act of bringing individuals to trial before international judicial bodies at Nuremberg and Tokyo for not just the crime of aggression and crimes of war, but also crimes against humanity,[1] represented a cursory attempt to move beyond the mere codification of IHL to the creation of a judicial IHL enforcement mechanism. The recognition of *jus cogens* law, and *erga omnes* obligations by the post-war military tribunals meant IHL enforcement had been at least partially wrestled from the exclusive jurisdiction of individual states and signaled the beginning of a renegotiation of the relationship between international criminal law and hitherto dominant post-Westphalian conceptions of state sovereignty. While some scholars interpreted the legacy of Nuremberg and Tokyo as providing a foundation for a paradigmatic shift away from state sovereignty based conceptions of international society (Cassese 1998, Hagan 2003: 29-30), this book will impart two key lessons that will demonstrate a need for greater engagement with the question of state interaction with international criminal justice bodies. First, triumphal interpretations of international criminal justice serve to obscure the continued dependency of international criminal justice regimes upon the state system and thus fail to adequately engage with the question of state compliance with tribunal

1 Nuremberg and Tokyo represented the first time individuals were successfully brought to trial for crimes against humanity; however, G.J. Bass points out antecedent, and unsuccessful, attempts at conducting international war crimes trials occurred following World War I when an effort was made to bring to trial Ottoman officials responsible for the Armenian genocide and the German Kaiser, who was presumed to be responsible for the outbreak of the First World War (2002: 58-146). Also, at Nuremberg the crime of genocide had yet to be defined and was therefore treated as a crime against humanity; however, the 1998 Treaty of Rome for the International Criminal Court established genocide as a distinct crime.

orders.[2] After all, Nuremberg and Tokyo's appeals to *jus cogens* law and *erga omnes* obligations did not translate into the creation of a permanent international judicial body with the authority to adjudicate crimes against humanity and violations of the laws of war. Instead, an international criminal justice regime only emerged in February 1993 when the UNSC adopted Resolution 808, which called for the creation of an international criminal tribunal to prosecute individuals for serious violations of IHL on the territory of the former Yugoslavia.[3] Second, increasing rates of compliance with international rules should not be interpreted as an indicator of regime legitimacy or norm internalization.[4] In the former Yugoslavia, state governments articulated a distinctly different understanding of compliance acts that focused on recasting wartime perpetrators as postwar victims. Moreover, it will be demonstrated in forthcoming chapters that compliance acts in relation to ICTY requests and orders occurred in the context of a complex bargaining process that relied heavily on the deployment of material incentives and disincentives by external actors and not an acceptance of the legitimacy of the ICTY's prosecutorial mandate.

## From Law Creation to Law Enforcement

UNSC Resolution 827 imbued the ICTY with a mandate to prosecute individuals for serious violations of IHL. IHL can be broadly defined as "...a branch of the laws of armed conflict which is concerned with the protection of victims of armed conflict, meaning those rendered *hors de combat* by injury, sickness or capture, and also civilians" (McCoubrey 1990: 1). It is thus distinct from *jus ad bellum* considerations, and focuses solely on *jus in bello*.[5] IHL is said to rest upon the assumption that "...the legitimate scope of military action is not unlimited and that those who are or have been rendered non-combatant are entitled to impartial humanitarian concern..." (McCoubrey 1990: 1). It is generally recognized that the legal codification of modern IHL began with the ratification of the first Geneva Convention in 1864, which established legal protections for non-combatants in times of war (McCoubrey 1990: 6); however, codes of conduct during armed conflict

2 Bassiouni and Cassese present state sovereignty and international criminal justice as mutually exclusive and as inherently in conflict (Bassiouni 2003a: 18, Cassese 1998: 11-17).

3 Four months after the adoption of Resolution 808 the Security Council passed Resolution 827, which established the International Criminal Tribunal for the former Yugoslavia.

4 Hurd makes a similar observation in his study of the United Nations Security Council (2007: 44).

5 The crime of aggression, which did not fall within the ICTY's prosecutorial jurisdiction, would fall within the former.

have been identified in the writings of Sun Tzu, Herodotus, Homer, and Plato.[6] Yet despite this historic recognition of the existence of IHL norms, attempts at norm enforcement through the establishment of a permanent international criminal tribunal in the early 20th century were never realized.[7] The interwar failure of the League of Nations to create a permanent international criminal court in the early 1920s for the purpose of bringing individuals to trial for violations of what Baron Descamps described as "the universal law of nations" is illustrative of the extent to which the concept of state sovereignty acted as a barrier to IHL enforcement in the years preceding the Second World War. The League of Nations was effectively blocked in its pursuit of an international criminal court by two legalist objections that were grounded in a defense of early 20th century conceptions sovereignty. The first of these objections held that individuals were not subjects of international law, while the second argued the proposed universal jurisdiction of the court was without legal foundation (Brown 1941: 119, McCormack 1997: 51-52). Rather than being perceived as a mechanism to facilitate conflict amelioration, during the inter-war years universal jurisdiction was regarded as presenting a significant threat to contemporary understandings of state sovereignty and was even decried as, "...a danger to the sovereign rights of states, perhaps even a menace to peace" (McCormack 1997: 51-52).

Legalist objections to the creation of international courts on the grounds of sovereignty were only muted during the course of the Second World War. Indeed, after the horrific atrocities committed across Europe by Nazi Germany were exposed during and after WWII, demands for the punishment of individuals involved in war crimes and other crimes against humanity became too powerful for states to ignore. McCormack notes, "the nature of some Nazi atrocities, even if not the scale or extent of them, was well known relatively early in the war. Consequently, discussion about the need for some form of international tribunal ...was widespread" (1997: 55). Moreover, the scale of Nazi atrocities prompted Justice Robert H. Jackson, the chief US prosecutor at Nuremberg, to note that

6 L.C. Green cites both Sun Tzu and Homer (1993: 19), Timothy L.H. McCormack notes Sun Tzu, Herodotus, and Plato make reference to the regulation of conduct during armed conflict (1997: 33-34).

7 Article 228 of the Treaty of Versailles called for the creation of an international military tribunal to prosecute Germans suspected of violating "the laws and customs of war." Meanwhile, the Treaty of Sèvres also included war crimes clauses which envisioned the prosecution of Ottoman officials for crimes against Armenians and British citizens during and preceding the First World War (G.J. Bass 2002: 134). However, in both cases attempts at prosecutions were largely unsuccessful. With regard to Germany an international tribunal was never established, and instead Germany was requested to initiate domestic proceedings against individuals suspected of committing war crimes during the First World War (G.J. Bass 2002: 58-105), while Britain "walked away" from pursuing war crimes prosecutions against Ottoman officials due to a fear of a nationalist backlash and acquiesced to the replacement of the Treaty of Sèvres (1920) with the Treaty of Lausanne (1923) which contained no provisions for the prosecution of war crimes (G.J. Bass 2002: 106-146).

the creation of the tribunal was legitimized through both the laws of humanity and the dictates of public conscience (May 2005: 35). The appeal to certain "laws of humanity" and "dictates of public conscience" at Nuremberg and Tokyo established the foundation for a new code of international law, the Nuremberg principles, that reconfigured the relationship between the individual, state, and international community, while also recognizing the doctrine of universal jurisdiction for certain crimes considered *jus cogens* (Bassiouni 2003a: 57-58, Bridge 1964: 1261, Broomhall 2003: 19). Despite Nuremberg and Tokyo being a manifestation of "victor's justice," Clark argues the postwar tribunals, "…firmly established in the legal consciousness the proposition that there are certain crimes which are of international concern or are crimes under international law" (1997: 185).[8] However, as previously mentioned, rather than heralding the emergence of an international criminal tribunal system, the onset of the Cold War effectively blocked planning for the creation of a permanent international criminal court.[9]

Nevertheless, the concept of universal jurisdiction combined with the rejection of state immunity enshrined in the Nuremberg principles remains relevant to IR scholars because these principles constitute a challenge to the post-Westphalian state system. By defining crimes against humanity as *jus cogens*, an *erga omnes* obligation on all governing authorities to investigate and prosecute such crimes either by local judicial institutions or before an international criminal tribunal was created (Bassiouni 2003a: 167-168, Broomhall 2003: 56). *Jus cogens* norms therefore establish certain norms of behavior, which restrict the actions of states within their own national jurisdictions (May 2005: 24). Violations of *jus cogens* norms on the part of a governing authority can oblige the judicial intervention of other states or international tribunals.[10] However, at this point it is important to emphasize that there exists no international judicial body imbued with a mandate to exercise universal jurisdiction. The subject of study in this book, the ICTY, was temporally limited to 1991-2005[11] and geographically limited to the territory of the former Socialist Federal Republic of Yugoslavia. Likewise, the International Criminal Tribunal for Rwanda (ICTR) was temporally limited to prosecuting serious breaches of IHL to a period which spanned a single year and territorially limited to a single state. Even the ICC cannot undertake prosecutions against non-

8 Donnelly attributes the contemporary UN human rights regime to a "decisive break" in perceptions of human rights that followed the Second World War (1986: 614-615).

9 Although the UN General Assembly resolved to freeze further discussion of an international criminal court until consensus could be reached on defining the crime of aggression in 1954 and 1957 (Bridge 1964: 1268-1269), Soviet bloc states challenged the creation of an international criminal court on the grounds an international criminal court would constitute a violation of state sovereignty (Bridge 1964: 1272).

10 Of course, this does not always take the form of an international prosecution as recognition of universal jurisdiction by national or state judiciaries could bring about the prosecution of third country nationals.

11 The ICTY's completion strategy prohibited the Tribunal from certifying new indictments after 2005.

Statute of Rome signatory states without referral by the UNSC, a process that grants *de facto* immunity from prosecution to states such as Russia, China and the United States.

*Ad Hoc Justice*

It was only in the 1990s, as the end of the Cold War coincided with the outbreak of genocide and ethnic cleansing in Bosnia-Herzegovina and Rwanda that international criminal tribunals emerged as mechanisms to confront what were perceived as challenges to both existing laws and conscience of humanity. Hagan points to a post-Cold War "opportunity structure" that included increased public awareness and activism in response to atrocities as acting as a catalyst for the reemergence of international criminal justice after nearly a half decade of dormancy (pp. 29-30). Kerr affirms the impact of growing public awareness on demands for justice when recalling how the explosive power of ITN television images broadcast in 1992 of the Omarska camp in Bosnia-Herzegovina, "reminiscent of Auschwitz and Belsen 50 years previously," stunned UNSC member states into adopting Resolution 771, which demanded an immediate end to violations of IHL in Bosnia-Herzegovina and called upon states and international organizations to begin collecting information on IHL violations across the former Yugoslavia (2004: 34).[12]

As the post-Cold War international community confronted the explosion of violence in the former Yugoslavia and Rwanda in the 1990s, *ad hoc* international criminal tribunals became the preferred option for policymakers reluctant to engage in more costly military intervention to prevent or halt attempts at genocide and ethnic cleansing (Scharf 1997: 30-36, Western 2004: 217-231, Williams and Waller 2002: 844); however, unlike their post-Second World War predecessors, the post-Cold War *ad hoc* tribunals could not depend on an occupying military force to carry out their orders, and instead a complex relationship was negotiated with states or in some instances territories under international civilian and military administrations that fell under tribunal jurisdiction. Despite the fact that the memory of Nuremberg was invoked before the UNSC at the ICTY's creation in 1993,[13] the historic memory of the post-Second World War tribunals is of limited utility when

12 Scharf also makes a similar observation (1997: 37-38).

13 Preceding the UNSC vote on Resolution 808 in February 1993, US Ambassador to the UN Madeleine Albright noted, "The Nuremberg Principles have been reaffirmed. We have preserved the long-neglected compact made by the community of civilized nations 48 years ago in San Francisco to create the United Nations and enforce the Nuremberg Principles" (Scharf 1997: 54). A decade later, however, Albright would recall a significant difference between the ICTY and the Nuremberg tribunal, "unlike the accused at Nuremberg, those suspected of war crimes in the Balkans were not surrendered leaders of a broken power" (2003: 182).

exploring the politics of compliance with international judicial bodies.[14] In 1994 the ICTY recognized this in its annual report to the UNSC:

> It is well known that the Allied Powers that set up the international tribunals at Nürnberg and Tokyo wielded full authority and control over the territory of Germany and Japan respectively and, in addition, had already apprehended the defendants when the trials commenced. Consequently, those tribunals did not need the cooperation of the defendants' national authorities or those of other countries for the prosecutors' investigations and collection of evidence (1994: 27).

As judicial proceedings at Nuremberg and Tokyo commenced only after the total military defeat of Germany and Japan, the post-Second World War military tribunals were not confronted with the task of securing custody of accused persons from adversarial states.[15] To be sure, the creation of a judicial body with limited temporal and territorial jurisdiction in the aftermath of an armed conflict where the vanquished parties were judged by representatives of the victorious states proved significantly less problematic than the abortive postwar attempt to establish a permanent international criminal court.[16] This was a lesson quickly learned by the postwar International Law Commission (ILC), which was tasked with drafting a statute for an international criminal court under the auspices of the United Nations, as the onset of the Cold War consigned the further development of an international criminal tribunal system to relative dormancy (Ferencz 1980: 15-16, Maogoto 2004: 6).[17]

Although there has been a deepening entrenchment of an international tribunal system since 1993, the interaction between the states and non-traditional sovereign entities over which international criminal tribunals exercise jurisdiction has not

14 References to the legacy of Nuremberg have become cliché in ICTY literature and among ICTY personnel with even former ICTY Chief Prosecutor Louise Arbour recalling the memory of Nuremberg was mentioned daily during her time in The Hague (Hagan 2003: 18). Meanwhile, differences between the UNSC established *ad hoc* tribunals and the post-World War II military tribunals remain understated.

15 Also, the prosecutorial focus of Nuremberg and Tokyo were on establishing responsibility for the crime of aggression. It should be noted that the crime of aggression was not crime for which an individual could be prosecuted before the ICTY.

16 That is not to say the establishment of the post-World War II tribunals was unproblematic as there was significant opposition to placing captured German elites on trial and instead various alternatives were proposed that envisioned mass executions. For a vivid discussion of the inter-allied debate concerning the fate of captured Nazis see G.J. Bass 2002: 147-205.

17 Although the International Law Commission was requested to draft a statute for a permanent international court in 1948, this project was put on hold during the Cold War. However, the project of IHL codification continued, examples include the four 1949 Geneva Conventions and its two 1977 Additional Protocols.

been adequately explored in existing scholarship.[18] It is an exploration of tribunal interaction with external bodies whose cooperation is necessary for the fulfillment of tribunal judicial mandates that will form the core of the following book.

*Explaining Compliance*

The relative absence of literature on state compliance with international criminal tribunal orders requires the creation of a research agenda that will address the relationship between international tribunals and territories over which tribunals exercise jurisdiction. While there is a growing wealth of literature that describes the legal precedents and obligations, which underpin international tribunals (Bassiouni 1992, 2003a, 2003b, Broomhall 2003, Cassese 1998), the interaction between international judicial bodies, states, intergovernmental organizations, and non-traditional sovereign entities requires further study. In fact, studies of state compliance with international legal obligations, which have long provoked intra-theoretical and inter-theoretical debate within and between the disciplines of International Relations (IR) and International Law (IL), remain on the periphery of international criminal justice scholarship.

In order to explain compliance and non-compliance with tribunal orders, this book will explore compliance with ICTY orders, on the part of states, intergovernmental organizations, and non-traditional sovereign entities in the former Yugoslavia. By limiting this study to the ICTY, we can explore compliance on the part of multiple actors that have all interacted with the same legal regime, the Statute of the Tribunal, which imposed a binding legal obligation upon all UN member states to cooperate with the ICTY and comply with Tribunal orders without "undue delay." The legal obligation to fully cooperate with the ICTY remained constant throughout the period of time under study, and should not be confused with compliance benchmarks articulated by third party enforcement agents that for the most part fell short of full cooperation and instead often demanded the transfer of individual suspects.[19] Moreover, assessments of state compliance were made annually by the ICTY, which submitted yearly reports to the UNSC on compliance on the part of both states and international organizations with a presence in the former Yugoslavia.

So as to fully explore the interaction between the ICTY, states, and the diverse range of actors over which the Tribunal exercises jurisdiction, this book includes five case studies and is divided into two constituent parts. Part I consists of the first three case studies and examines state compliance. Each case study includes an exploration of both the domestic and international politics of compliance so as to

---

18 There is a notable recent exception. Victor Peskin's *International Justice in Rwanda and the Balkans: Virtual Trials and the Struggle for State Cooperation* (2008). For more on recent scholarship see Lamont 2009: 339-346.

19 Article 29 of the Tribunal Statute outlines state obligations toward the Tribunal which go beyond the mere arrest and transfer of suspects and include a wide range of tasks that include the production of evidence and witness protection. See Appendix I.

help disentangle compliance causality. The subject of the first case study, Croatia, provides an opportunity to explore interactions between this newly independent state and the ICTY. The second case study pertains to Serbia, a state which has consistently failed to comply with ICTY orders. The third case study, Macedonia, offers a limited insight into the politics of compliance as the Macedonian state executed only a single arrest and surrender order, but nevertheless Macedonia's voluntary cooperation with the ICTY forms a stark contrast to the accompanying four case studies. The fourth case study introduces Part II of the book through an exploration of compliance on the part of a multitude of non-traditional actors that range from international peace enforcement missions to sub-state entities by taking into account Bosnia-Herzegovina. The complexity of securing compliance with the ICTY orders in Bosnia-Herzegovina arises from the fact that the ICTY is just one of various international actors that have played a significant role in the domestic politics of the postwar Bosnian state. In addition, Bosnia-Herzegovina also includes *de facto* mini-states, the Bosnian Serb *Republika Srpska* and the Federation of Bosnia and Herzegovina, which operate as virtually independent political communities. Finally Part II concludes with an examination of Kosovo's interactions with the ICTY. As with BiH, Kosovo is under international administration; however, unlike BiH, Kosovo lacks international legal recognition as a state.[20]

Before exploring the above case studies a review of existing tribunal scholarship will be presented. This will be accomplished by providing an overview of literature on the ICTY and theoretical interpretations of the emerging international criminal tribunal system; however, it is important to emphasize that this is not a study of the emergence of international criminal tribunals but rather a study of compliance with international criminal tribunal requests and orders. Because literature on international tribunals spans the fields of International Relations (IR) and International Law (IL), there will be an exploration of both IL and IR theoretical interpretations of compliance with international legal obligations.

## Tribunal Literature and Compliance: Bridging Theories of International Law and International Relations

The remarkable achievements of the ICTY, which included gaining custody of a majority of those indicted,[21] demonstrated the viability of international criminal

20 Kosovo's declaration of independence on February 17, 2008 falls after the period of time examined in Chapter 6 (1999-2008). Moreover, given the fact that all defendants under ICTY indictment were transferred to Tribunal custody preceding Kosovo's declaration of independence, the Republic of Kosovo will not be confronted with enforcing an ICTY arrest and surrender order.

21 As of December 2005, 161 individuals had been indicted by the ICTY and 131 had appeared before the court ("International Criminal Tribunal for the Former Yugoslavia: Key Figures of ICTY Cases", 2005).

tribunals as a mechanism for bringing war criminals to trial and facilitated both the entrenchment of international *ad hoc* tribunals and the eventual establishment of the International Criminal Court (ICC) (Western 2004: 240). Although the ICC's creation marked a fundamental turning point in the pursuit of international justice through legal means,[22] early scholarship on the ICTY was tinged with pessimism regarding the prospects for securing custody of accused persons from recalcitrant states. Illustrative of this pessimism was Scharf's quote from the ICTY's first chief prosecutor Richard Goldstone, who lamented, "perhaps the real yardstick for assessing the success of the [ICTY] is whether it leads to the establishment of a permanent international criminal court" (1997: 228). In 1997 securing state cooperation from the states of the former Yugoslavia was perceived to be a yardstick too far.

Even as late as 2002, Bass warned, "but with atrocities of such a nightmarish scale, and with a Western commitment that waxes and wanes, the outlook [for the ICTY] is still uncertain" (2002: 275); however, as of January 2009 only two out of 161 individuals indicted by the ICTY remained at large. The emerging post-Cold War international judicial infrastructure generated a growing body of IR literature that has attempted to explain the proliferation of international criminal tribunals. Not surprisingly, IR literature on IHL enforcement reflects the diversity of theoretical approaches within the field, which range from realist state-centric approaches that are dismissive of international criminal tribunals exercising independent compliance agency, to neoliberal institutionalist approaches which interpret compliance and non-compliance acts through self-interest and rational choice, to constructivist approaches that explain compliance through the lenses of norms and rule following.

### *Realism and Neorealism: International Justice or Realpolitik*

In describing a realist approach to international law, E.H. Carr references Hobbes' definition of law as command, *ius est quod iussum est* (1964: 176). Carr's conception of domestic law as arising from a domestic coercive order serves to mitigate prospects for the entrenchment of international law in the absence of a global sovereign. Morgenthau went on to modify Carr's pre-conditions for the existence of international law stating that it is only, "where there is neither a community of interest nor balance of power there is no international law" (1978: 282). Morgenthau's modification was necessitated by his observation that, "…during the 400 years of its existence international law has in the most instances been scrupulously observed"

22 The symbolic value of a former head of state standing trial in an ICTY courtroom as the Rome Statute entered into force on July 1, 2002 did not go unnoticed by international relations or international legal scholars. For example, Rachel Kerr describes scenes from the opening of the Milošević trial to begin her 2004 book on the ICTY, *The International Criminal Tribunal for the Former Yugoslavia: An Exercise in Law, Politics and Diplomacy* (2004: 1).

(1978: 281). Nevertheless, the realist focus on state survival and anarchy in the absence of a global sovereign leads realists to dismiss the prospect of state submission to the decisions of international tribunals in instances where perceived "vital" interests are at stake. As Schwarzenberger points out:

> In a system ultimately based on the rule of force, the Leviathans [states] cannot be expected to act with humility and moderation in matters of vital importance. As was emphasized in the Advisory Opinion of the Permanent Court of International Justice in the *Eastern Carelia* case, "it is well established in international law that no State can, without its consent, be compelled to submit its disputes with other States either to mediation or to arbitration or to any other kind of pacific settlement" (1941: 141).

Despite an historic record of state compliance with international law, realists contest that international law enforcement remains largely dependent upon *ad hoc* enforcement measures taken by powerful states. Morgenthau ominously warns that when international laws are violated, they are not always enforced, and when attempts are made at enforcement, they are not always effective (1978: 281-282). Evidence of the precarious and arbitrary nature of law enforcement within the international realm offered by realists includes the numerous violations of the Covenant of the League of Nations and Kellogg-Briand pact, both of which attempted to place legal restrictions on the use of force (Morgenthau 1978: 286-287). Thus, while realists recognize the existence of some form of international law, albeit under certain preconditions such as a community of interests or balance of power, compliance, non-compliance and international law enforcement are dictated by relative power distributions. Morgenthau emphasizes:

> There can be no more primitive and no weaker system of law enforcement…for it delivers the enforcement of the law to the vicissitudes of the distribution of power between the violator of the law and the victim of the violation. It makes it easy for the strong to both violate the law and to enforce it, and consequently puts the rights of the weak in jeopardy (1978: 298).

International law enforcement's dependency on the asymmetries of state power makes issues such as the question of legal rhetoric largely epiphenomenal and instead realists would suggest that we look toward the underlying distribution of state power to understand contemporary and past developments in international criminal justice.[23]

Neorealists, both offensive and defensive, also view international law as reflection of state power. Kenneth Waltz points to the distribution of material capabilities within the international system of states as shaping international order

23 Realists argue the resort to legal rhetoric serves as a pretext or disguise for acts motivated by the pursuit of power (Goldsmith and Posner 2005: 170-171).

(1979: 97-99), and identifies power, not international law, as the ordering principle in the international system (Waltz 1979: 97). Not surprisingly international criminal tribunals were not even mentioned in Waltz's *Theory of International Politics* (1979), nor did international judicial bodies warrant a mention in Waltz's reassessment of neo-realism after the Cold War (2000: 5-41). Mearsheimer also fails to directly engage with international criminal tribunals; however, it is evident Mearsheimer would be highly skeptical of the ability of international criminal tribunals to constrain state action. Mearsheimer posits international institutions "have minimal influence on state behavior" (1994-1995: 7). Grieco supports Mearsheimer's assertion by noting, "International institutions affect the prospects for cooperation only marginally" (1988: 488). Moreover, international institutions are argued to reflect the preferences of powerful states (Mearsheimer 1994-1995: 13, Waltz 2000: 20-21). Therefore, a realist explanatory hypothesis of compliance would identify relative power distributions as the explanatory phenomenon that explains compliance or non-compliance acts. Compliance on the part of a weaker state would reflect the successful projection of coercive power on the part of a more powerful state, while non-compliance would be symptomatic of a failure or an inability of a powerful state to project its power over large distances.

Realism's silence on international criminal tribunals is perhaps surprising given the realist emphasis on coercion can find affirmation in the observation that third party state enforcement measures were often attributed with facilitating the Tribunal's ability to secure custody of indicted individuals from the states of the former Yugoslavia. Realists can point to the linkage between international financial assistance or access to membership in international organizations and the handing over of indicted persons to the ICTY as the causal phenomena that explains why relatively weak states within the former Yugoslavia elected to cooperate with the Tribunal. Anecdotal evidence does seem to support the assertion that norms of international justice or the legally binding nature of the UN Charter are irrelevant to any discussion of compliance causality. Even former president of the ICTY, Antonio Cassese, highlighted the dependency of the Tribunal upon state cooperation in his 1997 report to the UN Security Council:

> If States…refuse to implement [the Tribunal's] orders or to execute [the Tribunal's] warrants, the Tribunal will turn out to be utterly impotent. Thus if greater respect is accorded to the authority of States than the need to deter gross abuses of human rights, this will place severe limitations on what the Tribunal can achieve (Report of the International Tribunal 1997: 44).

Goldsmith and Posner argue the Tribunal's subsequent lack of impotence was a mere reflection of the support of a single state, namely the United States (2005: 116). As will be highlighted in Chapter 2, coercion and inducements deployed by third party states can offer a power compliance narrative. Moreover, Chapter 3 will note Serbia's failure to meet a Washington imposed deadline for the transfer of Slobodan Milošević to The Hague, resulted in the United States not only suspending US$40 million in direct aid, but also casting negative votes in international lending institutions which effectively severed Belgrade's access to reconstruction assistance. Shortly after this decisive and expensive message was transmitted to Belgrade, Milošević was surrendered to the ICTY. However, while the preceding example provides support for a power-based approach to understanding state cooperation with the ICTY, there are also examples of financial incentives or penalties failing to induce cooperative outcomes such as the European Union's attempts to link the transfer of Ratko Mladić to Serbia's EU accession process.

Within the field of International Law, realists have found common ground with positivist IL scholars who share Carr's Hobbesian view of law within the framework of a coercive order. IL positivists are dismissive of prospects for the entrenchment of international law in absence of a global sovereign. Bassiouni appropriately cites Hobbes', *non veritas sed autoritas facit legem*, it is not rightness but authority that makes law, as part of the philosophical underpinnings of legal positivism (1992: 57). Scholars who concur with the preceding description of the relationship between power and law view international law to be part of a coercive order and argue that it is only "...made effective through the threat of state sanction" (Kerr 2004: 7). While IR realists and IL positivists who mitigate international law's ability to constrain state action can point to the historic failures of the Covenant of the League of Nations, the Kellogg-Briand pact, and the failure of the International Law Commission to establish a permanent international criminal tribunal during the Cold War, they cannot easily account for subsequent developments in the field of international criminal justice after 1993. After all, the establishment of the ICTY was followed by the creation of both the International Criminal Tribunal for Rwanda, the Special Court for Sierra Leone, and the Special Tribunal for Lebanon. Additionally, the coming into effect of the Rome Statute of the International Criminal Court was actively opposed by the United States and therefore cannot be dismissed as a tribunal dependent upon American power.[24]

An additional complicating factor for realist interpretations of international criminal tribunals is that realism's unit of analysis is the state. Thus, an exploration of Bosnia-Herzegovina and Kosovo defy realist assumptions regarding the state-centricity of the international legal order. Moreover, two underlying assumptions of the Nuremberg principles pose a direct challenge to realism's core underlying assumptions. The first is that war crimes are committed by individuals who deploy the apparatus of states in the commission of criminal enterprises. The second is that there exists *jus cogens* law and *erga omnes* obligations which states are unable to abrogate. With regard to the existence of *jus cogens* law, realism simply does not provide a framework for exploring ideational constraints upon state action. Mearsheimer's observation, "a state might destroy a defeated rival by killing most

24 Goldsmith and Posner argue the ICTY's "modest success in trying war criminals" was the result of "NATO's (and primarily American) military, diplomatic, and financial might" (2005: 116), which is consistent with Waltz's claim that the strength of an international institution reflects the strength and support of powerful states (2000: 20-21).

of its people" (2001: 151), provides a reminder of the extent to which realists are hesitant to criminalize statecraft.

The perceived realist denial of prospects for international legal structures to coalesce into a global judiciary and established precedents that constrain the international behavior of states has led realists to be derided by proponents of a more robust system of international criminal tribunals as advocates of an ideology of impunity disguised as *realpolitik*. Bassiouni, an international legal scholar and former head of the UN Commission of Experts that called for the creation of the ICTY, defines *realpolitik* as "the pursuit of political settlements unencumbered by moral and ethical limitations" (2003b: 190). *Realpolitik* according to Bassiouni "…may settle the more immediate problems of conflict, but, as history reveals, its achievements are … at the expense of long-term peace, stability, and reconciliation" (2003b: 190). However, Bassiouni fails to take note of the fact that Morgenthau does recognize certain international standards that serve to limit state behavior. Morgenthau writes, "if there was to be at least a certain measure of peace and order in the relations among such entities endowed with supreme authority within their territories and having continuous contact with each other, it was inevitable that certain rules of law should govern these relations" (1978: 280). Accountability *per se* is not incompatible with realist approaches to IR, after all the victor's justice of Nuremberg and Tokyo were not inconsistent with realist approaches to IR, but rather, the enforcement of IHL is limited by the asymmetries of state power. Thus, what realists hope to impart is that for a weak state to attempt law enforcement action against a more powerful adversary would bring catastrophic consequences upon the prospective law enforcer. Moreover, for realists there is no *erga omnes* obligation upon states to enforce IHL or even obey international law, the only *erga omnes* obligation that states assume is that of survival.

### *Liberalism: Tribunal Justice and Democratic Peace?*

Liberal accounts of international criminal justice suggest that democratic states are more likely to support the creation of international criminal tribunals (G.J. Bass 2002), but offer little insight into compliance. Bass observes, "Liberal states have taken a legalistic approach to the punishment of war criminals, even when so doing has greatly complicated international diplomacy…legalism seems to arise exclusively in liberal states…" (2002: 280). Although Bass recognizes securing custody of citizens of recalcitrant states has proven an obstacle that was in many instances insurmountable, Bass avoids attempts at explaining compliance or non-compliance acts. When the question of compliance is addressed by liberal theorists, it is assumed that compliance is most likely among a community of liberal democratic states.[25] For example, Moravcsik notes, "The most important preconditions for the creation of and compliance with the sort of highly refined

25 Burley defines liberal states as states with "…juridical equality, constitutional protections of individual rights, republican governments, and market economies based

regime norms found in Europe are strong pre-existing norms, practices and institutions of liberal democracy…" (1995: 184). Donnelly also credited, "a relatively homogenous and close sociocultural community" with sustaining a robust Western European human rights regime (1986: 623). Outside a community of liberal democratic states, Moravcsik suggests that we must fall back upon material incentives and disincentives to bring about illiberal state compliance with human rights regimes (1995).

There is also a significant body of IL literature which identifies domestic regime type as explaining compliance with international legal obligations (Burley 1992: 1907-1996, R. Fisher 1981; Henkin 1979). However, when it comes to explaining compliance, the liberal focus on regime type sheds little light on compelling compliance on the part of illiberal regimes. Moreover, there is disagreement within literature that links domestic regime type to compliance outcomes. In some cases all that is observed is that the less rules are respected within a state, the less likely it is that the state in question will respect international legal obligations (R. Fisher 1961: 1139). Note that this is a significant departure from Moravscik and Burley's identification of liberal democracy as an antecedent condition necessary to generate non-coerced compliance with international human rights regimes. Instead, according to Fisher all that is necessary is a state in which rules are respected:

> The situation in Congo vividly attests the weakness of governments whose officials do not respect law. In sharp contrast, the government of the Soviet Union is highly organized and rule-respecting. It is a mistake to think of that government as lawless and commanding obedience from its officials only at the point of a pistol. No one is holding a pistol to the head of the man who holds the pistol; that man is complying with rules (1961: 1139).

As the subsequent case studies cover multiple states with multiple regime types, we could expect compliance records to reflect regime type. However, as will be noted in our exploration of Croatia, Croatian cooperation with the ICTY deteriorated soon after the election of pro-Western democratic elites in January 2000. Moreover, the collapse of the Milošević regime in Serbia initially brought about a hardening of Serbian non-cooperation with the ICTY that was only effectively reversed following significant sanction on the part of the United States.

### *Neoliberal Institutionalism and an Atrocities Regime*

Neoliberal institutionalist IR scholars emphasize the role of regimes in facilitating cooperation between state actors (Axelrod and Keohane 1985, Keohane 1984, 1986, 1988, Keohane and Martin 1995, Keohane and Nye 2001; Krasner 1983)

---

on private property rights." Nonliberal states, according to Burley, are states that lack the above (1992: 1909).

and regard the emerging international tribunal system as an attempt to facilitate cooperation in a given issue area through the construction of an *atrocities regime* (Abbott 1999; Rudolph 2001).[26] The neoliberal conceptualization of the state as a unitary rational actor provides theoretical common ground with neorealists; however neoliberals and neorealists diverge in their analysis of the extent to which state behavior can or cannot be constrained by institutions or regimes. Krasner defines regimes as "sets of implicit or explicit principles, norms, rules and decision-making procedures around which actor's expectations converge in a given area of international relations" (Krasner 1983: 2). In regard to the issue area of atrocities and war crimes, IHL and international criminal tribunals can be viewed as both rules and procedures embedded within an emerging atrocities regime (Rudolph 2001). However, this image of international law as a means of facilitating inter-state cooperation led Reus-Smit to describe regime theoretic frameworks as almost purely functional in character (2004: 18).

For scholars of IL, neoliberal institutionalism's focus on regimes and compliance provides for a powerful response to an existential crisis within a discipline that emerged from a perceived inability to theorize compliance. Guzman wrote in the *California Law Review*, "…the absence of an explanation for why states obey international law in some instances but not in others threatens to undermine the very foundations of the discipline" (2002: 1826). Guzman went on to import the neoliberal institutionalist image of international law as a regulatory mechanism maintained by rational egoistic states through reciprocity and sanctions in an attempt to establish a framework for IL compliance theory.

Although the debate regarding why states comply with regime rules is relevant to explaining state compliance with ICTY orders, it must be noted that there exist four significant obstacles to applying neoliberal institutionalism to the subsequent study of compliance with ICTY orders. These obstacles include neoliberal institutionalist assumptions regarding regime consent, creation, reciprocity, and obligation. In regard to the first two obstacles, it is assumed that state subjects of legal obligations consented to abide by the rules of a given regime and participated in regime creation.[27] Therefore, state preferences are assumed to be reflected within the regime itself. Neither was the case in the former Yugoslavia. Compliance with ICTY orders was a legal obligation imposed by UNSC *fiat* upon the states of the former Yugoslavia and the states of the former Yugoslavia played no significant role in the drafting of the Tribunal Statute. In regard to reciprocity, neoliberal institutionalism assumes non-compliance decisions on the part of a single state inflict material costs upon other states. Although non-compliance with ICTY orders can inflict significant costs upon the ICTY itself, third party states are not materially harmed by a non-compliance act. The absence of cost is significant because rational games of coordination are left unable to explain third party state

26 Rudolph attempts to explain regime emergence and not compliance.

27 It should be noted that the extent to which regime rules reflect state preferences is said to reflect the relative power of a given state at the time of regime emergence.

enforcement of the ICTY Statute upon the states of the former Yugoslavia. The logic of reciprocity assumes defection by one state would inflict direct costs upon other states (Keohane 1986: 1-27), and the severity of retaliation inflicted upon the defecting state is assumed to reflect the level of harm inflicted upon states that remained compliant with regime rules (Keohane 1986: 12). In regard to obligation, neoliberal institutionalists and rational choice theorists do not assume the existence of an overriding obligation to comply with regime rules (Guzman 2008: 16-17; Keohane 1986: 19-20). Defection or non-compliance acts can be a rational choice for policymakers and are not dictated by moral imperatives. As a result the compliance method identified by neoliberal institutionalists to transform non-compliant behavior on the part of a recalcitrant state is identical to that of neorealism. Voluntary compliance, on the other hand, would be assumed to reflect rational self-interest.

*The Two Logics*

If we are to employ the dichotomy established by March and Olsen between the "logic of consequences" (LoC) and the "logic of appropriateness" (LoA), neoliberal institutionalism falls within the former along with neorealism (March and Olsen 1998, Risse 2001: 3). March and Olsen define the logic of consequence as presenting, "...political order as arising from negotiation among rational actors pursuing personal preferences or interests in circumstances in which there may be gains to coordinated action" (1998: 949). The logic of appropriateness is characterized as being rule-based. March and Olsen note, "Human actors are imagined to follow rules that associate particular identities to particular situations..." (1998: 951). The focus on perceived identities and rules will be discussed in more detail in the coming pages.

A LoC-based approach to international criminal tribunals would envision tribunals as acting an agent of states. International legal scholars Posner and Yoo support the LoC-based approach and suggest that the effectiveness of international criminal tribunals relies on prosecutors and judges remaining dependent upon the states responsible for their creation (2005: 1-74). Posner and Yoo posit:

> ... international tribunals can help states resolve disputes by providing information on the facts and rules of conduct. *But they must act consistently with the interests of the states that create them* (2005: 72).[28]

Posner and Yoo's conceptualization of the relationship between international tribunals and state interests is at odds with IL scholars such as Helfer and Slaughter

28 Emphasis added by author.

who argue that international tribunals are more effective when advancing principle over power (1997: 314), or in other words norms over interests.[29]

Posner and Yoo argue tribunals that are not closely controlled by states such as the ICC actually pose a threat to international cooperation because of the risk that an independent prosecutor or judges may infuse moral values, ideologies, or the interests of a clique of states into the work of the court (2005: 7, 73). This argument, however, is grounded on the assumption that moral or ideological imperatives hinder attempts at bringing an end to hostilities and raise costs imposed upon third party states.[30] If we are to accept the assumption that a global international criminal judicial infrastructure would actually increase costs upon states by prolonging conflict, then state support for international criminal justice defies rationalist explanation. Take for example the ICC's indictment of the Ugandan Lord's Resistance Army (LRA) leader Joseph Kony along with four senior LRA commanders. The ICC's indictments removed a powerful incentive for the LRA to enter into a peace settlement, amnesty. Catholic Archbishop John Baptist Odama illustrates the difficulties that have resulted from the ICC's indictments in posing the question, "how can we tell the LRA soldiers to come out of the bush and receive amnesty when at the same time the threat of arrest by the ICC hangs over their heads?" (Pelser 2005).[31] The cost of amnesty is significantly lower, at least in the short term, than that of prosecution, yet nonetheless, the ICC continues to enjoy the support of Statute of Rome signatory states.

*Norms, Rules and Legitimacy*

The constructivist focus on normative, ideational or social structures in IR (Kocs 1994, Kratochwil 1984, 1989, Shannon 2000, Wendt 1992, 1995, 1999) provides an alternative theoretical lens through which compliance with international criminal tribunal orders can be viewed. The compliance method identified by constructivists focuses on intersubjective processes of persuasion and shaming. Moreover, compliance with international law is a function of norm internationalization rather than the outcome of a rational weighing of material compliance costs. Table 1.1 outlines theories of IR and compliance methods explored up to this point.

---

29 Helfer and Slaughter along with Williams and Taft argue that prosecutorial independence from state actors is necessary for international criminal tribunals to carry out their judicial functions (Helfer and Slaughter 1997, Williams and Taft 2003).

30 For example, Williams and Taft claim that was precisely the absence of moral or ideological imperatives that prevented the ICTY from serving as a peace-building institution in the former Yugoslavia (2003: 225-233).

31 At the time of writing LRA interlocutors traveled to The Hague to enquire about the process of withdrawal of an ICC indictment. The LRA argues that an agreement with the Ugandan government to try war criminals domestically makes ICC prosecutions "redundant" (Glassborow and Eichstaedt 2008).

**Table 1.1 Compliance and IR theory**

| | Decision-making Process | Compliance Method | Explanations for Non-Compliance | IR Theories and Approaches |
|---|---|---|---|---|
| Logic of Consequences | Rational cost-benefit analysis | Coercion, inducements, use of force | Benefits of non-compliance > compliance costs | Realism, neo-realism, neo-liberal institutionalism |
| Logic of Appropriateness | Ideational, norm following | Persuasion, shaming | Competing norms, lack of norm internalization | Cognitive-sociological approaches, liberalism |

While LoC and LoA compliance methods have been juxtaposed in Table 1.1, they should not be construed as being entirely mutually exclusive. Table 1.1 is an organizational tool that has been provided to help provide clarity to multiple approaches to compliance established in existing scholarship. However, constructivist legal scholars do tend to imagine international norm-development as directly in conflict with state interest-based rational choice decision-making. Bassiouni notes that the history of IHL:

> … reveals the tension between norm-development which reflects the commonly shared values and aspirations of peoples irrespective of their diversity, and the political interests of states (2003a: 29).

On the other hand, Finnemore and Sikkink contend:

> … the current tendency to oppose norms against rationality or rational choice is not helpful in explaining many of the most politically salient processes we see in empirical research – processes we call "strategic social construction," in which actors strategize rationality to reconfigure preferences, identities or social context. Rationality cannot be separated from any politically significant episode of normative influence or normative change, just as the normative context conditions any episode of rational choice (1998: 888).

The forthcoming case studies will impart that rationality and normative context taken together provide for a deeper understanding of state compliance with ICTY orders than rational choice or constructivist approaches can provide on their own. LoC and LoA explanations for compliance are better represented by a continuum which would place purely LoC compliance or non-compliance acts at one extreme while purely LoA compliance or non-compliance acts would fall along the opposite extreme.

### *Norm Life Cycles, the Boomerang Pattern and Spiral Model*

Finnemore and Sikkink provide a useful model of what is described as a norm's life cycle that has significant implications for the study of compliance. The life cycle of a norm is said to consist of three-stages, norm emergence, norm cascade and norm internalization (Finnemore and Sikkink 1998: 887-917). The first stage, norm emergence, is characterized by norm entrepreneurs attempting to convince a critical mass of states to adopt a given norm. The second stage, norm cascade, describes a process by which certain states, norm leaders, attempt to convince other states, norm followers, to accept the new norm. The final stage, internalization, is marked by a new norm being "taken-for-granted" and no longer being the subject of debate (Finnemore and Sikkink 1998: 895). Thus, we can assume that weakly internalized norms, Stage I and II norms, would require substantial external persuasion to bring about compliance and non-compliance acts should be relatively common.[32] With regard to Stage III norms, we should find non-compliance acts as hardly occurring at all.

Yet contradictory normative behavior by states defies a linear progression of norm entrenchment. For example, while Croatia resisted cooperation with the ICTY, it was identified as being part of the group of "like-minded" states that pushed for the creation of the ICC (Bassiouni 2003a: 457). Also, although Finnemore and Sikkink concede new norms "never enter a normative vacuum but instead emerge in a highly contested normative space where they must compete with other norms and perceptions of interest" (1998: 897), the outcome of contests involving "new" norms coming into to conflict with preexisting norms requires further examination. After all, Kivimäki observes that states that rationalize non-compliance with human rights regimes often do so with appeals to the norm of state sovereignty (1994: 417).

Nevertheless, two complementary compliance models have emerged from Finnemore and Sikkink's exploration of norm life cycles. The first model, the "boomerang pattern" was developed by Keck and Sikkink and isolates domestic civil society as a causal mechanism which serves to mobilize external shaming processes through engagement with transnational advocacy networks (1998: 12-38). The second model, the "spiral model," builds on the boomerang pattern by tracing state responses to domestic and transnational civil society mobilization (Risse and Sikkink 1999: 1-38). Both models identify domestic and transnational civil society networks as acting to alter state behavior and necessitate an exploration of domestic and transnational civil society in the subsequent case studies so as to assess the explanatory power of the above models.

32 Sikkink and Walling point an increasing number of domestic, hybrid and international human rights trials as evidence of a "justice cascade" (2005) or Stage II of the above mentioned life cycle.

*Compliance and Legitimacy*

Because the ICTY's enforcement of IHL is restricted to the former Yugoslavia, the activities of the Tribunal are perhaps better described as imposed rather than norm-generating.[33] The ICTY was after all established by the UNSC under Chapter VII of the UN Charter and was imposed by legal *fiat* upon the former Yugoslavia. The ICTY was not a regime created by or directly consented to by the states under its prosecutorial jurisdiction.[34] Kratochwil argues that a perception of legitimacy with on the part of all parties involved in a particular exchange constitutes a precondition for an interaction to be considered a norm-based rule in the following analogy, "it is the lack of legitimacy of such demands that makes the acceptance of 'being robbed' as part of the normative discourse implausible, even if it is based on stable expectations" (1989: 53).

It is the question of legitimacy raised by Kratochwil which is almost completely ignored in rationalist IR scholarship.[35] To the extent that rationalist scholarship engages with the question of regime legitimacy, neorealists suggest rules and laws are legitimate if they reflect the underlying distribution of power, while neoliberal institutionalists assume legitimacy to be a reflection of functional benefits provided to states by adherence to a given rule or law. Revealingly, despite the similarities between neoliberal regime theory and international law that were identified by Slaughter, Tulumello, and Wood (1998: 367-397), substantial differences remain regarding conceptions of regime legitimacy. Within IL scholarship, the legitimacy of international regimes rests on the repeated equal enforcement of international law (Rudolph 2001: 686). Moreover, it is assumed that for the legitimacy of a given law to be maintained there can be little or no flexibility in its enforcement, while among neoliberal institutionalists the flexibility of regime rules is deemed to be essential for long-term regime survival (Rudolph 2001: 686).

Vinjamuri and Snyder refer to the body of literature that emphasizes cognitive legitimacy as the "emotional and psychology approach" to international justice and note that authors who utilize such an approach tend to argue that in order to prevent future atrocities an "emotional catharsis" among victims and an acceptance of responsibility by perpetrators must first be achieved (2004: 357). Despite the fact state compliance *per se* is not the central focus of literature on

33 Kratochwil makes a distinction between norm-based rules and commands noting that norm-based rules are said to be "...valid *erga omnes*, and are thereby quite different from commands" (1989: 53). In the case of the *ad hoc* tribunals the absence of consent on the part of belligerent states leads to the unfortunate observation that IHL enforcement has been by the Security Council rather than through an endogenous demand for enforcement.

34 It is of interest to note Sweden expressed concern regarding the ICTY's method of establishment through the UNSC and instead argued that the ICTY should have been established through a multilateral treaty and thus expressly consented to by the states of the former Yugoslavia (Scharf 1997: 54-55).

35 Pareto improving regimes are assumed by neoliberals to be legitimate.

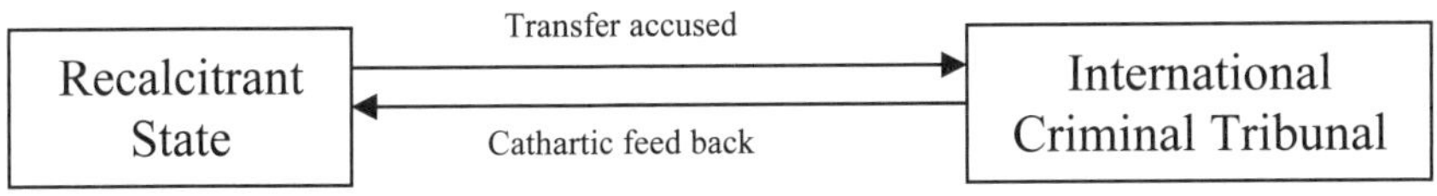


**Figure 1.1 Compliance feedback**

catharsis-based approaches to international criminal tribunals, there is an implicit assumption that tribunals, acting as the agent of victims, will enjoy significant support within post-conflict societies. Tribunals are also assumed to generate a justice constituency within post-conflict societies which will in turn pressure domestic elites into cooperating with international criminal tribunals. Although initial attempts at securing compliance may require third party enforcement, trial processes themselves are assumed to feedback to the recalcitrant state generating future voluntary compliance acts.[36]

In the early 1990s, proponents of the ICTY argued that cathartic feedback from international war crimes trials would heal "open wounds" that would otherwise remain a source of future conflict.[37] Neier suggested that it was the lack of justice in the former Yugoslavia following World War II that fed resentments which manifested in the early 1990s:

> The resentments that Serbs harbored against Croats for the unpunished crimes of the Ustasha state during World War II was a major factor in the catastrophic developments in the ex-Yugoslavia more than four decades later. Justice provides closure; its absence not only leaves wounds open, but its very denial rubs salt in them. Accordingly, partisans of prosecutions argue, peace without justice is a recipe for further conflict (1998: 213).

Williams and Taft also made a parallel argument when claiming that trials before an international court could have the effect of, "...laying bare to the Yugoslav people how they were manipulated through propaganda and coercion to commit savage acts on a massive scale" (2003: 238). This historical record is assumed to demystify destructive ideologies such as national chauvinism that serve to legitimize war crimes and reconstitute domestic norms.

Akhavan also argued that the much of the power of international criminal tribunals derives from cathartic feedback. Indictments certified by international tribunals are said to have a stigmatizing effect on indicted individuals and upon the states that fail to transfer them (Akhavan 2001). Thus, the stigmatizing effect of

36 Sikkink and Risse's spiral model illustrates how strategic acquiescence to human rights regimes can lead to norm internalization (1999: 17-35).

37 Of course the term "cathartic feedback" was not used within tribunal scholarship which emphasized the cathartic effect of international war crimes trials.

norm-breaking alone is assumed to facilitate state compliance.[38] It will, however, be noted in subsequent chapters that there is little evidence of individuals indicted by the ICTY being stigmatized within their local communities.[39] Instead, Ante Gotovina, Ramush Haradinaj, and Slobodan Milošević, to name just a few examples, have all seen their popularity increase following either their initial indictment or transfer to the ICTY. Tihomir Blaškić, a former Bosnian Croat commanding officer, was even enthusiastically greeted by Croatian government ministers after completing a nine year sentence for complicity in atrocities committed in Bosnia-Herzegovina (Pavić 2004). While the above examples are merely anecdotal, polling data from Croatia and Serbia appears to affirm a breakdown in Akhavan's stigmatization process. Despite the prosecution and conviction of Croats responsible for serious violations of IHL during the conflict in the former Yugoslavia, a large majority of Croats continued to believe that Croats did not perpetrate war crimes during the 1991-1995 conflict (Lalić 2002: 20; Lamont 2004: 61). More disturbingly, the percentage residents of the Republic of Serbia who accept Serb forces were involved in war crimes in Bosnia-Herzegovina, Croatia, and Kosovo decreased substantially since the beginning of the Milošević trial. For example, the percentage of Serbs who believed large numbers of prisoners were held by Bosnian Serbs in Bosnia-Herzegovina decreased from 36 percent in 2001, to 26 percent in 2004. Also, the percentage of Serbs who believe Serb forces besieged Sarajevo for over 1,000 days decreased from 53 percent in 2001 to 40 percent in 2004 (Belgrade Center for Human Rights 2005).

The assumption that international criminal tribunals can provide cathartic feedback relies heavily on the ability of international criminal tribunals to establish a historic record accessible to post-conflict societies. However, the practices of ICTY illustrates that the legal process may in fact serve as an impediment to the establishment of a historic record. First, acquiescence to state requests for the confidential submission of evidence may do more to obscure the past than provide clarity.[40] Moreover, those who are intent upon exposing historic records may

38 Finnemore and Sikkink argue, "We recognize norm-breaking behavior because it generates disapproval or stigma and norm conforming behavior either because it produces praise, or, in the case of a highly internalized norm, because it is so taken for granted that it provokes no reaction whatsoever" (1998: 892).

39 In fact, although there is no wider comparative study that empirically tests whether or not the phenomena of cathartic feedback exists, it is of interest to note indictments issued by the Tokyo Tribunal also seemed to lack the domestic stigmatizing effect. For example, the convicted Class-A war criminal and right-wing politician, Shigemitsu Mamoru, emerged from prison to become Japan's foreign minister from 1954-1956, while another war criminal convicted by the same tribunal, Kishi Nobusuke, was elected prime minister of Japan in 1957 (Dower 1999: 474). At this point, it must be emphasized that no ICTY convicted war criminal has returned to the former Yugoslavia to hold high public office.

40 Nataša Kandić of the Humanitarian Law Center's testimony at the ICTY in support of Florence Hartmann, who was indicted for contempt of court in August 2008, provides an illustration of the above (Nurković and Golčevski 2009).

find themselves subject to criminal prosecution. Second, the excruciatingly slow pace of international criminal investigations will inevitably permit a number of defendants to die natural deaths before they are ever brought to trial. It has even argued that the inability of the ICTY's Office of the Prosecutor (OTP) to bring charges against the Croatian leadership in a timely fashion meant that a historic record of Tuđman's role in the 1991-1995 conflict may never be established by the Tribunal. William and Taft write:

> ...the failure of the Office of the Prosecutor to act in a timely fashion on the indictment of Tuđman led to the loss of a significant historical record both for the international community, and the Croatian community. Undoubtedly the continued idolization of Tuđman among Croats regarding their role in the early Yugoslav conflict, arose not only from a strong sense of nationalism but also from a dearth of information regarding the specific aspirations and actions of Franjo Tuđman (2003: 219).

In addition to Tuđman, Croatia's wartime minister of defense Gojko Šušak died before an indictment could be brought against him for his role in the conflict, and Janko Bobetko, was only indicted in 2002 for crimes committed a decade earlier. Bobetko, too, died a natural death before his trial could begin. As a result of the inability of the OTP to bring charges in a timely fashion, Croatia's civilian political elite escaped prosecution, and the highest-ranking Croats to be tried were Croatian Army military officers and Bosnian Croat quislings of the Tuđman-era Croatian state. An additional factor that raises concerns regarding the ability of international criminal tribunals to establish an impartial historical record is the practice of sealing the records of cases of defendants who die before the court has reached a judgment. Williams and Taft lament, "...the failure of the Tribunal to make information accessible to the public greatly hampered its ability to serve one of the primary functions of justice – the establishment of an accurate historical record and the release of relevant information to the public" (2003: 219).[41]

If the focus of the debate is shifted from IHL enforcement to explaining demands for the creation of the ICTY, changing perceptions of what is and is not acceptable behavior on the part of belligerent parties during violent conflict perhaps has more explanatory power than a narrow focus on state interests. International criminal tribunals can be interpreted as not being the product of a hegemonic power harnessing international justice as just another tool for power amplification, but rather as emerging from a growing social awareness of the horrors perpetrated in the former Yugoslavia that violated all pre-existing norms

41 It is of interest to note that the Nuremberg Tribunal made a conscious effort to publicize its proceedings and even issued a 42 volume bilingual publication documenting the tribunal's work, while the failure of the Tokyo tribunal to transform Japanese opinion of Japan's role in the Second World War has been partly explained by the fact that the Tribunal never produced a comprehensive official record (Dower 1999: 453-454).

of appropriate behavior. This is consistent with a growing trend in IL scholarship which describes sovereignty as an evolving concept that is inclusive of obligations imposed upon states in return for recognition as part of the international community (Broomhall 2003: 59).

## Sovereignty Compromised?

There is an emerging consensus in both IL and constructivist IR literature that sovereignty "…is constituted by the recognition of the international community, which makes its recognition conditional on certain standards…" (Broomhall 2003: 43). These standards are codified in the form of international criminal law and represent the limits of state sovereignty (Broomhall 2003: 43). An interpretation of state sovereignty as constantly evolving permits the entrenchment of international criminal tribunals without mounting a zero-sum challenge to the Westphalian model of state sovereignty. While some scholars see sovereignty as not necessarily in conflict with an emerging criminal tribunal system either because sovereignty is the product of inter-subjective understandings among a community of states or because there is a perceived convergence between state interests and IHL enforcement, Cassese draws on practical experience as a former president of the ICTY to argue that the legal sovereignty afforded to states represents a continuing obstacle to IHL entrenchment. Cassese posits international criminal law cannot be effective so long as states retain certain aspects sovereignty that prevents tribunals from direct enforcement of their orders:

> So long as states retain some essential aspects of sovereignty and fail to set up an effective mechanism to enforce arrest warrants and to execute judgments, international criminal tribunals may have little more than normative impact (1998: 17).

Cassese presents international law entrenchment and the recognition of state sovereignty as almost mutually exclusive. In Cassese's words, effective international law enforcement mechanisms cannot exist in a world of states that value sovereignty over human rights.[42] Bassiouni provides a concrete example of a direct enforcement system for international criminal law:

> … a regime applicable to international judicial institutions which have the power of enforcing their orders and judgments without going through states or any other legal authority (2003a: 18).

42 Cassese also presents this dichotomy between sovereignty and human rights in his 1997 ICTY annual report to the United Nations Security Council (Report of the International Tribunal 1997).

The only historical examples of such a regime, according to Bassiouni, are the Nuremberg and Tokyo tribunals (Bassiouni 2003a: 18); however, these tribunals were only possible following the complete military defeat of the Germany and Japan which otherwise never would have voluntarily submitted to such a judicial body. More importantly, the Allied powers fell outside of the prosecutorial mandate of the postwar tribunals and were not willing to subject their conduct during the Second World War to international judicial scrutiny.

Because international criminal tribunals depend on states for their creation, the prospect for the emergence of a global direct enforcement tribunal system is neither expected nor seriously contemplated by policymakers. With regard to the existing permanent International Criminal Court (ICC), the Statute of Rome represents a deepening institutionalization of a limited international criminal tribunal system that depends on state cooperation. Furthermore, because the ICTY was an *ad hoc* tribunal with limited territorial and temporal jurisdiction, it was invested with significantly more authority in relation to the states over which it exercised jurisdiction than the ICC. For example, the ICC was not granted primacy over national courts. Contrast this with Article 9(2) of the ICTY's Statute:

> The International Tribunal shall have primacy over national courts. At any stage of the procedure, the International Tribunal may formally request national courts to defer to the competence of the International Tribunal (ICTY 2005).

The primacy clause has been the subject of much controversy as it presents a direct challenge to the sovereign jurisdiction of domestic courts. The tension between the primacy clause and domestic judiciaries has become more apparent following the death of Tuđman in Croatia and the fall of Milošević in Serbia as local prosecutors showed an increased willingness to launch proceedings against individuals either indicted or under investigation by the ICTY. In fact, the relationship between the ICTY and new the post-authoritarian regimes proved in some cases more problematic as new democratic elites confronted the legacies of their predecessors. In states where persons indicted for crimes against humanity were more popular than political elites, or in some cases were the political elites,[43] cooperation with an international tribunal posed a serious threat to the domestic political order.

*Compliance under Diffuse Sovereignty*

Over the course of the 1990s and 2000s, the ICTY interacted with multiple non-state actors. As two of the case studies are in fact under international administration, it will also be noted that international organizations in both Bosnia-Herzegovina and Kosovo have been criticized for non-cooperation with the Tribunal. Difficulties

43 For example, Slobodan Milošević was president of the Federal Republic of Yugoslavia and Ramush Haradinaj was prime minister of Kosovo at the time of their indictments by the ICTY.

have arisen as a result of conflicting interests between the ICTY, NATO, and the United Nations Mission in Kosovo (UNMIK). With regards to the latter two, the maintenance of stability has been prioritized over the investigation and prosecution of war crimes. However, when attempting to explore the causes of non-compliance in Bosnia-Herzegovina and Kosovo, it is important to recall that existing rationalist approaches to IR and even constructivist approaches, which Krasner labels sociological perspectives, offer little guidance on how to explain the behavior of entities that lack either legal sovereignty or the ability to act autonomously. Krasner points out:

> … [neo-realism, neo-liberal institutionalism and sociological perspectives] cannot analyze questions involving political entities that are not fully autonomous, much less those where territory and authority structures are not coterminous. Such entities, even if they are called states, are constrained not just by the power of other states but also by externally imposed domestic conditions (1995-1996: 147).

While neorealism and neoliberal institutionalism's inability to explore research questions involving "not fully autonomous" entities is self-evident, Krasner argues that the sociological assumption that the sovereign state is produced and reinforced by shared understandings and authority structures cannot account for states engagement in activities that undermine Westphalian understandings of sovereignty (1995-1996: 145-146). In regard to Bosnia-Herzegovina and Kosovo, assumptions regarding state compliance with international law in IR scholarship cannot be applied to entities whose governance structures are to varying degrees controlled by external actors. Chapter 5 will illustrate the extent to which the international community maintains direct control over domestic governance in Bosnia-Herzegovina through the Office of the High Representative and the Peace Implementation Council despite the fact Bosnia-Herzegovina maintained a legal identity as a sovereign state. Moreover, as will be demonstrated in Chapter 6, Kosovo's local institutions of self-government were prohibited from independent engagement with the ICTY, as cooperation with the Tribunal was deemed a "reserved competency" for UNMIK alone.[44]

## Introducing the Case Studies

The post-Cold War proliferation of international criminal tribunals brought about a diverse and growing body of tribunal scholarship; however, existing scholarship on international criminal tribunals largely neglects questions of compliance with tribunal orders and instead focuses on the historic-legal underpinnings of the

44 This point was emphasized in a personal interview with UNMIK spokesperson Alexandar Ivanko, November 8, 2007.

emerging tribunal system or consists largely of normative appeals for international justice which tend to emphasize the presumed therapeutic effect of war crimes trials on post-conflict societies (Akhavan 1998, 2001, Bassiouni 1992, 2003a, 2003b, Cassese 1994, 1998, Meron 1998, Neier 1998, Simpson 2007). The lacuna of literature on state compliance with tribunal orders represents a significant void in IR and IL literature given tribunal dependency upon state compliance can be found across the spectrum of post-Nuremburg international criminal courts. Post-Cold War international judicial bodies place legally binding obligations upon either UN member states, or in the case of the ICC signatories of the Statute of Rome, to cooperate with these institutions. In regard to the ICTY, Article 29 of the Tribunal Statute assigns to states a number of pre-trial tasks extending from assistance with Tribunal investigations to the enforcement of arrest and surrender orders.[45]

In order to test existing theoretical interpretations of compliance in IR and IL literature this book will explore both the domestic and international politics of compliance with ICTY orders. Article 29 encompasses a broad range of obligations which includes providing access to witnesses and documentation, and any study of compliance must acknowledge that although Article 29 obligations remained constant, compliance benchmarks articulated by third party enforcement agents changed over time and were often linked to the arrest and transfer of specified individuals. This study will examine compliance with Article 29 obligations and therefore seek to understand the conditions under which full cooperation can be expected. Before embarking on the case studies, it must also be noted that state provision of material evidence to the Tribunal can occur under a seal of confidentiality. Thus, in some instances non-compliance acts are never made public.[46] Arrest and surrender orders, on the other hand, offer a greater degree of transparency despite the fact the ICTY began issuing sealed indictments in 1997 against a number of accused who were considered a flight risk or resided in a state that did not recognize the jurisdiction of the Tribunal. This is because once a transfer to Tribunal custody took place, the seal of confidentiality was lifted. Because non-compliance and compliance acts are more easily identifiable when it comes to arrest and surrender orders, much of the following pages will focus on Tribunal efforts to secure custody of war crimes suspects.

The subsequent five case studies represent a diverse range of actors that were all subject to the same legal regime, the Statute of the Tribunal. The diversity of legal subjects requires this book to be divided into two constituent parts. The first three case studies more closely resemble the post-Westphalian model of a sovereign state: Croatia, Serbia, and Macedonia.[47] The latter two case studies, Bosnia-Herzegovina and Kosovo, encompass a state that existed under externally

45 See Appendix I.

46 This point was emphasized in a confidential interview with an ICTY legal officer, December 4, 2007.

47 In Chapter 4 it will be noted that while post-Ohrid accords Macedonia provided external actors with a significant supporting role for the peace agreement, Macedonia retained

imposed domestic governance structures and a territory administered by the United Nations that lacked international legal recognition as a state during the period of time under study.

Throughout the five case studies there will be an attempt to disentangle the domestic and international politics of compliance, while also exploring the extent to which compliance and non-compliance outcomes were dictated by utilitarian cost benefit calculus or normative obligation. Although all five case studies will include a discussion of the domestic and international politics of compliance, the first three case studies will also include an exploration of state legitimation and identity in order to assess the extent to which ideational structures shaped compliance decisions. Throughout the case studies there will also be a discussion of compliance and non-state actors, which will explore the extent to which non-state actors restricted government autonomy in relation to compliance and non-compliance decisions. Each chapter will then conclude with a discussion of the international politics of compliance.

---

sovereign control over its territory to a much greater extent than Bosnia-Herzegovina and Kosovo.

# PART I
# State Compliance

# Chapter 2
# Croatia: A Coercive Model for Compliance

## Introduction

In confronting the Republic of Croatia the ICTY was presented with the complex task of securing cooperation from a state that gained international recognition only a year preceding the UNSC's adoption of Resolution 827.[1] Although Croatia supported the creation of an international criminal tribunal for the former Yugoslavia, voluntary cooperation on the part of the Croatian state proved not forthcoming once the ICTY launched investigations into IHL violations committed by Croatian armed forces. Absent an in-country NATO security presence the OTP's investigations, and later prosecutions, were reliant on the assistance of the Croatian state for tasks such as the exhumation of mass graves, the collection of documentary evidence, and the arrest of war crimes suspects. Moreover, absent an international civilian administration, such as the Office of the High Representative in Bosnia-Herzegovina or the United Nations Missions in Kosovo, external actors lacked the ability to directly remove non-compliant state officials from office or impose domestic governance structures.[2] Nonetheless, by December 2005, the ICTY secured the transfer of all Croatian citizens indicted by the Tribunal for serious violations of International Humanitarian Law with the exception of Janko Bobetko, who died shortly after ICTY doctors confirmed the defendant's ill health in 2003.[3]

Chapter 1 outlined multiple causal pathways within IR and IL literature that could explain state compliance with ICTY orders that ranged from rationalist to norm-centric approaches.[4] In order to assess the former, the domestic and

---

1 Austria, Germany, Italy, Hungary, Sweden, and Switzerland recognized Croatia in January 1992. The United States established diplomatic relations with Croatia in August 1992.

2 One notable exception relevant to the period of time under examination was the UNTAES mission in Eastern Slavonia, which administered Eastern Slavonia for a transitional period of two years from January 15, 1995 to January 15, 1998. Established under UNSC Resolution 1037, UNTAES governed Eastern Slavonia until the region was returned to the Croatian state in 1998. One Croatian Serb accused, Slavko Dokmanović, was transferred by UNTAES to ICTY custody in 1997.

3 It should be noted that the ICTY indicted five Croatian citizens for war crimes committed within Croatia while 27 Bosnian Croats were indicted for war crimes committed in Bosnia-Herzegovina.

4 Literature which identifies norm internalization as a causal phenomenon emphasizes the transmission of international norms into domestic politics through exogenous

international politics of compliance must be examined with special attention to internal incentive structures along with material incentives and disincentives deployed by third party states to reward compliance and penalize non-compliance acts. The latter causal pathway requires an examination of the domestic politics of compliance with special attention to international criminal justice norm penetration of elites and civil society. So as to test rationalist and norm-centric explanatory hypotheses, this chapter will begin with a discussion of the domestic political context in which the ICTY attempted to secure state compliance. Interestingly, while regime type and elites changed during the first decade of interaction between the Croatian state and the Tribunal, episodes of compliance and non-compliance transcended Croatia's transition from presidential authoritarianism to parliamentary democracy. Moreover, throughout the period of time covered in this case study Croatian elites engaged in norm affirming rhetoric by both recognizing the jurisdiction of the ICTY[5] and supporting the establishment of a permanent international criminal court.[6] Next there will be an exploration of the domestic penetration of norms of international criminal justice. Because domestic civil society is identified in constructivist IR literature as a transmission belt for international norms (Finnemore and Sikkink 1998, Keck and Sikkink 1998, Sikkink and Walling 2005), special attention will be paid to Croatia's NGO community.[7] It will be emphasized that although an embryonic human rights NGO community emerged during the 1990s, powerful veterans' organizations proved more effective in pressuring elites to maintain non-compliance strategies.[8] Thus, social protest-based explanations for compliance with ICTY orders cannot explain the ICTY's tremendous achievements in Croatia. Instead, this chapter will demonstrate that there does appear to be a correlation between external coercion applied upon the Croatian state by third party states, primarily the United States (1996-1999) and European Union member states (2002-2006), and sporadic compliance outcomes. By dividing the international politics of compliance into four phases, it can be

transnational advocacy networks and endogenous civil society NGOs (Finnemore and Sikkink 1998).

5 Illustrative of Croatian norm affirmation of the ICTY are comments made by Ivan Šimonović before the UN General Assembly in 1998: "Let me reiterate Croatia's support for the efforts of the International Criminal Tribunal for the Former Yugoslavia to bring to justice all those responsible for war crimes and crimes against humanity. Croatia reiterates its view that cooperation with the Tribunal must be unconditional … " (Šimonović 1998: 8).

6 See for example, Croatia's statement delivered to the UN General Assembly in 1998 in which Croatia expressed strong support for the creation of a permanent international criminal court (*Statement Delivered by the Croatian Delegation* 1998).

7 Keck and Sikkink's "boomerang pattern" takes appeals by domestic NGO's within the norm violating state as a starting point for the mobilization of external shaming processes (1998: 12-14).

8 This is especially significant given the importance Sikkink and Walling attach to domestic NGOs in constructing the ideational context for war crimes trial processes (2005).

observed that rather than reflecting a change in domestic regime type or local elites, compliance acts reflected external incentives for compliance rather than exclusively endogenous preferences. However, before discussing the international politics of compliance, the domestic political context in which compliance and non-compliance decisions took place must first be established.

## Domestic Politics and Compliance

When the Socialist Republic of Croatia held its post-communist founding elections in 1990, multi-party elections were held within the context of a collapsing federal state and intensifying intra-Yugoslav republican conflict. Croatia's ruling communist party, the League of Communists of Croatia (*Savez komunista Hrvatske*, SKH), was challenged by Franjo Tuđman's Croatian Democratic Union (*Hrvatska demokratska zajednica*, HDZ), a party which Zakošek described as having a strong centralized leadership, internal cohesion, and a clear ethno-nationalist programmatic identity (2002: 30). The HDZ's centralized leadership structures allowed the party to quickly consolidate power around Tuđman following its electoral victory in 1990 through the ratification of the December 1990 "Christmas Constitution." Furthermore, the party's hold on power was amplified by the fact Croatian electoral law translated the HDZ's narrow electoral victory over the SKH into an absolute parliamentary majority in the Social Political Council, the dominant republican parliamentary decision-making institution (Lamont 2008b: 62).

In the aftermath of Croatia's June 1991 declaration of independence and subsequent outbreak of war, Croatia's regime type acquired an increasingly authoritarian hue as the Office of the Presidency, created in 1990, came to dominate all other institutions of government including the parliament and the judiciary (Lamont 2008b: 70). With regard to the parliament, the institution's role was almost entirely usurped by presidential advisory councils, in which policy decisions were made and presented to the legislature as *fait accompli* (Zakošek 2002: 113-114).[9] While neither the causes of the consolidation of authoritarianism nor the outbreak of war are the focus of this study, violent conflict and presidential authoritarianism embedded legacies that shaped the domestic political context of interaction between the ICTY and the Croatian state. For example, the centralization of powers around Tuđman and a small clique of advisors meant that there was relatively little debate regarding the ratification of the 1996 Constitutional Law on Cooperation with the ICTY. Additionally, the ejection of 150,000-200,000 Croatian Serbs in August 1995[10] meant that Serb victims of war crimes were no

9 Sikkink and Lutz argue centralized decision-making structures can be conducive to compliance (2000: 639).

10 Although 150,000-200,000 is a broad range, this is the figure quoted in the ICTY's initial indictment of Ante Gotovina (see *The Prosecutor v. Ante Gotovina* 2001).

longer members of the domestic political community and could not effectively engage in domestic advocacy for war crimes prosecutions targeting officials of the Croatian state. Meanwhile, predominately Croat victims of war crimes perpetrated by Serb forces mobilized with government support during the 1990s to demand the prosecution of ethnic Serb war crimes suspects.

*State Legitimation*

After Croatia's declaration of independence in 1991, the Tuđman-led government immediately sought international recognition of Croatian independence in order to affirm Croatia's status as a sovereign state. As a newly independent state, Croatia's ratification of human rights covenants was part of a larger effort to affirm Croatia's status as an independent state through membership in international institutions.[11] International legitimation was directly linked to domestic legitimation of the governing HDZ. Croatian membership in institutions such as the United Nations (UN) was perceived as a reaffirmation of state sovereignty and was enthusiastically received by domestic public opinion. In August 1992, the HDZ's triumph in parliamentary and presidential elections followed Croatia's admittance into the UN.[12] Furthermore, although Tuđman's authoritarianism meant that Croatia could not formally seek entry into either the EU or NATO, the perceived support of EU member states such as Germany was important in maintaining the legitimacy of the regime (Boduszynski 2001: 21). In addition, despite an inability of Croatia to formally negotiate membership into the EU or NATO, the extent to which Zagreb sought legitimation from European institutions can be illustrated by the fact that even in the absence of a formal EU accession process, in 1998 the Croatian government began to voluntarily harmonize new legislation with existing EU law (Office of European Integration 1999: 14).

While the HDZ's attempted to legitimize the new state through embedding Croatia in existing international covenants and treaties, the HDZ was also confronted with the task of de-legitimizing the Yugoslav *ancien regime*. It was through the linkage of the Yugoslav project to war crimes perpetrated by the Yugoslav National Army (*Jugoslovenska narodna armija*, JNA) on Croatian territory that what Kasapović later described as the "moral de-legitimation" of the Yugoslav project was promoted (2002: 293). For example, Croatian state television's labeling of JNA forces as, "*Yugo*-military greater Serbian aggressors" linked "Yugoslavia"

11 For example, as Croatia sought membership in the Council of Europe, Croatia signed the European Convention on Human Rights, the Framework Convention on the Protection for National Minorities, and the European Convention for the Prevention of Torture among others. Croatia became a full member of the Council of Europe in 1996.

12 Zakošek attributes the scale of the HDZ's electoral victory in August 1992 to the fact that elections were held shortly after Croatia won recognition as a member state of the UN (2002: 35).

to the Greater Serbian project.[13] In addition, the historic memory of war crimes committed by Josip Broz Tito's partisan forces in May 1945 was resurrected as a means of de-legitimizing the pan-Yugoslav partisan movement. Just as the Jasenovac memorial center, built on the site of a notorious concentration camp, came to symbolize the horrors of the World War II-era fascist Independent State of Croatia, (*Nezavisna država Hrvatska*, NDH), the resurrection of the memory of members of the NDH armed forces who were massacred by partisans at Bleiberg in Austria during May 1945 served to de-legitimize the Yugoslav state as it cast the state as having been the creation of a criminal enterprise (D.B. McDonald 2002: 170-172).[14] In fact, during the 1990s, Bleiberg became a pilgrimage site for officials of the Croatian state.[15] It is because of the nexus between regime illegitimacy and war crimes promoted in the 1990s that the initiation of ICTY investigations into major Croatian military operations was perceived not just as a threat to regime elites directly implicated in the investigations themselves, but as a threat to the legitimacy of the Croatian state as well.[16]

### *The Domestic Politics of Compliance 1996-1999*

The subversion of the rule of law through presidential control over judicial appointments and dismissals meant that a domestic legal regime underpinning ICTY arrest and surrender orders and state provision of complementary prosecutions and investigations was not a viable prospect during the 1990s. Domestic challenges to swift compliance with ICTY orders were overcome through extra-constitutional means rather than through an equal application of the arrest and surrender orders on the part of the Croatian state. The Office of the Presidency's interference in the judicial process meant the Croatian judiciary exercised little independence. Judges waited for clear signals from the presidency before reaching judgments in sensitive cases (Zakošek 2002: 30). This was particularly the case when it came to judicial decisions involving Croatian war crimes suspects or regime associates. Furthermore, the domestic legal foundation of the 1996 Constitutional Law on

13 Emphasis added by author (for more see Croatian Radio Television 2006).

14 Numerous publications detailing war crimes committed against surrendering Croatian fascist forces in 1945 were produced during the 1990s. For example, Darko Sagrak's *Zagreb 1941-1945* (1995). Furthermore, as the fascist NDH was the only "independent" Croatian state in modern history, attempts were made at rehabilitating the legacy of the Ustaša party's fascist regime. For example, Trpimir Macan, in the introduction to *Tko je Tko u NDH* [Who is Who in the NDH], edited by Marko Grčić, concluded "the Ustaša regime … was not criminal" (Grčić 1997: IX).

15 Media coverage of the commemoration of the Bleiburg massacre became an almost annual ritual following Croatia's declaration of independence (see for example Jutarnji list 2002: 2).

16 This linkage between state legitimacy and war crimes would become increasingly emphasized following the indictment of Ante Gotovina in 2001. See for example Lukić 2001.

Cooperation with the ICTY was even subject to legal challenge. Although the Constitution of the Republic of Croatia directly introduced international law into domestic legislation through Article 134, which states, "International agreements concluded and ratified *in accordance with the Constitution* … shall be part of the internal legal order of the Republic of Croatia…,"[17] Croatia's adoption of the Constitutional Law on Cooperation with the ICTY satisfied, "neither the procedure for amending the Constitution nor the procedure for enacting laws" (Josipović 2005: 188). As a result, despite Zagreb's demonstration of a willingness to comply with ICTY orders and establishing, "…a better record of cooperation and compliance with the Tribunal than the Federal Republic of Yugoslavia" (Report of the International Tribunal 1999: 27), the arbitrary means by which individuals were transferred to The Hague meant that there was no standardized process for the transfer of an accused to ICTY custody and instead ICTY indictments were responded to only on an *ad hoc* basis.

Tuđman's transfer of 17 Bosnian Croats to ICTY custody from 1996-1999 did not constitute an internalization of compliance. Quite the opposite, rather than ensuring the universal application of arrest and surrender orders, the Croatian government proved more willing to transfer those who lacked close political connections with the governing party or president. Zagreb also proved uncooperative in providing any form of assistance to ICTY investigations into war crimes alleged to have been perpetrated by the Croatian armed forces on Croatian territory. In terms of war crimes suspects, Zagreb's *ad hoc* responses to the transmission of arrest orders created a situation whereby war crimes accused found themselves at the center of a bargaining process which allowed some alleged war criminals to avoid transfer to ICTY custody for a substantial period of time. For example, while Tihomir Blaškić and Vinko Martinović[18] were voluntarily surrendered to The Hague, Croatian security services provided Ivica Rajić with a false identity and sent Rajić into hiding. In the case of Mladen Natelilić[19] and Janko Bobetko, arrest and surrender orders were initially denied upon the Croatian state's determination that the defendants were too ill to stand trial.[20]

Meanwhile, domestic war crimes proceedings held during and in the immediate aftermath of the 1991-1995 conflict almost exclusively targeted Croatian Serbs.

17 Emphasis added by author.

18 At the time of Martinović's indictment in December 1998 Martinović was already serving a prison sentence for a post-war murder unrelated to the ICTY indictment; however his transfer was considered voluntary in part because he instructed his attorneys not to challenge the transfer order issued by the Croatian Supreme Court.

19 Natelilić was also already imprisoned by Croatian authorities and was awaiting trial for unrelated criminal activities at the time of his December 1998 indictment by the ICTY for war crimes committed in Bosnia-Herzegovina; however, the Croatian government argued that because domestic proceedings had been delayed for reasons of ill health, Natelilić could not be transferred to The Hague.

20 After initial protests by the Croatian government, both Natelilić and Bobetko were examined by ICTY doctors in Croatia.

The OSCE reported that since 1991, the domestic courts certified over 1,700 war crimes indictments and secured over 800 convictions. A vast majority of these convictions involved members of Croatia's Serbian minority (OSCE 2002b: 1). Therefore, rather than representing an entrenchment of norms of IHL, many convictions were not consistent with internationally recognized human rights standards. Many Serbs were also tried *in absentia*. Furthermore, perhaps the most egregious example of the Croatian judiciary's ethno-centric interpretation of IHL occurred after Tuđman's death. Svetozar Karan, a Croatian Serb, was found criminally responsible for what the court referred to as the 500 year history of war crimes perpetrated by Serbs against Croats in the Gospić County Court (OSCE 2002b: 13).[21] Karan's conviction was symptomatic of the challenges that the Croatian judiciary faced in overcoming the legacy of Tuđman-era politically motivated judicial appointments and proceedings. Tuđman's subversion of the rule of law combined with a legacy of constitutional or legal nationalism, which Hayden defines as "...a constitutional or legal structure that privileges the members of one ethnically defined nation over other residents in a particular state" (2002: 655), illustrates just a couple obstacles to referring cases from the ICTY to the Croatian judiciary under Rule 11*bis*.[22] In the short term, *ad hoc* and extra-legal mechanisms through which Tuđman governed permitted both compliance and non-compliance with ICTY requests and orders that facilitated a bargaining process which allowed the Croatian state to extract material rewards for compliance acts; however, the long term effect of Croatia's *ad hoc* response to ICTY indictments was that following regime transition, the transfer of individuals indicted by the ICTY had become increasingly perceived as a political rather than judicial process.[23] Nevertheless, it must be emphasized that from 1993 to 1999, Croatia never challenged the legal status of the Tribunal itself and instead relied upon legal challenges to individual indictments and investigations. Failing the above, Zagreb also claimed a functional inability to comply with ICTY orders.

### *The Domestic Politics of Compliance 2000-2006*

The electoral defeat of the governing HDZ in parliamentary elections held in January 2000 resulted in the election of a six party coalition led by Ivica Račan's Social Democratic Party (*Socijaldemokratska partija Hrvatske*, SDP). The six party coalition's parliamentary success was quickly followed by the election of

21 This conviction was later overturned by the Croatian Supreme Court, which ordered Karan's re-trail in Karlovac. Karan was again convicted on other charges and sentenced to seven years imprisonment.

22 Rule 11*bis* of the Tribunal Statute permits the ICTY to refer cases back to state courts for prosecution (*Rules, Procedures and Evidence* 2007).

23 Personal interviews ICTY Outreach Office Zagreb, March 23, 2006. Personal interview with former Croatian foreign ministry official March 24, 2006. Also see Lamont 2004: 60-61.

opposition candidate and former HDZ Prime Minister Stjepan Mesić to the office of presidency. The HDZ's defeat in parliamentary and presidential elections created the perception among outside observers that the 2000 elections constituted the first step in bringing about a decisive break from Croatia's nationalist authoritarian past. Croatia's new found affirmation of ICTY jurisdiction into investigations of the Croatian Army's alleged role in war crimes committed on Croatian territory also appeared to signal a new cooperative attitude coming from Zagreb.

The change in government also marked a dramatic change in domestic regime type. The HDZ's defeat was followed by constitutional reforms aimed at stripping the Croatian presidency of powers accumulated under Tuđman (Lamont 2008b: 74). Croatia's transition to parliamentary democracy meant that cooperation with the ICTY could no longer remain dependent upon the outcome of *ad hoc* presidential decision-making processes, which previously monopolized compliance decisions, but rather would be reliant on parliamentary consensus. Croatia's transition to parliamentary democracy meant that government autonomy to bring out compliance had been significantly reduced.

As Croatia transitioned from presidential authoritarianism to parliamentary democracy, the HDZ's electoral defeat signaled an opportunity to improve cooperation between the ICTY and the Croatian state. After all, although Tuđman was willing to surrender individuals indicted by the Tribunal, Tuđman's government also obstructed ICTY investigations of war crimes perpetrated by Croat forces (Report of the International Tribunal 1999: 27). Representative of this initial optimism regarding the extent to which the reformist government in Zagreb was willing to confront war crimes committed by the previous regime was the OTP's acquiescence to the Croatian state taking the lead role in bringing former Croatian Army general Mirko Norac to trial for war crimes committed in Gospić. In early February 2001, Norac went into hiding and declared that he would only surrender to Croatian authorities under the guarantee that his trial be held under the auspices of the domestic judiciary and not transferred to The Hague. The guarantee sought by Norac was granted by the OTP on February 21, and Norac handed himself over to Croatian authorities (ICTY 2001).[24]

Račan's government also acted to adopt a parliamentary resolution affirming the government's commitment to cooperation with the ICTY and the Tribunal's jurisdiction over war crimes cases involving members of the Croatian armed forces (Declaration on Cooperation 2000). However, only months after the Norac crisis, the indictments of Rahim Ademi and Ante Gotovina, which were made public in July 2001, plunged the SDP-led coalition government into crisis. The contents of the Gotovina indictment proved particularly explosive as Gotovina was indicted for war crimes committed during the course of Operation Storm. In August

24 Mirko Norac was convicted before the domestic courts in 2003 and sentenced to 12 years imprisonment for war crimes committed in Gospić. Norac was also convicted in May 2008 for war crimes committed during the 1993 Medak Pocket operation in a case that was referred to the Croatian judiciary under Rule 11*bis*.

1995 Operation Storm effectively ended the war in Croatia, and terminated the existence of the Republic of Serbian Krajina, an ethnic Serb mini-state established on Croatian territory.[25]

A minor coalition partner, the Croatian Social Liberal Party (*Hrvatska socijalna libralna stranka*, HSLS) demanded non-compliance with the arrest and surrender request and a renegotiation of the Tuđman-era Constitutional Law on Cooperation with ICTY. Dražen Budiša, the HSLS' party leader, accused the ICTY of having indicted the Croatian nation for genocide in its indictments of Ademi and Gotovina (Lukić 2001). When Račan instead reaffirmed a commitment on the part of the Croatian government to continue to cooperate with the ICTY, despite not having acted to arrest Gotovina before the indictment was made public on July 25, 2001,[26] the HSLS left the governing coalition.

In addition to the departure of the HSLS from the governing coalition, Račan's government was also put under significant pressure by Croatia's large war veterans' organizations which organized massive rallies to protest the prosecution of members of the Croatian armed forces for violations of IHL before domestic and international courts. A February 2001 gathering in support of Norac took place in Croatia's second largest city Split attracted over 100,000 protesters and set the tone for subsequent demonstrations in support of Gotovina which were organized across the country throughout 2001-2002 (Lamont 2004: 60-61). The mobilization of veterans' organizations post-regime transition signaled to the Račan government the high domestic costs associated with compliance with ICTY arrest and surrender orders and guided Zagreb away from the norm-affirming rhetoric found in the April 2000 Declaration on Cooperation with the ICTY.[27]

### *Challenging Article 29 – The Bobetko Crisis*

In 2001 Račan's parliamentary government twice avoided a direct confrontation with both domestic public opinion and the ICTY. First in the context of the Norac indictment, which was left to the domestic judiciary, and second Račan avoided Gotovina's arrest after Gotovina went into hiding. Nevertheless the February and July 2001 crises exposed the government's vulnerability to populist opposition

---

25 Operation Storm also coincided with the removal of the Krajina Serb population.

26 The Gotovina indictment was initially confirmed on June 8, 2001 and shortly thereafter disclosed in confidentiality to relevant Croatian government ministers in an attempt to secure Gotovina's arrest before the indictment's publication. An arrest warrant for Ante Gotovina was issued by the Croatian Ministry of Justice on July 9, three weeks before the ICTY's indictment was made public. It was during the period of time that Gotovina went into hiding. It was also between June 8 and July 21 that Gotovina acquired a false passport under the name Kristijan Horvat. More on events that followed the ICTY's confirmation of the Gotovina indictment can be found in the *Prosecution's Response Opposing Gotovina's Request for Provisional Release* August 22, 2007.

27 It should be emphasized that Croatia would not deny its legal obligation to cooperate with the ICTY, but rather denied the legality of an individual indictment.

to compliance with ICTY orders. However, September 2002, brought with it an additional crisis when former head of the Croatian armed forces, Janko Bobetko, was indicted by the Tribunal. It was in response to the Bobetko indictment that Račan directly challenged the legality of an ICTY order and sought to renegotiate the relationship between the states of the former Yugoslavia and the ICTY. Račan's rejection of the Bobetko indictment on the grounds that domestic courts deemed the indictment to be illegal[28] was recognized by the Tribunal as an attempt to alter the relationship between states and the ICTY. In fact, the OTP reminded Croatia that compliance with Tribunal arrest and surrender orders was not "an optional regime" for states. Furthermore, the OTP warned that if states were to be the arbiters of the legality of indictments issued by the ICTY, then the effectively the Tribunal could no longer compel transfers (Decision on Challenge by Croatia 2002). Thus, in a strongly worded dismissal of Croatia's appeal of the Bobetko indictment, the Appeals Chamber found:

> Croatia's role in complying with [an arrest] request or order is the purely ministerial one of executing the warrants and carrying out such arrest and detention as ordered by the Tribunal. A State which is ordered to arrest or detain an individual pursuant to Article 29(d) has no standing to challenge the merits of that order (Decision on Challenge by Croatia 2002).

The failure of Croatia's appeal of the Bobetko indictment on procedural grounds led the Croatian government argue against Bobetko's transfer on grounds the defendant's health had substantially deteriorated. However, this objection too was dismissed by the OTP, which argued that it should be the ICTY which determines whether a defendant is too ill to appear before the Tribunal, not the state in question. The OTP also demanded that the defendant should be first surrendered to the ICTY and only then could the health of the defendant be assessed in The Hague by Tribunal doctors. Significantly, even after the failure of Croatia's legal appeals, Croatia never rejected the ICTY legal regime itself, but instead focused on efforts to reinterpret regime rules.

In October 2002, ICTY President Antonio Cassese reported Croatia's non-compliance to the UNSC (OSCE 2002a: 11). Following Cassese's report to the

28 Questions raised by the Croatian government in its appeal of the Bobetko indictment included: a) Does the [ICTY] Statute or the Rules provide for a right to appeal or to seek a review of a decision of a confirming Judge? b) If so, does Croatia have *locus standi* to make such an application? c) Was the prosecution under an obligation prior to issuing an arrest warrant to interview the proposed accused person? d) Should the confirming Judge have requested the prosecution to submit evidence which would demonstrate the necessity to arrest the accused? e) Should the confirming Judge have adopted a procedure less constraining than the issue of an arrest warrant if that other procedure could have served the same objective? In particular, if the accused satisfies the conditions for provisional release, does he nevertheless still need to be arrested? (Decision on Challenge by Croatia 2002).

UNSC a compromise was agreed between the Tribunal and Croatia which permitted Tribunal doctors to examine Bobetko's health in a Zagreb hospital. As Tribunal doctors confirmed Bobetko's health had in fact deteriorated, the ICTY agreed not to pursue Bobetko's transfer unless there was a significant improvement in the accused's health (Hartmann 2003). Bobetko's death in April 2003 brought an abrupt end to the crisis sparked by the September 2002 indictment. Although Bobetko's death brought the immediate crisis in the relationship between the Tribunal and the Croatian state to an end, the fact that the Račan government rejected the ICTY's demand Bobetko be served with the indictment[29] was interpreted domestically as a successful challenge to the ICTY.[30]

*From Non-Compliance to Compliance*

The return of the HDZ to government in November 2003 marked an end to the turbulence of that marred the Račan government's relationship with the ICTY. Despite the HDZ's vocal opposition to the transfer of Croatian Army officers under ICTY indictment while in opposition (Lamont 2004: 60), once the party returned to power in 2003, the HDZ engaged in norm affirming rhetoric that emphasized Croatia's legal obligation to cooperate with the ICTY. The HDZ's post-Tuđman party leader, Ivo Sanader, favored the pursuit of rapid EU and NATO membership (Lamont 2008b: 77) and viewed cooperation with the ICTY as a means by which Croatia could accelerate its accession into Euro-Atlantic institutions (Government of the Republic of Croatia 2005).

The priority which Sanader attached to improving relations with the ICTY can be illustrated by the fact that, along with other heads of government, Sanader contacted ICTY Chief Prosecutor Carla Del Ponte immediately after taking office in order to discuss ways Croatia could improve cooperation with the Tribunal. Sanader's government also enlisted the assistance of foreign intelligence agencies in the search for fugitive general Ante Gotovina.[31] More concretely, Sanader facilitated the surrenders of Generals Ivan Čermak and Mladen Markač, who were indicted and surrendered to Tribunal custody in 2004. Sanader's efforts to improve cooperation with the ICTY culminated in Gotovina's December 2005 arrest in Spain.

29 Although Bobetko's lawyers were eventually presented with the ICTY's indictment in March 2003, Bobetko's illness had progressed to a point that Račan avoided the prospect of having Bobetko served in person with the indictment.

30 Vladimir Šeks, an opposition HDZ Member of Parliament observed that Račan successfully transformed himself into "a leader of the Croatian Right" (Lamont 2004: 60-61). This transformation and apparent praise from a senior member of the HDZ did not prevent the SDP-led government from suffering electoral defeat to the HDZ in November 2003.

31 BBC correspondent Nick Thorpe provides a description of the role of UK intelligence in the search for Ante Gotovina (2005).

## International Justice and Civil Society

The preceding overview of Croatian state interaction with the ICTY highlighted domestic politics of compliance with ICTY orders; however, non-state actors also played an active role in compliance debates. The constructivist causal mechanisms of normative social protest or elite socialization could serve as non-material mechanisms to alter elite preferences. After all Finnemore and Sikkink argued that domestic civil society could utilize international norms of appropriate behavior to transform the preferences of domestic elites (1998: 893), and in the event access to local elites was blocked, Keck and Sikkink suggest NGOs could take their campaigns abroad to mobilize external shaming of elites (1998: 12-14).

In Croatia civil society served to harden non-compliance preferences.[32] While Croatian political elites engaged in norm-affirming rhetoric, even when challenging Tribunal jurisdiction over specific investigations, it was within civil society that more aggressive demands for a complete rejection of the ICTY's jurisdiction emerged. Mobilization against the ICTY on the part of segments of civil society was representative of widespread public distrust of the Tribunal and the belief that war crimes were not committed by Croatian armed forces during the 1991-1995 conflict (Lamont 2004: 60-62). While a prolific body of literature focusing on case studies of successful international norm internalization has emerged in recent years (Finnemore 1996, Finnemore and Sikkink 1998, Gurowitz 1999, Keck and Sikkink 1998, Klotz 1995, Lutz and Sikkink 2000, Sikkink 1993, Sikkink and Walling 2005), examinations of breakdowns in causal mechanisms identified in the literature remain lacking. In an attempt to explain the failure of international norms of international criminal justice to transform elite preferences, there will be an exploration of civil society and domestic institutional constraints to norm mobilization. However, first there will be a discussion of attempts by external actors to engage with domestic civil society and public opinion.

### *The ICTY and Transnational Advocacy*

Throughout the period of time under exploration in this case study external normative pressure was exerted by both the ICTY itself and transnational international human rights organizations. Such pressure took the form of attempting to open a domestic

32 When making reference to civil society, I am referring to a wide range of non-governmental actors that span from human rights organizations to veterans' groups. Civil society can never be described as a monolithic actor, and here I am simply observing that substantial non-governmental anti-ICTY mobilization reduced governmental autonomy to carry out arrest orders on behalf of the ICTY. Non-governmental in support of war crimes prosecutions did not have the effect of reducing governmental autonomy not to comply with ICTY orders.

debate on the recent past through engagement with and support for local human rights organizations. Unfortunately, the ICTY only belatedly engaged directly in this effort as a result of its failure to establish a regional Outreach Office until 2000.[33] Moreover, it was also only in 2000 that the Tribunal began to translate press releases into Serbo-Croatian (Power 2000: 22). The ICTY acknowledged its own image problem in its 1999 annual report delivered to the UNSC, which conceded, "The Tribunal is viewed negatively by large segments of the population of the former Yugoslavia" (Report of the International Tribunal 1999: 38). Because ICTY trials in The Hague were only accessible to a small minority within Croatia, widely accessible information regarding trial processes was filtered through domestic media outlets.

In the absence of ICTY outreach activities during the 1990s the state controlled media, which almost entirely monopolized television news coverage and also influenced coverage of events in the print media (Zakošek 2002: 29-30), was able to frame the Tribunal's activities in a manner that reflected non-compliance preferences of state elites. State involvement in undermining the legitimacy of international war crimes trials was facilitated through both state and private media, which launched aggressive attacks against the ICTY before a domestic audience that went effectively unchallenged by the Tribunal. Overall media coverage of the ICTY led an official of the ICTY Outreach Office in Zagreb to note that it was impossible for the Office to even attempt to counter campaigns of misinformation in the Croatian press.[34]

Although direct state control over the media was substantially weakened by legislation adopted in 2001 (Zakošek 2002: 131), intimidation of independent journalists proved an effective means of influencing war crimes coverage post-regime transition. For example, Freedom House found that independent media coverage of the ICTY was obstructed by a systemic campaign of intimidation against journalists. Freedom House's 2005 report on freedom of the press in Croatia noted:

> Government cooperation with the International Criminal Tribunal for the Former Yugoslavia (ICTY)... and other sensitive political issues are still difficult to cover for state-run and local media outlets. Several reporters were physically attacked this year, and one reporter claimed to have received death threats. There were no arrests for the 2003 shooting of a broadcaster owner and the car bombing of an influential publisher. Two separate incidents involving the harassment of journalists by the Counterintelligence Agency (POA) shocked

33 Even after the establishment of the ICTY's Outreach Offices in Zagreb, Sarajevo and Belgrade, these offices were only staffed with two full time professional outreach personnel. Personal interview with Alexandra Milenov of the ICTY Field Office in Belgrade, January 23, 2007.

34 Personal interview with a member of staff of the ICTY Outreach Office in Zagreb, March 23, 2006.

> media organizations. In November, a journalist came forward and stated that she was held against her will, threatened, blackmailed, and interrogated about the president's activities. Earlier in the year, four journalists filed complaints claiming that the POA had conducted surveillance against them and accused them of espionage because the journalists had reported on the whereabouts of an indicted war criminal. After each instance, the POA director was replaced (Freedom House 2005).

Even at times when the Croatian state expressed a compliance preference, state elites would find themselves the targets of intimidation from radical elements within civil society. For example, after Račan reaffirmed Croatia's commitment to cooperating with the ICTY, Dražen Pavlović of the Croatian Military Invalids of the Homeland War (*Hrvatski vojnih invalida iz domovinskog rata*, HVIDR-a), a prominent veterans' organization, issued a veiled threat warning that both Mesić and Račan would soon be "eating breakfast" with the recently assassinated Serbian prime minister Zoran Đinđić (Jutarnji list 2003). Pavlović's threat illustrated the extent to which segments of civil society acted as a mechanism that could force the involuntary defection of state elites expressing a compliance preference.[35]

*Civil Society: Veterans, Victims, and Human Rights NGOs*

Peskin and Boduszysńki point out that there was effectively no domestic pressure from civil society to investigate war crimes committed by the Croatian government during the 1991-1995 conflict, and instead the impetus for the investigation of war crimes was almost completely external (2003: 1123). The absence of a robust human rights NGO community may serve to explain the significant obstacles to conducting war crimes trials of prominent Croats suspected of serious violations of IHL whether domestic or international. Sikkink and Walling note that human rights NGOs can play a vital role acting as norm entrepreneurs bringing about domestic human rights trials and establishing the ideational context for international criminal tribunals (2005: 22-24). However, as many Latin American human rights NGOs to which Sikkink refers were initially composed of the direct relatives of victims of state human rights abuses (Sikkink 1993: 425), the ejection of the Krajina Serb community in 1995 serves to explain the relative absence of local NGO pressure groups demanding the prosecution of Croats responsible for war crimes as the victims of state human rights abuses are no longer members of the domestic political community.

35 Although the term involuntary defection was used by Putnam to describe domestic non-state actors blocking adherence or ratification of an agreement on the part of a state (Putnam 1988: 438), the term involuntary defection is used here to describe elements of civil society acting to block, impede or attempt to dissuade compliance acts on the part of a state.

To the extent that civil society did engage in the war crimes debate, major segments of civil society were intensely hostile to ICTY investigations committed by members of the Croatian armed forces. The early mobilization of civil society against the ICTY had a significant long-term impact on the subsequent development of the Croatian NGO community as the public war crimes debate was monopolized by advocacy groups with close links to the HDZ. In fact, an official from the ICTY Outreach Office in Zagreb recalled that despite an attempt in 2005 to engage with veterans' organizations through a conference on war crimes, veterans' organizations declined to participate out of lingering distrust of the Tribunal.[36]

As with the impetus for the prosecution of war criminals, NGO campaigns demanding investigations of war crimes committed during the 1991-1995 war were initially the outcome of external rather than internal *stimuli*. In fact, Croatian Serb victims of human rights abuses directed their campaigns toward public opinion in Western Europe and North America rather than attempt to engage public opinion within Croatia.[37] Although a domestic human rights NGO community began to emerge in the 1990s, it remained highly dependent upon foreign sources of funding from donors such as the US and UK Embassies in Zagreb, the US Agency for International Development, the European Commission and the Open Society Institute.[38] Furthermore, foreign-funded NGOs encountered substantial obstacles to operating in-country. One such obstacle was the fact that Croatian civil society was dominated by organizations that were not consistent with traditional concepts of NGOs and instead were often organizations of a distinct ethno-nationalist hue (S. Fisher 2003: 74-92).[39] The relative strength of anti-ICTY NGOs, primarily Croatian war veterans' and war victims' organizations, was the result of a decade of almost exclusive access to state funding and the recent memory or effects of armed conflict. Because many anti-ICTY NGOs are of a distinctly illiberal orientation, there should be a clear distinction made between domestically funded war veterans' organizations and more traditional conceptions of NGOs. Moreover, because compliance models which rely upon domestic civil society as part of a causal chain such as the "boomerang pattern" and the "spiral model" isolate human rights NGOs, non-compliance pulls exerted by other elements of civil society remains to be explored.

36 Personal interview with member of staff of the ICTY Outreach Office in Zagreb, March 23, 2006.

37 For example, *Amnesty International* initiated an international campaign in December 2004 demanding justice for Croatian Serbs murdered in 1991.

38 Data regarding funding of human rights NGOs collected by author.

39 S. Fisher notes that a number of ethno-nationalist NGOs even participated in a 1998 joint United Nations' and Croatian government sponsored NGO fair in Zagreb, which attracted the suspected war criminal Tomislav Merčep and his entourage of armed bodyguards (2003: 80).

Although much smaller in terms of membership when compared with victims' and veterans' organizations, human rights organizations with a Zagreb presence have attempted to engage domestic opinion with regard to war crimes issues; however, they have been unable to alter compliance preferences. More recently the human rights group *Documenta* has focused on the need to confront the legacy of mass atrocity through legal means. *Documenta* monitors and reports on domestic war crimes trials, and engages with a wider regional network of human rights NGOs.

Despite the emergence of an embryonic human rights community, local human rights NGOs faced negative media framing of their efforts to initiate a dialogue on the recent past. The Croatian Helsinki Committee for Human Rights (*Hrvatski helsinški odbor za ljudska prava*, HHO) noted even after Tuđman's death in December 1999, media defamation of NGOs continued in the local press (Croatian Helsinki Committee 2004). Furthermore, the HHO also pointed to evidence of Tuđman-era state involvement in media campaigns against NGOs:

> Attacks against non-governmental organisations at the end of [19]99 … were part of the special intelligence service action known as "Chameleon". The activities were undertaken in order to defame NGO[s] and the … opposition as well as some international organisations such as NED (Croatian Helsinki Committee 2004).

The same report also described how the newsweekly *Fokus* framed the motives of foreign funded NGOs:

> The bearers of the red star always disguise their violence under the mask of culture, under which, as a terrible stench carried by the wind, they spread their pseudo-culture or the so-called alternative culture. How much noise they made … during HDZ rule in order to infiltrate their morbid, drunkenly, and homosexual intoxicated programs [into Croatia]. Large quantities of money of *UN-(known) origin* was spent on spreading of all kinds of human perversities through their performances, concerts, films and media (Croatian Helsinki Committee 2004).[40]

While internationally funded human rights NGOs found themselves subjects of media campaigns of disinformation, such as those described above, Croatian war veterans' and war victims' associations were transformed into financial clients of the governing HDZ (Zakošek 2002: 128). Thus, despite complying with ICTY arrest and surrender orders during the 1990s and engaging in norm affirming rhetoric, the Croatian government was not confronted with the emergence of domestic actors that could challenge non-compliance acts or preferences. More consequentially, when the Croatian government sought to comply with ICTY orders, the state was confronted by significant opposition from veterans' and

40 Emphasis added by author.

victims' groups that retained the ability to mobilize public opinion against a given compliance act.

When Sanader's government articulated its commitment to locate, arrest, and transfer Ante Gotovina to Tribunal custody, Sanader risked provoking a wave of public protest that ultimately led Račan to abandon cooperation with the ICTY. However, because Sanader presided over the HDZ, which maintained close links with mainstream veterans' groups, the HDZ was able to quell public protest. Moreover, Sanader carefully framed the pursuit of Gotovina as consistent with his party's efforts to defend Croatia's role in the 1991-1995 conflict. While in opposition, the HDZ argued that the most effective way to defend Croatia's conduct during the war was by taking to the streets against Račan and Mesić. Once back in power, Sanader argued that a courtroom showdown between the OTP and legal defense teams representing accused Croats was the most effective means by which to challenge ICTY indictments (Lamont 2009: 19-21).

## The International Politics of State Compliance

Absent domestic pressure to either investigate war crimes committed by Croatian forces or comply with ICTY orders, the extent to which the ICTY would be able to compel cooperation reflected by the level of pressure which the US and EU member states were prepared to apply upon Croatia (Lamont 2008a: 129-142). As a result, the domestic politics of ICTY indictments and transfer processes only served to delay, not prevent, transfers. There are four distinct phases of Croatian interaction with the ICTY that are identifiable by the leading role of either the US and later EU member states in inducing compliance. The first phase lasted from 1996 until 2000 and begins with Croatia's ratification of the Constitutional Law on Cooperation with the ICTY. During Phase 1 compliance with ICTY requests and orders was the outcome of the US' linkage of bilateral military and financial assistance to the transfer of individuals under ICTY indictment. The second phase begins with the election of Croatia's first post-Tuđman government in January 2000 and lasted until March 2005 when the European Council froze Croatia's EU accession process as a result of ICTY Chief Prosecutor Carla Del Ponte's negative assessment of Croatian cooperation with the Tribunal. During this phase ambiguous signals from the US and internal divisions among EU member states were followed by an almost complete breakdown in relations between Croatia and the ICTY. During Phase 2 Croatian elites were confronted with significant public protest against cooperation with the ICTY and gradually adopted a more intransigent position toward the transfer of individuals to The Hague. The third phase begins with the suspension of Croatia's EU accession process in March 2005 and concludes in December 2005. It was during Phase 3 that the arrest and transfer of the last Croatian citizen sought by the Tribunal for serious violations of IHL, Ante Gotovina, occurred. It was also during this period that the progression of Croatia's membership negotiations was linked to Zagreb's full cooperation with the ICTY, which was defined in terms of Gotovina's arrest and transfer to Tribunal custody. The fourth phase constitutes a return to non-cooperation. Croatia, no longer pressured to maintain full cooperation with the ICTY, failed to satisfy OTP requests for documents relating to Operation Storm during 2008. Significantly, the four phases described above illustrate varying state reactions to an evolving international political environment. When compliance benchmarks were clearly articulated, compliance was forthcoming. However, the high domestic costs associated with compliance meant that absent clearly articulated compliance benchmarks, non-cooperation would remain the preferred policy option of local elites.

### *Phase 1: Tuđman and the ICTY*

Despite the fact ICTY investigations, albeit at this point not indictments, targeted individuals within Tuđman's government, Peskin and Boduszysńki pointed out that, "Tuđman would be more forthcoming in handing over indicted war crimes suspects than would his democratic successors who pledged increased cooperation" (2003: 1124).[41] While it can be argued that Croatian compliance with ICTY orders during the 1990s was a reflection of the absence of ICTY indictments targeting regime elites, it should be noted that the ICTY also failed to indict Federal Republic of Yugoslavia regime elites until May 1999, yet Belgrade's recalcitrance proved significantly less malleable. Moreover, even though the ICTY's 19 indictments transmitted to the Croatian judiciary between 1995 and 1999 targeted members of the Bosnian Croat armed forces known as the Croatian Defense Council (*Hrvatska vijeće obrane*, HVO), during the war in Bosnia-Herzegovina there was little distinction between the HVO and the regular Croatian Army (*Hrvatska vojska*, HV). In fact, not only did Zagreb exercise effective command and control over the HVO, HVO officers could be promoted into the ranks of the HV itself.

### *The United States and the Coercive Model*

Compliance with ICTY orders which antagonized Tuđman's own regime elites can be explained by the dependency of the Tuđman regime upon US military, intelligence, and financial support both during and after the war in Croatia. Absent US pressure to transfer Bosnian Croat officers indicted by the ICTY, the Tribunal's orders would have remained unenforced by the Croatian state. During the 1990s, the US exercised significant leverage over Zagreb. In fact, as Croatia found itself isolated in Europe in the aftermath of Operation Storm, the close relationship Tuđman's government enjoyed with the US became increasingly important to a regime that feared international isolation.

---

41 This observation was made prior to the return of the HDZ to government in November 2003.

Because the US viewed the Croatian Army as a means by which the US could exert pressure on Bosnian Serb forces without direct US military involvement in Bosnia-Herzegovina (US Department of State 1995, Holbrooke 1999: 73), the US was prepared to provide Zagreb with substantial material support. Moreover, Camp Pleso, a military hospital, was established at Zagreb's international airport and quickly transformed into a hub for US logistical support activities in the region. Franjo Tuđman's son and former head of Croatia's intelligence services, Miroslav Tuđman, later described the relationship between Croatian and US intelligence services as a partnership in which the US provided Croatia with intelligence on Serb activities (Gutman and Barry 2001: 30).

As the conflict in Bosnia-Herzegovina intensified, the US began to assume a role in transforming the Croatian Army into an effective fighting force that could eventually end the war in Croatia and in neighboring Bosnia-Herzegovina (Gutman and Barry 2001: 30). US assistance proved vital in altering the balance of power on the ground between Croatian and Serb forces in the months immediately preceding the Dayton Peace Agreement. When the Croatian Army launched offensive military operations in 1995, US Foreign Service Officer Robert Frasure reminded the Clinton administration's chief negotiator Richard Holbrooke:

> We "hired" these guys [Croatia] to be our junkyard dogs because we were desperate. We need to try to "control" them. But this is not time to get squeamish about things. This is the first time the Serb wave has been reversed. That is essential for us to get stability, so we can get out (Holbrooke 1999: 73).

The extent to which US assistance described by Frasure proved effective was highlighted in a 2001 US Department of Defense commissioned report:

> In the space of 1 year, with the help of a US consulting firm, Military Professional Resources, Inc. (MPRI), with unusually strong political support from the top, and with adequate funding, the Croatians built a force that drove the Serbs out of their territory. They surprised not only their enemies but the rest of the world as well (Braddock and Chatham 2001: 21).

Furthermore, this same report suggests that the Croatian Army which "drove the Serbs out" was almost entirely the creation of MPRI: "Croatia's success was the result of exceptional circumstances including *not having an existing military* to resist changes that made for effective training" (Braddock and Chatham 2001: 21).[42]

The US was also cognizant of the fact ICTY investigations had been initiated against senior Croatian civilian and military officials for their conduct in military operations that prepared the ground for Dayton. Andrija Hebrang, a former minister of defense, recalled that US General Wesley Clark personally transmitted a warning to the Croatian government in 1998 that the ICTY had initiated investigations and

42 Emphasis added by author.

intended to issue indictments regarding war crimes committed by Croatian forces in 1995 (Hebrang 2005: 20).

A coercive model for cooperation emerged as the *modus operandi* for Croatian state interaction with the Tribunal in February 1996 when US Assistant Secretary of State for Human Rights John Shattuck first informed the Croatian government full cooperation with the ICTY was a pre-condition for future US military and political assistance. Compliance conditionality was also established in regard to US support for Croatian relations with the IMF, World Bank, and NATO's Partnership for Peace program (Granić 2005: 140).[43] Within two months of Shattuck's visit to Zagreb the Constitutional Law on Cooperation with the ICTY was adopted by the Croatian parliament.[44] While the threat of freezing relations had the desired effect of Croatian ratification of the Constitutional Law on Cooperation with the ICTY, it would require further inducements to bring about the actual transfer of Bosnian Croats indicted by the Tribunal. The transfers of accused persons required additional pressure by the US in the form of a renewed threat to block US-Croatian bilateral relations in the event the ICTY's most wanted Bosnian Croat fugitive, Dario Kordić, was not transferred to the ICTY.[45] After the US informed the Croatian government of the costs of non-compliance, Dario Kordić was transferred to The Hague (Granić 2005: 160). It was during Kordić's transfer to ICTY custody what former Croatian foreign minister Mate Granić described as a "coercive model" of cooperation with the ICTY crystallized. The coercive model of cooperation operated under the assumption that only external pressure was an effective means to bring about Croatian state cooperation with the ICTY (Granić 2005: 160).

The coercive model for cooperation is entirely dependent upon the willingness of external actors to impose costs upon recalcitrant states. While the US was prepared to exercise significant coercion to secure the transfers of Bosnian Croats to ICTY custody in 1996 and 1997, by 1998 the US proved significantly less

43 US compliance demands upon Croatia reflected the fact that the ICTY exercised an important function in US foreign policy toward to the former Yugoslavia in part because of the Tribunal's potential ability to marginalize recalcitrant nationalist politicians and military elites (Hazan 2004: 52). It was in 1994 that the US seconded 22 intelligence analysts and legal professionals to the ICTY, an act which was credited with giving the Tribunal a capability to begin investigations that could lead to indictments. With regard to the Tribunal's creation, the US actively began planning for an international criminal tribunal for the former Yugoslavia in 1992 when State Department officials from the Legal Advisors Office, the Bureau of Human Rights and Humanitarian Affairs, and the Bureau for European and Canadian Affairs were tasked with planning for an international court to prosecute war criminals in the former Yugoslavia (Western 2004: 228).

44 The Constitutional Law on Cooperation with the ICTY was ratified by the Croatian parliament on April 19, 1996.

45 Robert Gelbard informed Croatian Foreign Minister Mate Granić that the United States would freeze relations with Croatia if Dario Kordić along with other Bosnian Croats were not surrendered to the ICTY. Gelbard noted that should Tuđman comply, the US would remain a "reliable ally" of Croatia (Granić 2005: 160).

willing to coerce Croatian compliance. Given Zagreb's initial reaction to ICTY indictments against lower ranking Bosnian Croats, the US had reason to fear that subsequent indictments targeting senior officials within Tuđman's government could threaten US-Croatian relations, and more importantly the ability of the US to maintain its military presence in post-Dayton Bosnia-Herzegovina.[46] Although whether Washington acted to shield Zagreb from non-compliance costs during 1998 and 1999 remains unclear, it is of interest to note that following Croatia's refusal to transfer Natelilić in 1999 the US was portrayed by *Vjesnik*, a pro-government daily, as having behaved like "an ally" at the UNSC in assisting Croatia avoid international sanction for non-compliance with an ICTY arrest and surrender order (Vjesnik 1999).[47]

### *European Union Member States and the ICTY*

Meanwhile, throughout the 1990s, EU member states proved less able to influence Croatia's strategic behavior. Although the EU attempted to engage the newly independent Croatian state through an initiation of negotiations for a Cooperation Agreement in 1994, Croatia's Operation Storm resulted in the EU freezing further negotiations on the agreement (Office of European Integration 1999: 40).[48] The termination of negotiations for a Cooperation Agreement effectively ensured Croatia's exclusion from the EU accession processes until January 2000. An additional consequence of Operation Storm was that Croatia found itself excluded from the EU's PHARE program, but Croatia maintained its Autonomous Trade Agreement with the EU. Significantly for Zagreb, renewal of the Autonomous Trade Agreement was not linked to cooperation with the ICTY, while on the other hand economic assistance from the United States was in 1996 and 1997 linked to Croatia's fulfillment of ICTY arrest and surrender orders.

It is important to point out that while the US took an early interest in supporting the ICTY and was thus prepared to periodically exert considerable coercive pressure upon the Croatian government to comply with arrest and surrender orders, particularly from 1996-1997, EU member states were initially highly skeptical of the Tribunal. European skepticism was exacerbated in June 1994, when the US seconded 22 specialists to the Tribunal which included Defense Department

46 The US military not only maintained a "national support element" in Croatia but also utilized Croatian ports on the Adriatic to support US troop deployments in Bosnia-Herzegovina. The US military also utilized supply routes across northern and central Croatia. For more on Croatia's supporting role in Operation Joint Endeavor see Fontaine 1997-1998.

47 Before Croatian non-compliance was to be reported to the UN, US ambassador to Croatia, William Montgomery, held a consultative meeting with Mate Granić, Croatia's foreign minister (Vjesnik 1999).

48 The EU-Croatian Cooperation Agreement was modeled on the 1993 EU-Slovene Cooperation Agreement, which marked the first step toward Slovenia's EU accession.

and CIA analysts along with legal professionals. Although the seconded personnel provided the ICTY with the capability to conduct investigations and produce indictments, in private EU member states expressed a hostile response to this overt act of US support for the Tribunal. Former ICTY spokesperson Christian Chartier was warned by an unnamed Western European diplomat, "This is unacceptable. Your Tribunal is infiltrated by the CIA!" And, former ICTY president Judge Antonio Cassese recalled European governments asking, "Why are you accepting all these Americans?" (quoted in Hazan 2004: 53). Skepticism of the Tribunal in Western European capitals reflected Europe's priority being the restoration and maintenance of peace in the former Yugoslavia, and not the pursuit for alleged war criminals.[49]

### *Phase 2: Challenging the Tribunal*

As previously mentioned, Tuđman's death and the subsequent triumph of opposition parties in both parliamentary and presidential elections held in January 2000 was initially welcomed as an opportunity for Croatia to intensify cooperation with the ICTY. The end of single party HDZ governance and the election of a six party coalition led by the SDP resulted in a dramatic reorientation of Croatian foreign policy, which for the first time since independence prioritized accession to the EU (On the Accession of the Republic of Croatia 2002). Zagreb's formal pursuit of EU membership meant that the EU could exert new-found leverage in the form of conditionality, which was unavailable to the EU during Tuđman's authoritarian presidency. However, Račan's government's expectation of rapid integration into the EU, similar to that of Slovakia following the electoral defeat of the authoritarian Mečiar in parliamentary elections in 1998, was quickly diminished. EU member state ratification of the Stability and Association Agreement (SAA), which was signed in May 2001, proved to be a much slower process than Zagreb initially expected.[50] Moreover, the EU transmitted ambiguous signals regarding the costs of non-compliance with ICTY orders from July 2001 to March 2005 because of significant internal divisions among member states regarding the extent to which Croatian membership negotiations should be effected by non-compliance with the orders of a non-EU institution.[51] The UK government proved most critical of Croatian non-compliance and observed, "Croatia has failed to respect and honour

49 For more on European efforts to end the war in the former Yugoslavia see Chapter 3.

50 Although the SAA was ratified by Croatia in October 2001, the ratification process was not completed by EU member states until February 2005.

51 States which argued for EU membership to be linked with cooperation with the ICTY included the United Kingdom, the Netherlands, Denmark and Sweden. The above states refused to ratify Croatia's SAA following Račan's refusal to transfer Janko Bobetko, whereas Central European states such as Austria and later the new Eastern European member states argued that compliance with ICTY orders should not be linked to Croatia's pursuit of EU membership. Personal Interview, March 24, 2006.

its regional and international commitments to co-operate fully with the ICTY" (Foreign and Commonwealth Office 2003: 167). Croatian non-compliance resulted in the UK suspending parliamentary ratification of Croatia's SAA. Meanwhile, following the UK decision to suspend SAA ratification, German Chancellor Gerhard Schroeder, offered strong support for Croatia's membership bid without even mentioning the Bobetko crisis (Croatian Government 2003).

*Enforcement Ambiguity and Non-Compliance*

Ambiguous signals transmitted from EU member states regarding the costs of non-compliance (Massari 2005: 268-269) were followed by an almost complete breakdown in relations between Croatia and the Tribunal. Croatia's rejection of the Bobetko indictment, which the Račan government described as "...legally and politically unacceptable to the Republic of Croatia..." (OSCE 2002a), marked a new low point in Croatia-ICTY relations. Absent the clear threat of sanction, which compelled Croatian cooperation with the ICTY in 1996 and 1997, Croatian elites began to rhetorically defend Croats indicted for war crimes for domestic political gain. Although it had been clearly articulated Croatia's invitation to join the NATO alliance was contingent upon full cooperation with the ICTY,[52] the US too was unwilling to effectively coerce Croatia's post-Tuđman elites into compliance. Furthermore, unlike Serbia, Croatia did not face the prospect of securing annual certification of being in full cooperation with the ICTY on the part of the US Secretary of State.[53]

Although Bobetko's death in April 2003 brought an end to the immediate crisis, Croatia's continuing failure to cooperate with the Tribunal led the UK to adopt a stance that would eventually be accepted by other EU member states. This was the clear linkage between EU membership and cooperation with the Tribunal agreed to among EU member states at the December 2004 European Council.[54] The UK had previously argued, "if Croatia wishes to show full respect for the rule of international law and highlight its commitment to European values and standards ..., the government must resume full cooperation [with the Tribunal] as soon as possible" (Foreign and Commonwealth Office 2003: 168). In fact, in March 2003, it was the growing threat of EU sanction that led the Račan government to present

52 In 2002, a report issued by a NATO parliamentary assembly meeting in Istanbul condemned Croatia's failure to transfer Bobetko to the ICTY (Salihbegović and Trkanjec 2002), and at the 2004 NATO summit in Istanbul, Croatia's invitation to join the NATO alliance was linked to full cooperation with the ICTY (*Istanbul Summit Communiqué* 2004).

53 See the *Foreign Operations, Export Financing and Related Programs Appropriations Act 2006, Section 563.*

54 At the December 2004 European Council the onset of Croatia's accession negotiations were directly linked to "full cooperation" with the ICTY (European Council 2004).

Bobetko's lawyers with the ICTY indictment, an act the government had previously rejected. Račan's direct challenge to the ICTY led one Western diplomat to lament, "it is not even necessary to extradite Bobetko to The Hague, but it is important that [Račan] accepts the competency of the tribunal and receives the indictment."[55] In other words, it was more important that Croatia continue to engage in norm affirming rhetoric than actually carry out its legal obligations toward the Tribunal. Here, it is argued that while EU internal divisions encouraged non-compliance with the Bobetko arrest and surrender order, it was also the undermining of the normative underpinning of international justice by the US Bush administration through its aggressive pursuit of an Article 98 agreement to exempt US citizens from transfer to the International Criminal Court that transmitted an unintended signal to Croatian elites that cooperation with international criminal tribunals was after all an optional regime.

*Article 98: Contradictory Norms?*

The opposition of the US to the ICC in the early 2000s created uncertainty amongst Croatian policymakers as to whether the US would continue to support the work of the ICTY.[56] In fact, as a result of the American Servicemember's Protection Act, Croatia found itself subject to the loss of military assistance from the US because of its failure to conclude an Article 98 agreement with the US, and not because of Croatian non-cooperation with the ICTY. Although not directly related to the issue of cooperation with the ICTY, ratification of an Article 98 agreement was viewed as intrinsically linked to Croatian defiance of the ICTY because they both related to questions of state obligations to cooperate with international judicial bodies. Furthermore, the US appeared to undermine the legitimacy of international war crimes trials when US Ambassador to Croatia, Ralph Frank, declared before an audience of Zagreb University students, "We believe that war crimes cases should be tried by the affected countries themselves, when possible, not by a new international court" (Frank 2004). Although Frank pointed out that because the ICTY was a Chapter VII creation of the UNSC and not established through a multilateral treaty, Croatia remained obligated to cooperate with the Tribunal, statements such as "the United States is not a signatory to that treaty [the Rome Statute]. And I point out that neither Russia nor China is a signatory either, if you think we are alone on that" (2004) introduced contradictory norms into the compliance debate. As the Bobetko crisis erupted concurrent to US demands for Croatia's ratification of an Article 98 agreement, compliance with arrest and surrender orders from an international tribunal was increasingly perceived as

55 Quoted in Hedl 2002.

56 Personal interview, March 24, 2006. Moreover, in an interview with the Croatian daily *Vjesnik*, US Ambassador to Croatia, Ralph Frank publicly denied speculation that in return for Croatia's signing of an Article 98 agreement with Washington, the US would "forget" Croatia's outstanding obligations toward the ICTY (Lopandić 2004).

voluntary response to material incentives rather than a binding obligation under international law.

*Phase 3: Compliance*

In November 2003 the return to power of Tuđman's HDZ under the leadership of Ivo Sanader marked the beginning of a period of rapprochement between the Tribunal and the Croatian state. Despite Sanader's robust rhetorical support for individuals indicted by the ICTY (Sanader 2001: 121), Croatia's EU accession was increasingly threatened by the linkage of cooperation with the ICTY to the launch of formal membership negotiations. Although the new HDZ government signaled an increased willingness to cooperate with the Tribunal after the European Council conditioned the start of Croatian accession negotiations on full cooperation with the ICTY in December 2004, it was not until March 2005 that attempts to locate Gotovina acquired the urgency necessary to bring about an arrest. March 2005 was significant because it was at this time EU membership negotiations were scheduled to begin; however, as a result of a negative assessment of Croatian cooperation on the part of the ICTY's OTP, negotiations were indefinitely postponed until Croatia was certified by the Tribunal as being in full cooperation.[57]

It must be pointed out that it is impossible to overstate the impact of EU conditionality on transforming the relationship between the Tribunal and the Croatian state. After the EU's cancellation of membership negotiations, Croatian intelligence services began to closely monitor Gotovina's relatives in Croatia in an attempt to locate the fugitive general,[58] and on October 3, 2005 ICTY Chief Prosecutor Carla Del Ponte informed the EU General Affairs and External Relations Council that Croatia was in full cooperation with the Tribunal after having received assurances from Zagreb that Ante Gotovina had been located in Spain. Del Ponte's assessment of Croatian cooperation permitted the Council to approve the onset of Croatia's accession negotiations (European Council 2005b). However, it should be emphasized that Croatia's pursuit of EU membership and cooperation with the ICTY were contingent upon a pre-existing elite consensus that favored rapid integration into Euro-Atlantic institutions.

57 At the December 2004 meeting of the European Council, the Council agreed on opening accession negotiations with Croatia on March 17, 2005 "provided that there is full cooperation with the ICTY." On March 16, 2005 the General Affairs and External Relations Council (GAERC) determined that EU accession negotiations with Croatia should be postponed until Croatia was deemed as being in full cooperation with the ICTY (European Commission 2005: 3).

58 Gotovina's location was revealed through electronic surveillance of communication between the accused and his wife, who remained in Croatia (Kočić 2007).

*Phase 4: Where are the Documents?*

In 2008, after the commencement of the Gotovina trial in The Hague, Zagreb was once again alleged by the OTP to have violated its obligations to assist the Tribunal in securing access to evidence. In June 2008, the OTP requested the Trial Chamber hearing the Gotovina case order Croatia to produce evidence demanded in its Artillery Document Request. The Trial Chamber in turn ordered Croatia to "intensify and broaden" its investigation into the whereabouts of the requested documents and to provide any documents discovered to the prosecution (Order in Relation to the Prosecution's Application 2008). However, unlike in 2005, when the ICTY's effort to secure a single individual was supported by the EU, which established a compliance benchmark linked to the transfer of Gotovina, in 2008 the Tribunal was engaged in an effort to secure access to documents that Zagreb claimed did not exist. Thus, despite making reference to Croatia's failure to produce evidence requested in the prosecution's Artillery Document Request in its report to the United Nations Security Council (Report of the International Tribunal 2008), the dispute between Zagreb and the OTP did not result in European Union intervention. Instead, the European Commission's 2008 *Accession Progress Report* took note of Croatia's failure to produce the artillery documents and requested the Croatian state undertake an investigation into the whereabouts of these documents without articulating the consequences of non-compliance (European Commission 2008: 15). In 2009 ICTY Chief Prosecutor Serge Brammertz noted that despite question Croatian cooperation in relation to OTP access to missing documents, it remained a question for the EU to, "...decide about the political weight to give the assessments we are making" (MacDonald 2009).

## Conclusions

Although Croatia's transfer of individuals indicted by the ICTY provides strong support for rationalist approaches to compliance, a closer examination of Croatia's interaction with the Tribunal raises the question of why Croatian elites engaged in international justice norm affirming rhetoric in the absence of domestic mobilization to support international war crimes trials during the 1990s. Zagreb even provided diplomatic support for the creation of a permanent international court throughout the late 1990s concurrent to its legal challenge to the ICTY's jurisdiction over Operation Storm. Even though the gap between norm affirmation and compliance was only closed by third party enforcement agents, Zagreb's pursuit of membership in a wide range of international organizations meant that Croatia was also prepared to accept a wide range of international human rights commitments as a price for membership into the international community.

The liberal focus on explaining compliance outcomes through an exploration of endogenous constraints suggests Croatia would have maintained a policy preference for non-compliance unless external incentives or disincentives altered the domestic cost-benefit equilibrium facing domestic elites. The reinforcement of non-compliance preferences by societal actors illustrates the importance of understanding limitations to government autonomy in bringing about compliance outcomes in an issue area as salient as war crimes. However, while domestic incentive structures serve to explain the time lag between the certification of Tribunal indictments and the actual transfer of war crimes suspects, transfers were brought about through external intervention on the part of third party enforcement agents.

An elite consensus that favored rapid integration into Euro-Atlantic institutions allowed the EU, on the principle of conditionality, to secure Croatian compliance with ICTY orders only after internal divisions between member states were overcome, and the EU clearly articulated the linkage between cooperation with the ICTY and EU membership. Within months of the EU freezing Croatia's accession process, Ante Gotovina was transferred to ICTY custody. In the case of Janko Bobetko, Croatia's rejection of an ICTY order was a response to ambiguous signals regarding the costs of non-compliance from the EU and a perception that US foreign policy no longer prioritized cooperation with international criminal tribunals. In sum, Croatia demonstrates that when confronted with non-compliance on the part of a state seeking entry into international organizations and the maintenance of strategic relationships with third party states that are prepared to take enforcement action in support of an international criminal court, rationalist enforcement mechanisms can prove effective in altering non-compliant behavior. However, as the 2008 dispute between Zagreb and the OTP pertaining to the provision of evidence illustrates, cooperation will only continue as long as third party enforcement agents remain willing to impose costs upon defiant states.

# Chapter 3
# Serbia: The Politics of Denial

## Introduction[1]

On February 26, 2007 the International Court of Justice (ICJ) delivered its judgment in the case of *Bosnia-Herzegovina v. Serbia and Montenegro* and found Serbia[2] "...failed in its duty to co-operate fully with the International Criminal Tribunal for the former Yugoslavia...," and emphasized, "this failure constitutes a violation by [Serbia] of its duties as part of the Dayton agreement, and as a Member of the United Nations, and accordingly a violation of its obligations under Article VI of the Genocide Convention" (*Bosnia-Herzegovina v. Serbia and Montenegro* 2007: 161).[3] The ICJ's judgment in *Bosnia-Herzegovina v. Serbia and Montenegro* highlighted what was a decade and a half long record of non-compliance on the

1 Parts of Chapter 3 previously appeared in Christopher Lamont "Contested Sovereignty: The International Politics of Regime Change in the Federal Republic of Yugoslavia" *Journal of Communist Studies and Transition Politics*, 25(2/3), 2009, 181-198.

2 Before exploring Serbia's interaction with the ICTY, it must be noted that the former Yugoslav republic of Serbia, has undergone substantial transformation during the first 15 years that followed the 1991 collapse of the Socialist Federal Republic of Yugoslavia (*Socijalistička federativna republika Jugoslavjia*, SFRJ) and did not acquire an international legal identity as an independent state until 2006. Between 1991 until 2006 Serbia transitioned from being a constituent republic within the SFRJ to a constituent republic within the SRJ and then to a constituent republic within the State Union of Serbia and Montenegro (*Državna zajednica Srbija i Crna Gora*, SiCG) before becoming an independent state, the Republic of Serbia. Despite Serbia's former status as a constituent republic within the SRJ and later the SiCG, the focus of this study will be on the Republic of Serbia itself. This is because the Republic of Serbia dominated the SRJ, in which Montenegro functioned as Serbia's junior partner until Montenegrin president Milo Đukanović broke with the Milošević regime in 1997. After Đukanović's break with Milošević, Montenegro became a *de facto* independent state and adopted an independent foreign and economic policy. In fact, the ICTY published separate assessments of compliance for Montenegro and Serbia while both were member republics of the SRJ and later the SiCG. For the purpose of clarity Serbian foreign policy will be referenced by Belgrade's international legal identity during the period of time in question. Thus, when exploring Serbian foreign policy from 1992 until 2002, the actor referenced will be the SRJ, while from 2002 until 2006 the actor will be referenced as SiCG. From 2006 to present, the actor referenced will be Serbia.

3 Bosnia-Herzegovina filed suit against Serbia and Montenegro for violating the Genocide Convention in 1993. After hearing oral arguments from representatives of Bosnia-Herzegovina and Serbia and Montenegro, the International Court of Justice found that Serbia violated its obligations under the Genocide Convention to prevent genocide

part of multiple Belgrade governments. Moreover, the ICJ judgment, which found Serbia's failure to cooperate with the ICTY not only to be a breach of the Dayton agreement and multiple UNSC resolutions but also a breach of the Genocide Convention, failed to bring about Serbia's "full cooperation" with the Tribunal.

Given Serbia's record of non-cooperation, this chapter will explore both the domestic and international politics of Serbian state cooperation with the ICTY as a narrow focus on international politics offers only a partial picture of Serbia's troubled relationship with the Tribunal. This chapter will begin with a discussion of the politics of state legitimation, which will highlight Serbia's foreign policy divergence from other successor states of the former Yugoslavia. Belgrade neither secured international recognition for the newly established Federal Republic of Yugoslavia (*Savezna republika Jugoslavija*, SRJ),[4] nor demonstrated an aversion to international sanction.[5] Second, there will be an exploration of the domestic politics of compliance, which will be followed by an examination of the role of civil society and transnational advocacy networks in order to assess the impact of non-state societal actors on compliance decisions. Next, there will be a discussion of the international dimension of Serbia's troubled relationship with the ICTY. Here, it will be noted attempts at conflict resolution on the part of the Contact Group, which brought about the 1995 Dayton agreement and the 1999 Rambouillet agreement, led to an abandonment of attempts to coerce Serbian compliance with ICTY arrest and surrender orders so as not to antagonize the Milošević regime (Williams and Scharf 2002: 202). Coercion was, however, utilized by the United States and European Union member states against post-Milošević Serbian governments from 2000 until 2007 with limited success. Finally, this chapter will seek to explain why coercion, coupled with incentives that proved effective in bringing about Croatian compliance with ICTY Article 29 obligations, failed to produce a similar outcome in Serbia. After all, it was the linkage of EU accession to cooperation with the Tribunal that brought about the arrest of Croatian general Ante Gotovina in December 2005, yet a similar linkage failed to compel Serbia to surrender Ratko Mladić.

---

in Srebrenica and by failing to cooperate with the International Criminal Tribunal for the former Yugoslavia (*Bosnia-Herzegovina v. Serbia and Montenegro* 2007).

4 Dušan Lazić noted that as of 1999 the SRJ was not a full member of any major political, economic or financial organization including, but not limited to, the UN, the OSCE, the Council of Europe, the IMF, the World Bank, the WTO or Interpol (1999). In fact, the SRJ only gained admittance to the United Nations as a member state in November 2000 (see United Nations General Assembly Resolution A/RES/55/12, 2000).

5 The inability of a series of UNSC resolutions (UNSC Resolutions 757, 787 and 820) which imposed a trade embargo upon the SRJ to have a discernible impact on Belgrade's war in Bosnia is just one example of a lack of aversion to international sanction. Pevehouse and Goldstein provide additional support for this observation in a time series study which revealed "...Serbian actions toward Kosovo were not affected by international actions toward Serbia" (1999: 538-546).

## Domestic Politics and Compliance

Unlike Croatia, which saw new elites assume power preceding the collapse of the Yugoslav federal state, Serbia experienced regime continuity from 1987, when Slobodan Milošević assumed control of the League of Communists of Serbia (*Savez komunista Srbije*, SKS), until October 5, 2000. The ability of the Milošević regime to survive a crisis in legitimacy, which proved lethal to the League of Communists' hold on power in neighboring Yugoslav republics, was attributed to Serbian nationalist grievances being incorporated into SKS ideology through a campaign that de-legitimized the Titoist ethno-federal division of the Yugoslav state creating an illusion of regime change despite continued SKS rule (Malešević 2002: 188-189, Vladisavljević 2002). Milošević's transformation of the SKS into the Socialist Party of Serbia (*Socijalistička partija Srbije*, SPS), an ethno-nationalist populist political party, effectively destabilized nascent opposition political movements and secured regime survival in multi-party elections held in 1990. Although the subsequent outbreak of war and deepening ethnification of Serbian politics and society have been well documented elsewhere (Cohen 2002: 102-133, Gordy 1999, Pavlaković 2005: 13-54, Ramet 2005: 125-142), Belgrade's rejection of the emerging post-cold war regional consensus which favored economic and political integration into Euro-Atlantic and international organizations requires further discussion.

### *State Legitimation*

Domestic regime continuity was reflected in SRJ foreign policy as Belgrade claimed inheritance of the international legal identity of the SFRJ (Aćimović 1994: 413-424, Kreća 1994: 399-412, Libal 1997: 138-139) and maintained ties with non-aligned bloc countries in the UN General Assembly (Granić 2005: 47).[6] Belgrade's claim to SFRJ continuity meant that Belgrade was absent from campaigns led by Croatia and Slovenia, which were often described during 1991 as rebel republics,[7] to gain international recognition and membership in

---

6 The SFRJ was one of the founding members of the non-aligned bloc of countries, and Belgrade hosted the first Non-Aligned Movement summit in 1961. Moreover, Petković noted Belgrade enjoyed strong support amongst Non-Aligned Movement member states at a ministerial summit held in 1991. Once the war in Bosnia-Herzegovina erupted, divisions emerged within the Non-Aligned Movement as predominately Muslim states advocated a harsher line against Belgrade. At the movement's Jakarta summit, Belgrade was described to have been in the "doghouse." Nonetheless, at Jakarta, the Non-Aligned Movement did not debate the Yugoslav crisis out of a fear that such a debate would divide the Movement between Muslim and non-Muslim states (Petković 1992: 7-8).

7 Take for example, the title of an article that appeared in *The New York Times*, "Conflict in Yugoslavia: Yugoslavia's Army Issues Ultimatum to Rebel Republic," on June 30, 1991 (Tagliabue 1991: 1).

international organizations.[8] Although Badinter Commission explicitly rejected Belgrade's claim to SFRJ continuity and deemed the SRJ to be a new state (Libal 1997: 138-139), the SRJ remained unwilling concede the question of continuity. The SRJ continued to claim inheritance of the legal identity of the SFRJ because international recognition of continuity was perceived to strengthen Belgrade's claim that the conflicts in Croatia and Bosnia-Herzegovina constituted civil wars as opposed to international conflicts (Aćimović 1994: 415, Libal 1997: 139). Moreover, Michael Libal, former head of the Southeast European Department in the German Foreign Ministry, suggested Belgrade hoped an acceptance of SFRJ continuity would retroactively invalidate the Badinter Commission, thus removing the legal basis for the recognition of Yugoslavia's successor states (1997: 139). Nevertheless, the prospect for the actual recognition of SRJ-SFRJ continuity was virtually non-existent as UNSC Resolution 757 rejected Belgrade's claim to SFRJ continuity and UN General Assembly Resolution 47/1 rejected the SRJ's claim to inherit the membership status of the SFRJ and went on to state the SRJ must apply for membership as a new UN member state (Kreća 1994: 399-412).[9]

### *The Domestic Politics of International Institutions*

Although Croatia and Slovenia's campaigns for recognition met with significant resistance from the United Kingdom and France, Germany's declaration of an intention to unilaterally recognize the two republics (Crawford 1995: 1-34) meant that during the course of 1992 Bosnia-Herzegovina, Croatia and Slovenia would secure international recognition and eventual acceptance into the UN as member states.[10] While all three republics sought integration into international organizations, Croatia in particular perceived membership in international organizations as both a reaffirmation of independence and a means of securing state survival (Granić 2005: 11-46, 153).[11] The SRJ, on the other hand, prioritized the establishment of *ad hoc* bilateral relations outside the context of international organizations (Lazić 1999). Moreover, rather than attempt to negotiate membership into international organizations,[12] the SRJ embarked on a campaign to de-legitimize existing institutions, from which Belgrade found itself excluded, through its

8 For more on Croatian efforts to secure international recognition and membership in international organizations see Granić 2005.

9 Belgrade did not to apply for United Nations membership as a new member state until after the collapse of Milošević's regime in October 2000.

10 Macedonia faced significantly greater difficulty gaining international recognition as a result of a Greek diplomatic campaign against the use of the geographic term Macedonia in the official name of the new state. See Chapter 4.

11 Libal argued that during 1991, when Croatian armed forces were suffering losses at the hands of the Yugoslav National Army, Zagreb sought to secure an internationalization of the conflict in the former Yugoslavia (1997: 38), while Belgrade characterized the conflict as an internal matter.

12 See footnote 3.

claim international organizations represented a threat to SRJ state sovereignty. International organizations, according to the SPS' 1992 party program, "openly engage in the internal affairs of sovereign states in opposition to the general principal of sovereign state [UN] member non-interference..." (Socialist Party of Serbia 1992). More sinisterly, international organizations were characterized as being part of a "New World Order" of "imperialist character" that sought to secure the "...domination of the West over the East and South" (Socialist Party of Serbia 1992). The SPS' challenging of the emerging post-cold war neo-liberal economic consensus was even utilized as a means of contextualizing the intra-Yugoslav conflict unfolding in the early 1990s. Take for example Milošević's closing statement at the first party congress of the SPS:

> The crisis facing Yugoslavia, which is exposed to the pressure of conservative and disintegrative forces, as well as the presence of such forces in Serbia herself, have made it necessary and justified to bring together socialist, i.e. left-wing forces, ideas and people in order to preserve peace and secure progress and social development. Peace and economic and cultural progress, the fruits of which will be equally enjoyed by all citizens, are the essence of our new party's commitment at this moment. Our longer-term commitment is to create a society without economic exploitation and without political hierarchy (1990).

Examined in the context of SPS party ideology, it is perhaps not surprising to note that Serbia and Montenegro were the only former Yugoslav republics to oppose the very establishment of the ICTY in 1993. The SRJ rejected UNSC Resolution 827, which established the ICTY, on the basis that the UNSC's actions violated the principle of state sovereignty (Kerr 2004: 37). Interestingly, however, in a letter transmitted to the United Nations Secretary General and the President of the UNSC, the SRJ sounded a conciliatory note by expressing a willingness to prosecute its own citizens responsible for serious violations of International Humanitarian Law before national courts (Vukasović 1994: 12). Once the ICTY was established, it is worth noting the SRJ's rejection of legally binding commitments to comply with UNSC Resolution 827 violated Article 16 of the Constitution of the SRJ, which automatically incorporated international law into domestic legislation (Fatić 2002: 67). This contradiction, needless to say, did not have an impact on SRJ policy toward the Tribunal as the domestic judiciary functioned as an appendage of the Milošević regime.

From 1996 to 1997, there was a brief rapprochement between the SRJ and the European Union during which time the SRJ was granted autonomous trade preferences by EU member states (Janjević 1999: 5). In fact, during this period of time, SRJ deputy foreign minister Radoslav Bulajić argued for the SRJ's reintegration into the global economy and Yugoslav membership into the World Trade Organization and the International Monetary Fund (1997: 7). However, the intensification of violence in Kosovo in 1998 resulted in the EU revoking its trade agreement and imposing a robust trade sanctions regime upon the SRJ which included the freezing of SRJ assets in EU member states (Janjević 1999: 5). In response, Belgrade negotiated an alternative preferential trade agreement with Moscow and sought integration into an undefined Russian led union with Belarus (Jovanović 1999-2000: 26-31).

*State Legitimation and Identity*

Even after the collapse of Milošević's authoritarian regime in October 2000, and the launch of EU efforts to integrate Belgrade into its Stability and Association Pact for Southeastern Europe, many Serbian elites continued to view international institutions with hostility and presented building closer ties with Russia as an alternative to EU integration. Vojislav Šešelj, the head of the Serbian Radical Party, which in 2007 was Serbia's largest parliamentary political party, perceived Serbia to be a "defender" of Russian interests in Southeastern Europe. Take for example Šešelj's description of Serbia's relationship with the Russian Federation, "Serbia tirelessly defends the fatherland. And Russia sleeps. We also defend Russia and at the same time try to awaken her" (Šešelj 2006). The SRS party program also presented an alternative foreign policy orientation which envisaged Serbia building closer ties with Russia, China, Japan, India along with "Arab states" and the "states of South America" (Serbian Radical Party 2001). As the SRS remained the largest single parliamentary political party from 2000 to 2007, there could be no political consensus in support of integration into the European Union along the lines of the broad cross party consensus for rapid integration into Euro-Atlantic institutions that emerged in post-Tuđman Croatia.[13]

*State Legitimation and Ethnicity*

An exploration of domestic legitimation must also take into account that throughout the 1990s a single ethnic community, namely ethnic Serbs, monopolized control over all state organs at the expense of sizable domestic ethnic minorities. The exclusion of domestic minorities from political life during the 1990s resulted in the construction of national or state interests along exclusively ethnic lines, hence the campaign to establish an ethnically defined Greater Serbia.[14] An illuminating example can be found in a comparison of the 1990 SPS party program, which

13 After Kosovo's February 2008 declaration of independence, Belgrade sought to forestall Kosovo's recognition as an independent state. Although the EU has not linked Serbia's accession process to recognition of Kosovo's independence, the EU's role in providing assistance to Kosovo's post-independence political institutions through EULEX has introduced a complicating factor in EU-Serbian relations.

14 Trust in the ICTY is much higher amongst Serbia's ethnic minorities than amongst ethnic Serbs (Institute for Social Sciences 2004: 12). This was potentially significant as according to the last pre-war census conducted in 1991 ethnic Serbs only comprised 66 percent of the total population of the Republic of Serbia. Ethnic Albanians comprised

committed the party to acting to secure continuity of the socialist system and acting to block Serbia's integration into the international economy, to the Second Congress of the SPS, which framed the conflict in Yugoslavia as an inter-ethnic conflict. The SPS party program adopted at the Second Congress did not disguise a commitment to create a Greater Serbia and promised to take into consideration the concerns of Serbs in Croatia and Bosnia-Herzegovina and secure their "right" to be territorially integrated into the SRJ (Socialist Party of Serbia 1992).

The ethnification of politics also undermined the norm of international justice. It is of interest to note that six years after the collapse of the Milošević regime, ICTY Chief Prosecutor Carla Del Ponte argued that the very concept of the rule of law remained alien to Serbian political culture (B92 2006). Del Ponte's observation is reinforced by Obradović who noted in 1994:

> However, outside the circle of specialists in this field, in the broader public opinion, these obligations of the state, their scope and the reasons for their establishment, are not always completely clear. This is particularly the case within the better part of public opinion in the FR Yugoslavia, where, ... the prevailing understanding is that since Serbs have been attacked by Croats and Muslims and are "biologically endangered" as they say – all means for their defense are permitted, and therefore, ... it is superfluous to discuss responsibility for war crimes. And it is particularly superfluous and unjust for this responsibility to be discussed by the International Tribunal (1994: 24).

Ethno-nationalist mobilization not only resulted in norms of justice being exclusively applied to "biologically endangered" Serbs, but undermined the rule of law within the SRJ. In addition, Milošević's consolidation of power in the 1990s completely undermined even the appearance of constitutionalism. When exploring the foreign policy of the SRJ, it is important to note that Milošević dominated the foreign policymaking process while occupying the office of president of Serbia, despite a constitutional division of powers, which delegated control over foreign policy to the federal structures of the SRJ.[15]

---

Serbia's largest ethnic minority at 17 percent of the population, followed by ethnic Hungarians representing 3.5 percent of the population (Republic of Serbia Census 1991).

15 Although Milošević occupied the office of president of Serbia from 1990 until 1997, and president of Yugoslavia from 1997 until 2000, Milošević's power did not derive from a constitutional division of powers between the two offices but rather from extra-institutional bases of support that crystallized around the regime in the 1990s. Thus, from 1990-1997 the Yugoslav presidency was a largely ceremonial office, while actual power was exercised by the Serbian president; however, from 1997 to 2000, this arrangement was reversed. Significantly, this *ad hoc* and extralegal foreign policy-making process would return to haunt Milošević. It was the Republic of Serbia which transferred him to the ICTY in contravention of SRJ law which explicitly reserved questions of extradition to the federal and not republican governments (Fatić 2002: 69).

*The Domestic Politics of Compliance 1993-2000*

In 1993 the SRJ robustly opposed the very establishment of the ICTY on the grounds the Tribunal Statute violated SRJ state sovereignty (Kerr 2004: 37). Although as a signatory to the 1995 Dayton agreement Milošević accepted an obligation to cooperate with the Tribunal, the SRJ failed to comply with ICTY orders throughout the 1990s.[16] Despite this failure to cooperate with the Tribunal, Milošević was rewarded for acting as a peace-broker at Dayton through the removal of UN economic sanctions imposed during the wars in Croatia and Bosnia-Herzegovina (Williams and Scharf 2002: 164-167). Absent any significant external or domestic demand for cooperation with the Tribunal, Milošević was able to effectively ignore the existence of ICTY indictments against SRJ citizens.[17] The result was not a single ICTY annual report from 1996 until the collapse of the Milošević regime in 2000 found SRJ cooperation with the Tribunal to be satisfactory. The Tribunal was unable to challenge Serbian non-compliance and in the words of the 1999 ICTY annual report to the UNSC, "for a considerable period of time, the international community failed to respond adequately to the challenges to its authority by the Federal Republic of Yugoslavia" (Report of the International Tribunal 1999: 26). Although the international politics of compliance will be discussed in detail shortly, at this point it should be noted that SRJ non-compliance with Article 29 obligations resulted in multiple referrals of Belgrade to the UNSC. In response to one such referral the UNSC adopted Resolution 1207 in November 1998, which demanded the SRJ's "immediate and unconditional execution" of ICTY arrest orders, but did not include any form of punitive measures in the event Belgrade ignored the Security Council's demands. Despite an intensive campaign by the OTP to highlight SRJ non-cooperation, in 1999 the ICTY reported:

> None of these demands brought any concrete improvement in the attitude or behaviour of the Federal Republic of Yugoslavia and none was supported by effective action to compel such change until the situation in Kosovo had deteriorated dramatically (Report of the International Tribunal 1999: 27).

The ICTY would have to wait until a change in regime was brought about in the SRJ before any realistic attempt at securing the transfer of ICTY indictees could be made.

---

16 An exception to this would be the transfers of Dražen Erdemović and Radoslav Kremenović to ICTY custody in March 1996 for questioning by the OTP over Srebrenica (ICTY 1996). However, as Erdemović had not (yet) been indicted at the time of his transfer to The Hague, and Kremenović was remanded back to the SRJ, Milošević was able to claim this act did not constitute a precedent for future cooperation (G.J. Bass 2002: 256).

17 The first three SRJ citizens indicted by the ICTY were Mile Mrkšić, Miroslav Radić, and Veselin Šljivančanin, who were indicted for grave breaches of the Geneva Conventions, war crimes and crimes against humanity on October 26, 1995.

Nevertheless, during 1996 there were two transfers from the SRJ to Tribunal custody. Because the SRJ's rejection the ICTY's claim to exercise jurisdiction over the territory of the SRJ was reinforced by the position of the domestic judiciary, which considered the transfer of an SRJ citizen to the ICTY to be an unconstitutional act, Belgrade faced significant difficulties in publicly explaining the transfers of Dražen Erdemović and Radoslav Kremenović.[18] Therefore, when these compliance acts occurred they were characterized as *sui generis* events. For example, when Erdemović and Kremenović were transferred to ICTY custody, their lack of SRJ citizenship was said to provide the legal basis for the transfer.[19] The need for Belgrade to articulate a legal basis for the transfer of these individuals that did not take into account the Tribunal Statute illustrates the extent to which non-compliant behavior was internalized as legitimate within the SRJ. Moreover, the internalization of the norm of state sovereignty, as articulated in the foreign ministry's legal challenge to the ICTY, restricted the scope for compliance on the part of Serbia's post-Milošević elites in the aftermath of the collapse of the Milošević regime in October 2000.[20]

While the events surrounding the Kosovo conflict will be discussed in greater detail shortly, here it will be noted that the escalation of violence in Kosovo during 1998 once again made Milošević the focus of international efforts to contain violent conflict in the former Yugoslavia and the Tribunal's efforts to secure cooperation from the SRJ were largely ignored by Contact Group member states. Concurrent to efforts to find a negotiated settlement to the Kosovo crisis, the United States and the United Kingdom worked to build a consensus within NATO for the use of force against the SRJ should efforts to secure a negotiated settlement over Kosovo fail (Williams and Scharf 2002: 183-184). The subsequent indictment of Milošević by the Tribunal during NATO's Operation Allied Force brought an abrupt end to Tribunal access to the SRJ. In the aftermath of NATO's air campaign,

18 Dražen Erdemović and Radoslav Kremenović were former members of the Bosnian Serb armed forces who contacted Western media, in particular *ABC News*, during 1996 with details of the Srebrenica massacre. Erdemović confessed to taking part in the massacre on the direct orders of superiors (Engelberg 1996). Both Erdemović and Kremenović expressed a preference to voluntarily surrender to ICTY custody; however they were arrested by SRJ authorities on March 2, 1996 for crimes committed in Srebrenica. An official of the US Embassy in Belgrade at the time expressed a fear that Erdemović and Kremenović were arrested so as to prevent their surrender to ICTY custody (Engelberg 1996). However, on March 30, 1996 the SRJ transferred the two war crimes suspects to the Tribunal.

19 One of the more creative rationalizations offered for Erdemović's transfer to the ICTY was that he was "on lend" from the SRJ to the ICTY and thus his presence in The Hague was not tantamount to an extradition (Čičić 1996). And, as previously mentioned, the fact the Erdemović and Kremenović transfers preceded their indictments by the ICTY, Belgrade was able to argue the transfers were not precedent setting.

20 Polling data from the *Belgrade Center for Human Rights* indicated that from 2003-2005 an average of just 15.6 percent of the population supported cooperation with the ICTY because cooperation would be "just."

the ICTY was referred to by the SRJ's foreign minister as a "NATO Tribunal" and was characterized as being an instrument of US foreign policy (Jovanović 1999-2000: 29). Interestingly, while Belgrade attempted to de-legitimize the ICTY, the SRJ filed suit against NATO member states at the International Court of Justice (ICJ), charging alliance members with having committed the crime of genocide (Jovanović 1999-2000: 29). Before the ICJ dismissed Belgrade's suit, the SRJ's foreign minister argued that unlike the ICTY, which was characterized by Belgrade as a political court, the ICJ was a legitimate forum in which a state could seek "justice" (Jovanović 1999-2000: 29).

*Domestic Politics of Compliance 2000-2006*

Despite the initial optimism that followed the collapse of Milošević's government in October 2000, a change in domestic regime type did not bring about an immediate change in state policy toward the Tribunal.[21] The dimming prospects of regime change having a transformative effect on Belgrade's non-cooperation with the ICTY were highlighted in March 2001 by Morton Abramowitz in testimony given before the US Senate Subcommittee on European Affairs. Abramowitz testified:

> Belgrade has yet to detain and transfer a single indictee to the Hague Tribunal. It has plagued the work of the Tribunal's Belgrade office with bureaucratic obstacles. And President Koštunica's hostile public statements have left no doubt about his attitude toward cooperation with the Tribunal in general, and the effort to have Milošević face charges in the Hague in particular. Earlier this week, one indictee did go the Hague – a Bosnian Serb of dual nationality – and Mr. Koštunica's government was eager to emphasize that his surrender was "voluntary" and entailed no change in policy. I think we should take them at their word (2001: 13).

Although Milošević was surrendered to the ICTY within months of Abramowitz's testimony, overall cooperation between the Tribunal and the SRJ was deemed at these hearings to be identical to pre-1998 levels (Bang Jensen 2001: 19). In fact, Milošević's 2001 transfer to the ICTY was the outcome of external coercion which produced a domestic political contest between the Yugoslav president Vojislav Koštunica and Serbian prime minister, Zoran Đinđić. No political consensus in favor of cooperation with the ICTY emerged from the Milošević transfer as illustrated by the fact that Milošević's surrender to the Tribunal was not immediately followed by the transfer of other senior SRJ citizens under ICTY

21 The Milošević-era president of the Republic of Serbia, Milan Milutinović was indicted by the ICTY along with Milošević in 1999. Milutinović remained in office as president of Serbia after the collapse of the Milošević regime creating a situation whereby the new reformist government was tasked with bringing about cooperation with the ICTY while Milutonović occupied the Serbian presidency.

indictment.[22] Moreover, a legal framework for the transfer of accused persons to ICTY was not established because Milošević's transfer was affected by the Republic of Serbia as oppose to the SRJ (Fatić 2002: 69).

*Understanding the Domestic Politics of Non-Compliance after Milošević*

Although post-authoritarian elites in both Serbia and Croatia confronted substantial populist opposition to compliance with ICTY orders, the domestic political environment in Croatia proved more favorable toward compliance for four reasons. First, in regard to Croatia, Sanader's reform of the post-authoritarian Croatian Democratic Union meant that the radical right was left without an anti-system parliamentary political party that could electorally benefit from populist appeals for non-compliance with Article 29 obligations or attempt to utilize parliamentary procedure to obstruct compliance. As a result, a clear parliamentary consensus in favor of cooperation with the ICTY was more easily negotiated in the Croatian parliament given the fact that as of November 2003 not one major political party actively opposed Croatian state compliance,[23] whereas in Serbia there remained a significant anti-ICTY parliamentary bloc. In Croatia there also existed a clear parliamentary consensus in support of EU accession. Therefore, once compliance with Article 29 obligations and EU accession were explicitly linked by the European Council in December 2004, residual parliamentary opposition to cooperation with the Tribunal evaporated.

Second, in the Croatian context, ICTY indictments were much fewer in number and never targeted civilian political elites, i.e. the leaders of major political parties, former presidents, and government ministers. Therefore, Croatian Prime Minister Ivo Sanader and President Stjepan Mesić could dismiss any link between the indictments against Croatian military personal and the overall legitimacy of military campaigns undertaken by the *ancien regime*. In Serbia, however, indictments were certified not only against former presidents, ministers, and military elites, but also the leader of an opposition political party, Vojislav Šešelj, making any attempt to localize guilt around individuals much more difficult than in Croatia. Also, by targeting civilian and military elites of the SRJ, and not just regime surrogates, ICTY indictments threatened not only indicted individuals, but large segments of the SRJ ruling elite. As a result in post-Milošević Serbia, compliance with ICTY orders proved highly polarizing within the Serbian parliament. Delegates from

22 It will be noted in an exploration of the international politics of compliance that the domestic power contest between the Yugoslav president and Serbian prime minister was itself precipitated by intense United States coercive pressure to surrender Milošević to the ICTY.

23 Even the Croatian Party of Rights, which experienced significant internal turmoil that resulted in the expulsion of a number of senior members, only expressed muted opposition to ICTY indictments against Croatian Army officer when compared to previous years.

the SRS and the SPS openly questioned Serbian obligations *vis à vis* the Tribunal. Furthermore, parties which supported state cooperation with the ICTY, such as Zoran Đinđić's Democratic Party (*Demokratska stranka*, DS), only did so for pragmatic reasons such as gaining international financial assistance or normalizing Serbia's relationship with the European Union and the United States.[24]

In the aftermath of October 2000 entrenched elites in Belgrade sought to maintain a policy of non-compliance with Tribunal orders. These elites stretched from Milošević-era military appointees such as Nebojša Pavković, who remained head of the Yugoslav Army until 2002, to the SRJ's first post-Milošević president, Vojislav Koštunica. Against this backdrop, Serbia's republican government led by Prime Minister Đinđić sought to fulfill outstanding obligations to the Tribunal as a means of bringing the SRJ closer to the European Union. However, because Koštunica occupied the SRJ presidency, Đinđić was forced to secure Milošević's transfer to The Hague extra-judicially (Fatić 2002: 69). From the office of the Yugoslav presidency, Koštunica was able to obstruct cooperation with the ICTY through his power base among recalcitrant nationalists in the Yugoslav Army and the Supreme Defense Council.[25] Meanwhile, Đinđić attempted to construct a support base within the Republic of Serbia's Ministry of the Interior (Edmunds 2003: 29). Although Đinđić supported SRJ fulfillment of ICTY obligations and the transfer of all individuals under ICTY indictment to The Hague, the continued presence of Milošević-era regime associates within Serbia's security services ultimately brought about Đinđić's assassination in an operation code-named *Stop The Hague* (CSCEb 2003: 12).

Third, during the Milošević-era, legislation enabling cooperation with the ICTY, such as Croatia's 1996 Constitutional Law on Cooperation with the ICTY, was not ratified leaving the very question of state obligations to comply with Article 29 obligations the subject of domestic political debate amongst post-authoritarian elites. Because Croatia established a legal framework for compliance, Croatia's post-Tuđman elites inherited a domestic legal regime that favored compliance.[26] In contrast, the Serbian parliament's May 2002 adoption legislation establishing a domestic legal framework for cooperation with the ICTY even included a clause

24 The only notable exception was the Liberal Democratic Party, which entered parliament in January 2007, and advocated cooperation with the Tribunal in order to "change Serbia's image." Personal interview with Andrej Nosov of the Youth Initiative for Human Rights, Belgrade, January 23, 2007.

25 The Yugoslav Army appeared to have been effective in shielding one of the ICTY's most wanted war crimes suspects, Ratko Mladić from arrest in the years following the collapse of the Milošević regime in October 2000. For a period of time preceding May 2002, Ratko Mladić was alleged to have been housed at the behest of the Yugoslav Supreme Defense Council in Yugoslav Army barracks near Belgrade (Wood 2006).

26 Although a legal regime for compliance was created, in practice ICTY indictments were responded to by the Croatian state on an *ad hoc* basis. See Chapter 2.

denying the ICTY jurisdiction over indictments issued by the Tribunal after the entry into force of the Law on Cooperation with the ICTY.[27]

Fourth, organized crime's penetration of state security services amplified the ability of recalcitrant civil servants and the security services to obstruct compliance. After all, during the 1990s Serbian elites did not cultivate formal institutional structures, buttressed by an independent judiciary, but rather relied upon informal personal relationships with the state security apparatus and organized crime. The latter moved overtly into the political process during the second half of the 1990s as underworld figures formed political parties and contested elections. One of these figures included Milošević's wife, Mirjana Marković, who established her own political party, the Yugoslav United Left (*Jugoslovenska udružena levica*, JUL), which was essentially a vehicle for the facilitation of criminal activities that ranged from embezzlement to murder (Palariat 2001: 911-912, Sekelj 2000: 62). Furthermore, the notorious paramilitary figure Željko Ražnjatović established a political party known as the Party of Serbian Unity. The nexus between politics and organized crime resulted in the Serbian political environment becoming an increasingly violent forum as the assassinations of former Serbian President Ivan Stambolić, Prime Minister Zoran Đinđić, and assassination attempts against prominent opposition politician Vuk Drašković serve to illustrate.[28]

### *Pragmatic Compliance*

Rather than symbolize an acknowledgement of Serbia's legally binding obligations to cooperate with the Tribunal, arrests and transfers of ICTY suspects from 2000-2003 occurred in the context of a domestic power contests between elements of the new regime loyál to Zoran Đinđić and elements of the *ancien regime* that retained influence and control over state security services. The assassination of Zoran Đinđić in March 2003 occurred in the context of this power struggle and was followed by the arrest and transfer of individuals to ICTY custody on the part of the Serbian government. It was after Đinđić's assassination that the Serbian government requested the ICTY bring forward the indictments of former Milošević-era security chiefs Franko Simatović and Jovica Stanišić (CSCEa 2003: 6). However, rather than interpreting the Simatović and Stanišić's transfers as a compliance act, it is important to point out that Belgrade merely took advantage of an opportunity to do away with the two individuals who constituted a threat to

27 Article 39 of the Yugoslav Law on Cooperation with the ICTY stated that any individual indicted by the Tribunal subsequent to the entry into force of the Law on Cooperation with the ICTY would be tried by the domestic courts violated the primacy clause of the ICTY Statute. In April 2003, the Law was subsequently amended to confirm ICTY jurisdiction over all war crimes cases.

28 The list of public figures extends far beyond the examples noted above and includes government ministers, police officials, *nouveau riche* business elites, and regime affiliated criminals (Branković 2002: 211-212).

the post-Đinđić government under Zoran Živković. The manipulation of the ICTY for domestic political purposes led Bang-Jensen to conclude, "…no pattern of cooperation with the Tribunal ever emerged even after war crimes suspects began to arrive from Serbia in The Hague" (CSCEb 2003: 6). Eric Witte of the Coalition for International Justice also pointed out that as late as 2003, there was almost no attempt to conceal non-compliance on the part of Belgrade, and even Ljubiša Beara, who was publicly indicted by the ICTY in 2002, maintained his entry in the local telephone directory (CSCEb 2003: 14).

Although non-compliance did not end with the Milošević regime, there has been an effort on the part of post-Milošević governments to encourage voluntary surrenders following Koštunica's brief marginalization from 2002-2004. After the establishment of the State Union of Serbia and Montenegro, the federal presidency was substantially weakened leading Koštunica to focus his attention on securing the late Zoran Đinđić's office of Serbian prime minister.[29] With Koštunica temporarily out of office and Pavković removed as head of the armed forces in 2002, ICTY suspects began to "voluntarily surrender" to ICTY custody at the encouragement of the Serbian government. While the Croatian government proved willing to arrest ICTY fugitives on its territory who were hidden by elements loyal to the *ancien regime* such as Ivica Rajić, the Serbian government sought to encourage voluntary surrenders and, with the notable exceptions of Slobodan Milošević, Franko Simatović, Jovica Stanišić, Zdravko Tolimir, and Radovan Karadžić, sought to avoid transferring suspects to Tribunal custody against their will, or at least absent the appearance the accused's transfer was voluntary. In fact, after Koštunica's electoral triumph in 2004 parliamentary elections, his party emphatically declared, "…arrests were not an option for the Democratic Party of Serbia" (Holliday 2005: 2). The necessity for transfers to the Tribunal to appear to be voluntary stems from the ICTY's lack of popular legitimacy within Serbia, which will be explored in greater detail below. This absence of legitimacy limits the effectiveness of external coercion as successive Belgrade governments argue the domestic costs of compliance prevent the state from carrying out arrest and transfer operations (Holliday 2005: 1-5).

## International Justice and Civil Society

As in Croatia, the impetus for the prosecution of domestic elites and the members the local armed forces was almost completely external. Despite episodes of anti-Milošević social protest in 1991, 1996 and 2000, Serbian civil society largely failed to mobilize public opinion in support of the prosecution of SRJ nationals suspected of serious violations of IHL. It must also be emphasized there were significant barriers to advocacy groups either domestic or international from directly engaging with Serbian public opinion because the domestic media reinforced the

29 Koštunica became prime minister of the Republic of Serbia following parliamentary elections held in 2004.

perception of Serb victimhood during wars waged by Belgrade across the former Yugoslavia.[30] In fact, when asked to compare Serb victimization to that of other ethnic groups within the former Yugoslavia, 81 percent of respondents believed Serbs were the most victimized ethnic group during the conflict in the former Yugoslavia (Belgrade Center for Human Rights 2005). Although the media's role in reinforcing the perception of Serb victimization during the conflict in the former Yugoslavia has been well documented elsewhere (D.B. McDonald 2002), it should be noted that many of the same journalists who engaged in spreading hate speech through the media under Milošević have been rehabilitated in post-Milošević Serbia.[31]

Moreover, in post-Milošević Serbia, Serbia's largest parliamentary political party, the SRS, utilized both the traditional media and the Internet to remind the electorate of atrocities perpetrated against ethnic Serbs. In fact, on the SRS website a link was provided to video footage of atrocities committed by Croats and Bosnian Muslims against Serb populations in Bosnia-Herzegovina and Croatia.[32] In addition, as of August 2006, the official website of the Serbian Government included a highly detailed study of "Albanian Terrorism and Organized Crime in Kosovo-Metohija," which attempted to link the Kosovo Liberation Army to Al Qaeda (Serbian Government 2003: 26-29). Rather than confront the legacy of Serbian state involvement in the conflicts that followed the collapse of the Yugoslavia, successive governments have been engaged in a campaign to gather evidence of war crimes committed by other warring parties in order to de-legitimize proceedings against indicted Serbs before the ICTY. For example, in 2005, Serbian Prime Minister Vojslav Koštunica declared that Serbs had been the victims of "the greatest ethnic cleansing after the Second World War" as a result of Croatia's 1995 Operation Storm (Serbian Government 2005). Furthermore, during government sponsored commemorations of the Operation Storm, Serbian officials failed to mention that the ICTY indicted three Croatian Army generals for their part in the Operation.[33]

### *The ICTY and Transnational Advocacy Networks*

Negative perceptions of the ICTY remained persistent in the years following the collapse of the Milošević regime and were symptomatic of the Tribunal's failure to directly engage with public opinion in Serbia. It should be noted that during

---

30 Polling data collected by the *Belgrade Center for Human Rights* affirms this observation (2005).

31 Personal interview with Andrej Nosov of the *Youth Initiative for Human Rights* in Belgrade, January 23, 2007.

32 The short film *Istina* [Truth] was available for download on the Serbian Radical Party's official website as of 2006: [www.srs.org.yu].

33 Personal interview with Alexandra Milenov of the ICTY field office in Belgrade, January 23, 2007.

the 1990s the ICTY invested minimal effort in engaging with Serbian public opinion, in contrast to substantial effort invested by the Tribunal in engagement with North American and Western European media.[34] As mentioned in Chapter 2 the Tribunal failed to initiate outreach programs until 1998 and it was not until 1999 that the Tribunal employed staff able to answer reporters' questions in Serbo-Croatian.[35] The failure of the Tribunal to effectively engage in outreach activities may have damaged the ICTY's ability to mobilize public support for international war crimes trials especially as the above described victim-centered propaganda went unchallenged. However, it is impossible to empirically test whether or not Tribunal outreach during the 1990s would have had a transformative effect on public opinion given the fact local media was for the most part monopolized by regime surrogates.

As previously noted, Keck and Sikkink's "boomerang pattern" depends on local civil society acting to mobilize transnational civil society. Absent local mobilization, the causal pathway identified by Keck and Sikkink lacks a crucial antecedent condition (1998: 13). The failure to mobilize social protest within Serbia itself may serve as a more plausible explanation for the absence of a domestic justice constituency than Obradović's 1994 observation that Serbs find international tribunals particularly unjust. After all, during the 1990s Serbian elites often appealed to human rights norms despite their widespread violation. Even Slobodan Milošević attempted to legitimize the actions of the SRJ through appeals to human rights. In a 1991 speech to the Serbian parliament, Milošević declared, "If the human rights of Albanians really were threatened in Kosovo-Metohija, we certainly would not hesitate to protect them" (1991).[36] Moreover, it was Belgrade that made one of the earliest appeals to the 1948 Genocide Convention during the wars in the former Yugoslavia. A 1992 Yugoslav Government memorandum noted:

> … we regret to inform the Organization of the United Nations, … that Croatian authorities and their paramilitary and illegal armed forces have committed, in 1991 and early 1992, for the second time in the past 50 years, the crime of genocide against the Serbian people in Croatia (Memorandum of the Government of Yugoslavia 1992).

---

34 In the ICTY's 1995 annual report to the UNSC the Tribunal included a section on "The Tribunal and World Public Opinion," which detailed coverage of the ICTY by major Western news outlets, such as *The New York Times* and *Le Monde*, while including only a single paragraph on "sporadic" contact with media based in Belgrade and Zagreb (Report of the International Tribunal 1995: 36-40).

35 Personal interview with Alexandra Milenov of the ICTY field office in Belgrade, January 23, 2007.

36 Of course Milošević's norm affirming rhetoric was inconsistent with the conduct of Serbian security forces, which were involved in a brutal campaign of repression of in Kosovo that followed the revocation of Kosovo's status as an autonomous province.

The 1992 Memorandum also appealed to United Nations member states to take action against perpetrators of genocide, although it stopped short of explicitly calling for the creation of an international criminal tribunal (Memorandum of the Government of Yugoslavia 1992).

Belgrade's appeals to norms of human rights suggest Belgrade sought to avoid being seen as violating human rights norms, even at the height of the Bosnian and Croatian wars. Polling data accumulated by the Belgrade Center for Human Rights confirms respondents accept the statement "a war criminal is a criminal regardless of nationality" (2005). Thus, although the percentage of Serbian citizens who agree with the statement "a war criminal is a criminal regardless of nationality" decreased from 84 to 73 percent from 2004 to 2005, the percentage of Serbs who either completely agree or mostly agree with the above statement represent an overwhelming majority of respondents (Belgrade Center for Human Rights 2005).

In Serbia the ICTY faced significant challenges from the domestic media and elements of civil society. The impetus for the establishment of the Tribunal was external and did not emerge from the demands of local civil society.[37] Furthermore, media hostility toward the Tribunal throughout the 1990s created an environment in which war crimes committed by non-Serbs were profiled in the domestic media in an attempt to de-legitimize Tribunal indictments and proceedings against Serbs. In response to these challenges, ICTY outreach efforts in Serbia, while more substantial than those that existed in Croatia, remained largely inadequate as a means of transforming public opinion in part because international actors favored rationalist methods of bringing about compliance over normative engagement.[38]

### *Civil Society: Human Rights NGOs and the Ethno-Nationalization of Civil Society*

There was almost no domestic pressure from civil society to investigate war crimes committed by Serb forces during the conflicts in the former Yugoslavia and the impetus for war crimes investigations and prosecutions was largely external.[39] In explaining the relative lack of a domestic demand for international justice, Alexandra Milenov of the ICTY Belgrade Field Office noted that the

37 This is despite the fact that ICTY proceedings have included trials against individuals accused of war crimes committed against Serbs, see for example the Haradinaj *et al.*, Orić and Gotovina *et al.*, trials.

38 It should also be noted international actors at times even contributed to Serbian perceptions that war crimes had not been perpetrated by Serbs. In fact, genocide denial by international actors such as US Secretary of State Warren Christopher's statements denying the actions of Serb forces constituted genocide were directly incorporated into domestic war propaganda (Williams and Waller 2002: 839).

39 The Humanitarian Law Center and the Helsinki Committee are examples of NGOs which have demanded the investigation of war crimes perpetrated by Serb forces and the prosecution of perpetrators.

failure to establish an Outreach Office in the early years of the Tribunal was a serious error and believed contact with local NGOs to be an important element of the Tribunal's work in the region.[40] The ICTY Office in Belgrade maintained contacts with both domestic human rights groups and victims organizations. Although human rights organizations which focus on war crimes committed by Serb forces are few in number, they include the Humanitarian Law Center, the Belgrade Center for Human Rights, Youth Initiative for Human Rights, and the Women in Black. Activists from the Youth Initiative for Human Rights and Women and Black have been subjected to violent intimidation by nationalist organizations such as Obraz. Moreover, seven years after the collapse of the Milošević regime, the Humanitarian Law Center noted that rather than act to protect human rights activists, state security organs continue to view human rights activists as enemies of the state (Humanitarian Law Center 2007).

Although anti-war groups emerged in the 1990s, such as the Women in Black, anti-regime mobilization was stunted in the 1980s. Bieber observed human rights organizations were subsumed by groups that focused on the defense of national or collective rights over individual human rights such as the Kosovo Serb movement (2003: 83). In fact, Slobodan Milošević's rise to power in the SKS was the result of Milošević's receptivity to the demands of what was essentially a civil society grassroots movement of Kosovo Serbs (Vladisavljević 2002). On the other hand, non-nationalist civil society was largely marginalized in the early- to mid-1990s (Bieber 2003: 83). Additionally, the attribution of the collapse of the October 2000 Milošević regime to civil society movements should not be interpreted as a signal that a non-nationalist civil society has become increasingly robust in post-Milošević Serbia. In fact, as Bieber points out, the *Otpor* movement, credited with bringing down the Milošević regime, destroyed its own *raison d'être* through its success because the organization was highly dependent upon foreign sources of funding, which was for the most part discontinued after October 2000 (2003: 87). Thus, in post-Milošević Serbia, as in post-Tuđman Croatia, civil society was unable to mobilize social protest against state non-compliance decisions, and instead, anti-ICTY advocacy groups dominated the domestic compliance debate.

## The International Politics of Compliance

Absent a domestic preference for compliance or domestic social protest that could serve to alter pre-existing preferences of local elites, the extent to which Belgrade cooperated with the ICTY would be dictated largely by external variables. However, unlike Croatia, external coercion and incentives proved far

---

40 Personal interview with Alexandra Milenov of the ICTY field office, Belgrade, January 23, 2007.

less effective in transforming Serbian state preferences during the period of time under examination. In the words of Serbian military analyst Aleksander Radić:

> For many years Serbia's relationship with The Hague was characterized by Serbia's presumption it could maneuver its way around the condition of arresting Mladic … This has been one of the greatest follies of the Serbian government because time has shown that the West won't change its position. There is also a lot of interest inside Serbia among powerful people to protect Mladic (*Russia Today* 2009).

As will be noted shortly, despite third party enforcement agents having secured the transfer of a number of high profile Serbian war crimes suspects, at the time of writing Ratko Mladić remained at large. Before an attempt is made to draw conclusions regarding why external material incentives and disincentives proved less effective in altering state behavior in the case of Serbia the international political context in which Belgrade interacted with the ICTY must first be established.

### *Phase 1: From Pariah State to Peace Partner*

The now infamous images of concentration camps established by Bosnian Serbs at Omarska and Keraterm broadcast worldwide during 1992 had a transformative effect on how the international community perceived the war in Bosnia-Herzegovina and eventually shocked the United Nations Security Council into adopting Resolution 827 in 1993.[41] Yet despite the fact the establishment of the ICTY was brought about in response to war crimes perpetrated by Serb forces during the conflict in Bosnia-Herzegovina (Kerr 2004: 34), the Milošević regime never faced substantial coercive pressure to comply with ICTY orders. At the time of the Tribunal's creation, the Bosnian war was at its height and the priority of international diplomacy in the region was to bring the conflict to an end rather than support the work of the Tribunal (Gow 1997, Williams and Waller 2002).[42] The ICTY's efforts to secure custody of Radovan Karadžić and Ratko Mladić, who were both indicted in July 1995, were further complicated by the fact that the Tribunal was viewed as a threat to peace in the region by international mediators, such as Cyrus Vance and David Owen, who were attempting to broker an end to the war (Williams and Waller 2002: 843). Matias Hellman of the ICTY Registry recalled many states that supported Resolution 827 never expected the court to

41 Croatian foreign minister Mate Granić explained how images of Serb-run concentration camps emerging from Bosnia had a transformative effect on perception of Belgrade in the international community (Granić 2005: 72).

42 Matias Hellman also noted that in the early years the Tribunal struggled to survive as an institution as many states that supported the creation of the Tribunal did not expect the ICTY to actually function. Personal interview with Matias Hellman of the ICTY field office in Sarajevo, January 16, 2007.

function as anything more than a "paper tiger."[43] And, as if in confirmation of Hellman's observation, war crimes suspects on the territory of the SRJ were granted *de facto* immunity from ICTY indictments after international mediators rejected attempts by the Bosnian delegation at Dayton to include the SRJ in a robust ICTY compliance regime that would have included the re-imposition of economic sanctions should the Tribunal determine Belgrade was in non-compliance (Williams and Scharf 2002: 163).

The *de facto* immunity granted at Dayton to ICTY accused residing in the SRJ began to take shape in early 1995, when the United States adopted what was referred to as the "Milošević strategy," which entailed a lifting of economic sanctions against the SRJ in return for Milošević pressuring the Bosnian Serb leadership into accepting a peace agreement (G.J. Bass 2002: 232).[44] The perceived need to engage the Milošević regime in order to bring about an end to the Bosnian war led to the almost complete marginalization of the ICTY in 1995 (Williams and Scharf 2002: 161-166). Even before 1995, Milošević was perceived in Europe as moderate within the Serbian political spectrum and as an important player in any potential peace settlement, which explains the hostile response in European capitals to a 1994 attempt by the US to give the ICTY the investigative capability necessary to begin issuing indictments (Hazan 2004: 53).[45] Despite Milošević's role in the initiation of violent conflicts in Croatia and Bosnia-Herzegovina, the summer of 1995 brought about an acceptance that Milošević's SRJ must be accommodated in any peace settlement even if this meant keeping Mladić and Karadžić out of ICTY custody. The extent to which Milošević was embraced as a peacemaker in the former Yugoslavia cannot be overstated. Silber observed:

> Just three years after Secretary of State Lawrence Eagleburger had named Milosevic a suspected war criminal, the Serbian president was in Dayton being praised as a peacemaker. When the Dayton Agreement was signed in September in Paris, President Bill Clinton applauded Milosevic and shook his hand. As Clinton said, quoting the late Israeli prime minister Yitzhak Rabin, "You cannot

43 Personal interview with Matias Hellman of the ICTY field office in Sarajevo, January 16, 2007.

44 The pragmatic need to engage with the SRJ despite earlier declarations by US officials that Slobodan Milošević was a "war criminal" stemmed from the belief that because previous attempts to negotiate directly with the Bosnian Serb leadership under Radovan Karadžić ended in failure, the most effective way to bring about an immediate end to hostilities was to bypass the Bosnian Serb leadership and negotiate directly with Belgrade (G.J. Bass 2002: 232; W. Bass 1998: 101). W. Bass emphasized the key role Milošević played in forcing Bosnian Serb elites to acquiesce to Dayton by noting that for the Bosnian Serbs the Dayton agreement represented an imposed peace (1998: 102).

45 For more on the reaction of Western European states to US assistance to the ICTY in 1994 see Chapter 2.

> negotiate peace only with friends." Washington, with its newly formed Balkan pragmatism, had met its match in Milosevic (Silber 1996: 63-64).

At Dayton, Milošević agreed to the US brokered peace agreement and the UN sanctions regime against the SRJ was dropped. Absent the diplomatic backing of either the United States or European Union member states, the ICTY could not independently sanction non-compliance on the part of Belgrade. As mentioned in Chapter 1 the only institutional mechanism through which the Tribunal could request sanction was through referral to the UNSC. The UNSC in turn could take any measure under Article 41, short of the use of force, or invoke Article 42, for the use of force against a non-compliant state (Kerr 2004: 138). However, it must be pointed out that punitive action has never been taken by the Security Council against non-compliant states.

Although the Dayton agreement obliged the states of the former Yugoslavia to cooperate with the ICTY, a clear signal was transmitted by international mediators that the removal of sanctions would not be linked to cooperation with the Tribunal. In fact, the European Union's representative at Dayton, Carl Bildt, made clear war crimes conditionality would not be part of any post-Dayton order by warning the Bosnian Muslim delegation not to even mention war criminals during the course of peace negotiations (G.J. Bass 2002: 242). Moreover, although the ICTY indicted three SRJ citizens for the 1991 Vukovar hospital massacre, Mile Mrkšić, Miroslav Radić, and Veselin Šljivančanin, there was no attempt by European Union member states to pressure Belgrade into transferring the three accused to The Hague (G.J. Bass 2002: 242). Quite the opposite, non-compliance was rewarded when the European Union extended an Autonomous Trade Preference regime to the SRJ absent a commitment to cooperate with the ICTY on the part of the Milošević government.[46] The result of the above described international concessions to Belgrade was a period of SRJ economic growth that saw the US dollar value of SRJ foreign trade increase by 42 percent between 1996 and 1998 (OECD 2003: 23). Meanwhile, in neighboring Bosnia-Herzegovina, NATO reaffirmed the international community's *laissez faire* approach to international criminal law enforcement. NATO's first commander in Bosnia, Admiral Leighton Smith, appeared on Bosnian Serb television to reassure Radovan Karadžić and Ratko Mladić that NATO, "did not have the authority to arrest anybody" (W. Bass 1998: 107). Further underlining NATO's commitment not to enforce ICTY arrest orders, a NATO spokesperson explained to Bosnian Serbs that IFOR, "…is not a police force and will not undertake police duties" (Meštrović 1997: 23).[47]

---

46 Nosov compared the EU's embrace of Koštunica in 2006 as a pro-European reformer to that of the EU's embrace of Milošević in 1996 as a regional peacemaker. Personal interview in Belgrade, January 23, 2007.

47 For more on NATO's failure to arrest individuals indicted by the ICTY during 1996 and the first half of 1997 see Chapter 5.

*Phase 2: The Kosovo Crisis and War with the West*

Events in Kosovo during 1998 and 1999 transformed the relationship between the ICTY, the United States, European Union member states, and the SRJ. At Rambouillet, the international community brought together representatives of the SRJ and Kosovar Albanians in an attempt to secure a negotiated settlement to the increasingly violent conflict in Kosovo. While Kosovar Albanians pushed for the inclusion of a binding ICTY compliance regime into the Rambouillet agreement,[48] the Serbian delegation redlined any mention of the ICTY. For the most part, international mediators at Rambouillet sided with Belgrade and only permitted the inclusion of existing obligations to cooperate with the Tribunal into the final agreement (Williams and Scharf 2002: 196-201). Williams and Scharf observed:

> ... the delegates ... seemed to be under the impression that the Serbian government did not intend meaningful cooperation with the Yugoslav Tribunal no matter which provisions were included in the accords, and thus it was unnecessary and inconvenient to propose such specific principles that would give the Serbian delegation an opportunity to object to the accords (2002: 202).

Belgrade did not need this opportunity to object to the agreement. The SRJ abandoned Rambouillet on the grounds Belgrade could not accept a NATO led mission within its borders.[49]

The failure of the parties to come to an agreement at Rambouillet marked the beginning of NATO's Operation Allied Force. The initiation of hostilities in March 1999 and the subsequent indictment of Slobodan Milošević in May 1999 by the ICTY crystallized a policy of regime change that was supported by both the United States and European Union member states (Albright 2003: 502, Williams and Scharf 2002: 207). The indictment of Slobodan Milošević along with the SRJ military high command during Operation Allied Force meant that a post-Kosovo rehabilitation of the Milošević regime, similar to that which took place post-Dayton, could not take place without directly undermining the ICTY's first indictment of a head of state. While decisions of when and whom to indict lay outside the scope of this book, it should be noted that the timing of Milošević's indictment was precipitous as an indictment before the SRJ delegation's rejection of Rambouillet could have made conflict inevitable by making it difficult for the United States and European Union member states to negotiate with a Belgrade government led by Milošević. Moreover, the US even expressed a preference that Milošević himself

48 A binding compliance regime would have required the SRJ to transfer ICTY accused on its territory to the Tribunal as condition for the cessation of hostilities in Kosovo.

49 Belgrade also objected to the inclusion of the word 'peace' in the Rambouillet agreement (Albright 2003: 405-406).

be present at Rambouillet (Williams and Scharf 2002: 194-195).[50] It was only after the collapse of Rambouillet and the onset of NATO's air campaign that Milošević was indicted by the Tribunal for war crimes in Kosovo.[51] Nevertheless, ICTY Chief Prosecutor Louise Arbour claimed that there was considerable anger within NATO as a result of her decision to indict Milošević (G.J. Bass 2002: 313).[52] Even though there was a fear that the Milošević indictment could prolong the Kosovo conflict, US Secretary of State Madeleine Albright appeared to welcome Arbour's decision and made clear that the US saw the ICTY as having further legitimized the NATO campaign against the SRJ:

> We believe that the indictment actually shows the validity of our campaign … We had said all along that the behavior of the Serb authorities and Milosevic himself in Kosovo was unacceptable in terms of how we deal with situations like that at the end of the twentieth century (National Public Radio 1999).

Furthermore, the transfer of Milošević to the ICTY became a pre-condition to the ending the diplomatic isolation of the SRJ, which effectively locked-in a demand for SRJ cooperation with the ICTY through a policy of regime change (Albright 2003: 500). Albright stated that the SRJ:

> …[had] an obligation to turn [Milošević] over and I think that it is very important that we see a future for a democratic Serbia which could rejoin the community of nations if it followed through on its obligations … to turn an indicted war criminal over to the Hague (National Public Radio 1999).

In support of the US' campaign to push Milošević "out of power, out of Serbia and in the custody of the war crimes tribunal" Madeleine Albright and German Foreign Minister Joschka Fischer adopted a strategy that combined economic sanctions with engagement with opponents to Slobodan Milošević in Serbia itself to help bring about a change of regime in Belgrade (Albright 2003: 500). In the face of almost complete isolation within Europe and the United States' commitment to a policy of regime change, the SRJ increasingly turned to Russia and China for

50 In fact, given the presence of senior Serbian officials such as Milan Milutinović, who was later indicted by the ICTY, indictments against Milošević regime officials would have likely precluded SRJ participation in Rambouillet. Interestingly, Williams and Scharf note that despite a desire on the part of an unnamed US government official to have Milošević attend Rambouillet, Milošević feared the existence of a sealed ICTY arrest warrant and therefore chose not to attend so as not to risk arrest (2002: 194).

51 Slobodan Milošević would not be charged with genocide in Bosnia-Herzegovina and violations of IHL in Croatia for another two years.

52 While Arbour gives the impression the US opposed her indictment of Milošević, Williams and Scharf claim Arbour was reluctant to indictment Milošević and only did so after a meeting with a US State Department official who asked for Milošević to be indicted (2002: 206-207).

financial and diplomatic assistance. In regard to Russia, the SRJ even proposed Yugoslavia's accession to a new state that was to be formed through a merger of Belarus and Russia, in effect transforming the SRJ into a Russian province (Lazić 1999).

In June 1999 Belgrade agreed to withdraw from Kosovo under an agreement brokered by Marrti Ahtisaari and Viktor Chernomyrdin and a NATO led international peacekeeping force moved into the province. UNSC Resolution 1244 established the legal foundation for an international security presence in Kosovo; however the Security Council failed to put in place a regime that would secure the ICTY access to SRJ territory outside of Kosovo (Williams and Scharf 2002: 208). Because France and Russia opposed any attempt by the Security Council to specifically address the question of continued SRJ non-compliance with ICTY obligations (Williams and Scharf 2002: 208), there was little expectation Belgrade would provide any meaningful cooperation with the Tribunal absent regime change.

*Phase 3: The US, the EU and Post-Milošević Serbia*

After the collapse of the Milošević regime in October 2000, the EU raised the prospect of EU membership for the SRJ;[53] however, unlike in Croatia where there existed an elite level consensus in favor of integration into the EU and NATO, Serbia's political elite remained divided along the lines of two competing visions of Serbia's place in the international community. Absent a consensus for EU accession in Belgrade, EU conditionality would prove significantly less consequential to bringing about Serbian compliance than in the context of Croatia. Instead, it was the threat of direct sanction by the United States which trigged a domestic political crisis between Đinđić and Koštunica in 2001 that resulted in the transfer of Slobodan Milošević to ICTY custody.

*Explaining Compliance and Rationalizing Non-Compliance*

After the collapse of the Milošević regime, the initial position of the first post-Milošević president of the SRJ, Vojislav Koštunica, regarding the ICTY was a continued denial of Tribunal jurisdiction (Abramowitz 2001: 7). Despite public opposition to cooperation with the Tribunal, it was during early 2001 the most spectacular transfer of an SRJ accused to the ICTY occurred, that of Slobodan Milošević. Milošević's transfer to the ICTY, while having occurred in the context of a domestic political conflict between the Yugoslav president and the Serbian prime minister, was the direct result of coercive pressure applied by the

53 Although at the Feira European Council meeting in June 2000 all Western Balkans states were described as potential candidates for EU membership, it was only in the immediate aftermath of the collapse of the Milošević regime that the Council extended an invitation to the SRJ to begin the Stability and Association process.

United States, which threatened to use its votes in the IMF to block Belgrade's access to international financial assistance during the crucial period of time in the immediate aftermath of the collapse of the Milošević regime. Furthermore, SRJ was the subject of US legislation that required an annual certification by the US Secretary of State of Serbian compliance with Article 29 obligations. This certification process, which relied on disincentivizing non-compliance through the threat of financial sanction, proved far more consequential in bringing about the arrest and surrender of individuals indicted for war crimes than the more long-term incentives subsequently offered by the European Union such as the linkage of Stability and Association Agreement negotiations to cooperation with the ICTY. This was because rather than providing for a long-term incentive for cooperation, the US was willing to impose significant and immediate costs upon the SRJ for non-compliance as failure to secure US certification meant that not only would Serbia lose access to direct assistance from the US, but the US could also use its votes in the IMF and World Bank to block financial assistance to Serbia from international lending institutions.

After Milošević's transfer to the ICTY, Serbia once again failed to comply with Article 29 obligations and overall cooperation with the Tribunal once again deteriorated as the United States proved less willing to coerce Belgrade into surrendering the remaining ICTY indictees on the territory of the SRJ. While the linkage of EU accession to compliance with Article 29 obligations did not bring about immediate arrests,[54] by 2005 the Serbian government increasingly perceived the presence of ICTY fugitives on its territory as a liability and began to actively encourage persons indicted for war crimes on the territory of Serbia to voluntarily surrender themselves to the Tribunal.[55] However, Alexandra Milenov of the ICTY field office in Belgrade noted that these surrenders were always characterized as "patriotic" acts and no mention was ever made of the contents of the ICTY indictments against persons accused of war crimes.[56] Furthermore, in instances where voluntary surrenders were not forthcoming, such as with regard to Ratko Mladić, the Serbian government failed to take action to bring about an arrest.

Despite the characterization of voluntary surrenders as patriotic acts on the part of the state, the rationalization of non-compliance on the part of Belgrade evolved from a complete rejection of Tribunal jurisdiction to that of acceptance of obligations imposed by the Tribunal Statute. As of 2007, the Belgrade government's public rationalization of non-cooperation with the Tribunal consisted largely of arguments which identified functional law enforcement difficulties, such as an inability to locate ICTY suspects, instead of a rejection of legal obligations toward

54 As previously mentioned, in 2003 arrests were carried out in response to the assassination of Zoran Đinđić.

55 Koštunica opposed carrying out arrests in support of the ICTY, but his party, the DSS, was willing to encourage voluntary surrenders.

56 Personal interview with Alexandra Milenov of the ICTY Field Office in Belgrade, January 23, 2007.

the Tribunal that were voiced as late as 2001. The transformation in Belgrade's rationalization of non-compliance with Article 29 obligations illustrates that post-Milošević governments were concerned about the perception of non-cooperation inflicting costs upon Belgrade. However, also in 2007, Serbian government officials suggested that despite a change in rhetoric, the transfer of ICTY accused remained dependent upon an extralegal bargaining process linked to the negotiation of a final status agreement for Kosovo. For example, Aleksandar Vasović quoted an anonymous government official as describing Mladić as an asset and stating, "We can get him and hand him over easily but only when we get Kosovo-related assurances from major powers, specifying what Serbia and Kosovo Serbs will receive in return" (2007).

### *Ratko Mladić, Radovan Karadžić, and the End of Conditionality?*

In the case of Ratko Mladić, the Serbian state denied that it was in non-compliance with Article 29 obligations and instead argued it was unable to locate the accused. The nuance in Serbian government descriptions of a non-compliance event suggests that the there was a desire to avoid being seen as not complying with state international legal obligations, which was absent from 1995-2002. However, the ICTY countered that the Serbian state was actually aware of Ratko Mladić's location and Mladić could be arrested and transferred to The Hague by Belgrade.[57] As previously mentioned, the European Union adopted a policy that linked the start of Stability and Association Agreement talks with Belgrade to the handing over of the remaining ICTY fugitives on Serbian territory including Ratko Mladić (European Council 2003). Yet the incentive of SAA and EU candidacy proved insufficient to bring about Serbian compliance. Recall that in the case of Milošević, compliance only occurred after the costs of non-compliance, denial of access to financial assistance, was clearly transmitted to Belgrade; however, in the case of Mladić the only cost associated with non-compliance was a delayed initiation of SAA talks. Moreover, Belgrade hoped that the EU would allow Serbia to progress toward EU membership even in the absence of Mladić's transfer. Given Serbia's long-term prospect of EU accession, the incentive of SAA proved unable to bring Serbia into compliance with Tribunal orders. Furthermore, a significant bloc of EU member states, led by Italy and Austria opposed the linkage of cooperation with the ICTY to Serbia's EU accession process and actively lobbied the European Council to decouple Serbia's EU accession process from cooperation with the ICTY (Brunnstrom 2007).[58]

Following January 2007 elections in Serbia, which saw the Serbian Radical Party gain the largest bloc of votes, an increasing number of EU member states

57 Confidential interview January 24, 2007.

58 As of February 2008, only the Netherlands demanded Serbian compliance with ICTY arrest and surrender orders are maintained as a pre-condition for signing an SAA with Belgrade (Dicker and Leicht 2008).

saw the immediate re-launch of Serbia's EU accession process as a means of strengthening "pro-European" political parties in Serbia ahead of Kosovo's recognition as an independent state (B92 2007a) and the linkage between Mladić's arrest and the onset of SAA talks was temporarily abandoned.[59] There were also significant expressions of concern on the part of the Serbian government that Serbia's fragile post-Milošević institutions risked collapse under the weight of an increasingly assertive Serbian far right. The signing of Serbia's SAA and Interim Agreement on Trade and Trade-related issues on April 29, 2008, just weeks before parliamentary elections that were called in the aftermath of Kosovo's February 2008 declaration of independence reflected growing concern among EU member states regarding the electoral appeal of the SRS. However, despite Belgrade's continued attempts to decouple ICTY cooperation from its EU accession process, The Netherlands sought to maintain the EU's linkage of further progress toward membership to the arrest and transfer of Ratko Mladić (Lobjakas 2008).

The arrest of Radovan Karadžić on July 21, 2008 was brought about by intense pressure on the part of the EU, in particular the Dutch government, for Serbia to arrest and transfer remaining war crimes suspects residing on its territory. Radovan Karadžić, the former president of the Bosnian Serb republic, assumed a false identity under the pretence of being a new age guru and was arrested in Belgrade five months after Kosovo's declaration of independence. While EU foreign policy representative Javier Solana hoped Karadžić's arrest would be enough for the ICTY to declare Serbia as being in "full cooperation" with the Tribunal (Walker 2008),[60] the Netherlands continued to insist upon the arrest and transfer of Ratko Mladić. At the time of writing there is a question over how long EU conditionality will remain in place, as there is significant pressure from within the EU for an abandonment of the linkage between Mladić's arrest and Serbia's EU accession.

## Conclusions

Serbia's interaction with the Tribunal often proved contentious and, as of 2009, Serbia never achieved "full cooperation" cooperation with the Tribunal. In attempting to coax an unwilling state into compliance with Article 29 obligations, the ICTY relied heavily upon third party enforcement during the post-Milošević period, which produced sporadic compliance events. Unlike in neighboring Croatia, where the partnership between the EU and the ICTY in the form of conditionality brought about Croatian compliance with the Tribunal orders, Serbian

59 The resumption of SAA negotiations followed the arrest of Zdravko Tolimir on May 31, 2007, and the ratification of the SAA was to be contingent on full Serbian cooperation with the ICTY.

60 Of course, full cooperation defined in Article 29 of the Tribunal Statute goes far beyond the arrest and transfer of individual accused and includes obligations for states to fully cooperate in the provision of evidence.

non-compliance with not just Article 29(d) and (e) obligations, but also (a), (b) and (c), persisted despite a change of domestic regime and the linkage established between eventual EU membership and cooperation with the Tribunal. Despite a decade of non-compliance, the OTP argued that the continued application of coercive pressure is necessary to bring about Serbian cooperation. Because third party enforcement proved effective in bringing about Croatian compliance, Carla Del Ponte advocated a similar approach be taken by the EU, "…the Croatian case demonstrates that if the EU sticks to its principles it can achieve a lot" (B92 2006). Del Ponte's comparison of Serbia with Croatia, however, obscures divergent ideational and material incentives operating within the two states that have proven consequential to compliance outcomes.

In regard to ideational incentives, Belgrade's appeals to countervailing norms made the rationalization of compliance acts considerably more difficult for Serbian governments. Whereas Croatian elites engaged in international criminal justice norm-affirming rhetoric throughout the 1990s, Belgrade initially rejected the ICTY regime and appealed to countervailing norms. The antecedent condition which amplified the effectiveness of third party enforcement identified in the Croatian case study, an acceptance of legal obligation, was absent with regard to Serbia throughout much of the time under examination. Thus, while Croatian elites were able to internally rationalize coerced compliance acts as the fulfillment of pre-existing legal obligations, when it came to rationalizing transfers from Serbia to the ICTY, Serbian elites instead framed transfers as pragmatic responses to external coercion. Meanwhile, domestic material incentives for non-compliance were much stronger in Serbia and included recalcitrant security services, which were responsible for the murder of Zoran Đinđić in 2003. There was also significant opposition to cooperation with the ICTY amongst parliamentary political parties. The absence of a broad cross-party parliamentary consensus for EU accession made the eventual establishment of a linkage between ICTY cooperation and EU membership less likely to transform state compliance preferences.

It is important to emphasize that it is not argued here that material incentives are not consequential to compliance, but rather that how states rationalize compliance and non-compliance acts can either serve to amplify or dilute material incentives for compliance. Endogenous material incentives locked-in a non-compliance preference that was not transformed by domestic or transnational civil society even after the collapse of the Miloševic regime in October 2000. Instead of a domestic "boomerang effect" mobilizing third party enforcement, the ICTY was left to directly appeal to both the US and EU member states to apply pressure upon Belgrade. As a result of Belgrade's challenging of the emerging international criminal justice regime during the 1990s, even when post-Milošević local elites sought to comply with ICTY orders, domestic opposition to the ICTY served to block compliance acts.

# Chapter 4
# Macedonia: Voluntary Compliance?

## Introduction

The Republic of Macedonia[1] reluctantly declared independence in 1991 as Yugoslavia's western republics of Slovenia, Croatia and Bosnia-Herzegovina departed the federation amid violent conflict; however, unlike in Yugoslavia's western republics, war did not breakout on the territory of the Republic of Macedonia until 2001, a decade after the dissolution of the Yugoslav state and eight years after the UNSC established the ICTY. As a result, the period of time and number of arrests and transfers covered in this case study are significantly shorter and lower than with regard to Chapters 2, 3, 5, and 6. ICTY investigations and indictments targeting Macedonian citizens only emerged after 2001 and the transfer of individuals to ICTY custody occurred in the context of post-Ohrid Framework Agreement (OFA) international engagement in Macedonia.[2] Furthermore, only two Macedonian citizens were indicted by the Tribunal, Ljube Boškoski and Johan Tarčulovski, and only Tarčulovski was transferred to the Tribunal by the Macedonian state.[3]

Nonetheless, despite a lacunae of arrest and surrender orders addressed to the Macedonian government, Macedonia represents an important case study, as Skopje was never found to be in non-cooperation with the Tribunal. In fact, every ICTY annual report, which dealt with the question of Macedonian cooperation with the Tribunal, included a positive assessment of Macedonian interaction with the ICTY (Report of the International Tribunal 2002: 40; Report of the International Tribunal 2003: 54; Report of the International Tribunal 2004: 70; Report of the International Tribunal 2005: 37; Report of the International Tribunal 2006: 21). Macedonian cooperation with the ICTY stands in contrast to the previous two case studies, which demonstrated a pre-existing preference for non-compliance with regard to the enforcement of arrest and surrender orders. Macedonia, therefore, presents us with an example of first order compliance with international legal obligations stemming from Article 29 of the Tribunal Statute, unlike Croatia and

1 For the purpose of clarity, I refer to the Republic of Macedonia by name which it uses to describe itself.

2 The Ohrid Framework Agreement was agreed to by ethnic Albanian and Macedonian political parties in August 2001 and ended the brief Albanian-Macedonian civil conflict.

3 Boškoski was a dual Croatian and Macedonian citizen and resided in Croatia at the time of his indictment for war crimes committed during the conflict in Macedonia. Thus, Boškoski was arrested and transferred to ICTY custody by Croatian authorities in 2005.

Serbia.[4] Fisher's observation, "Short of military defeat, governments might be unwilling to allow their officers to be punished by an international authority" (R. Fisher 1981: 88-89), does resonate with previous case studies as Belgrade and Zagreb resisted cooperation with the Tribunal, albeit eventual compliance was not necessitated by military defeat. Rather when Belgrade and Zagreb complied with ICTY orders, compliance was the outcome of rational interest based calculations, or what March and Olsen described as a "logic of consequences" (1998). Moreover, tools relied upon by external actors to either induce or coerce cooperation, after a state was found to be in non-compliance with standing legal obligations, were dependent upon a logic of consequences in guiding recalcitrant elites toward compliance. Chapter 2 demonstrated that Croatian cooperation with the ICTY was largely dependent upon a pre-existing elite preference for integration into Euro-Atlantic structures coupled with third party enforcement action, while Chapter 3 noted that although a combination of third party coercion and inducements were relied upon to bring about compliance on the part of post-Milošević Serbia, Serbian non-compliance preferences proved less malleable to external incentives and disincentives. What makes Macedonia unique among the case studies is that coercive threats, such as denial of access to international financial assistance or the canceling of EU accession talks, were not needed to transform non-compliant behavior because Skopje promptly arrested and transferred Johan Tarčulovski to Tribunal custody following his 2005 indictment.

As Chapters 2 and 3 illustrated, ICTY compliance decisions must be contextualized within the broader foreign policy preferences of the target state. Recall in the case of Croatia, Zagreb's post-Tuđman foreign policy preference for integration into Euro-Atlantic institutions amplified the effectiveness of EU and NATO accession conditionality, while in the case of Serbia the absence of consensus for integration into Euro-Atlantic institutions diluted the effectiveness of conditionality. While Zagreb's preference for rapid integration into the EU and NATO emerged only after the death of Franjo Tuđman, throughout the 1990s Skopje voluntarily enmeshed the Macedonian state within a complex web of international institutional arrangements which saw external actors assume control of state security functions. Skopje's weakness and encirclement by more powerful neighbors, metaphorically labeled the "four wolves" (Ackermann 1999: 71) led Macedonia to seek security within international institutions long before violent conflict broke out in 2001 (Ackermann 1999: 84). Moreover, Skopje's receptivity to an in-country international presence, first on the part of the UN and later on the part of NATO and the EU, illustrates the extent to which Macedonia relied on external actors to ensure state survival at a time when hostile neighboring

4 First order compliance refers to a state respecting standing rules, in this case pre-existing legal obligations to cooperate with the ICTY. Second order compliance would pertain to a state complying with an arrest and surrender order only after being found to be in non-compliance of the Tribunal Statute. For more on first and second order compliance see R. Fisher 1981: 28-29.

states harbored territorial ambitions over the embattled former Yugoslav republic (Ackermann 1999: 71; Rossos 2006: 110-113). It will be argued that Macedonian compliance must be viewed in the context of a decade long engagement with international actors, with the UN even assuming responsibility for border control functions and security through the United Nations Preventative Deployment Mission to Macedonia (UNPREDEP). UNPREDEP was then succeeded by NATO and EU security missions in Macedonia which molded the Macedonian state's interactions with external actors such as the ICTY.

In order to explore compliance causation this chapter will begin with an exploration of the domestic politics of compliance. It will be noted Macedonia's acceptance of the 2001 OFA, which ended the brief civil conflict, marked a watershed moment in shaping the identity of the Macedonian state as Macedonia accepted its transformation from nation-state into a decentralized multi-ethnic state (Brunnbauer 2002: 4). While UNPREDEP provided security pre-1999, the security of the post-Ohrid Macedonian state was guaranteed by both NATO and the EU, and the domestic political order was stabilized by the inclusion of ethnic Albanian political parties into coalition governments. Before turning to an exploration of the international politics of Macedonian cooperation with the ICTY, it must again be emphasized that unlike Croatia and Serbia, only two ICTY indictments were issued against Macedonian citizens and four investigations were referred back to the Macedonian judiciary by the Tribunal, which meant the question of enforcing arrest and surrender orders never achieved the political salience, domestic or international, that was observed in the previous two case studies.[5] In our discussion of the international politics of compliance it will be noted that Macedonia was an extremely weak state, which did not possess an armed forces at independence and found itself reliant upon assistance from the United States and the European Union for security. While Macedonia's vulnerability brought Skopje into a close relationship with the United States, Macedonian compliance cannot alone be explained by relative power distributions. After all, Croatia found itself dependent upon US assistance during the 1990s, yet compliance on the part of various Zagreb governments could not be described as automatic. Although the fragility of the Macedonian state contributed to compliance outcomes, it will be argued here that Macedonia's decade long engagement with international actors and the implementation of the OFA established a political context that made compliance with ICTY requests and orders acts of rule following as opposed to the outcome of a prolonged decision-making process in which the costs of non-compliance were weighed against the costs of compliance.

---

5 The ICTY requested five cases under investigation by the Macedonian judiciary to be transferred to the Tribunal: the NLA leadership case, the Mavrovo road worker case, the Lipkovo water reserve case, the Ljuboten investigation, and the Neprošteno investigation. Of these cases and investigations, only the Ljuboten investigation resulted in prosecution before the ICTY (ICTY Press Release 2002).

## The Domestic Politics of Compliance

Parallel to elections held in Bosnia-Herzegovina, Croatia, and the Federal Republic of Yugoslavia (Serbia and Montenegro), Macedonia held its first post-communist multi-party elections in November and December 1990. Macedonia's 1990 elections resulted in a nationalist coalition of four parties, led by the Internal Macedonian Revolutionary Organization – Democratic Party for Macedonian National Unity, (*Vnatrešno Makedonska Revoluciona Organizacija-Demokratska Partija za Makedonsko Nacionalno Edinstvo*, VMRO-DPMNE), winning the largest bloc of parliamentary seats and the communist successor party, the Social Democratic Union of Macedonia, (*Socijaldemokratski Sojuz na Makedonija,* SSM), winning the second largest bloc of parliamentary seats (Perry 1997: 233). As in Croatia, during the 1990 elections party cleavages broke down along the question of independence. The VMRO-DPMNE advocated Macedonian independence while the SSM favored salvaging a Yugoslav state in an attempt to prevent Slovenia and Croatia from seceding from the federation.[6] Despite the nationalist bloc's narrow victory, Kiro Gligorov of the SSM won appointment by parliament as president.[7] In the months preceding the outbreak of war in 1991, Gligorov along with Bosnian President Alija Izetbegović, attempted to prevent the dissolution of the Yugoslav state through the promotion of an inter-republican compromise that would have created a Yugoslav confederation (Poulton 2000: 175-176). However, the Gligorov-Izetbegović proposal was rejected by Belgrade and failed to prevent the outbreak of violent wars of secession in Slovenia and Croatia (Libal 1997: 33).[8]

### *Independence, Insecurity and the UN*

Macedonia became an independent state in November 1991, albeit reluctantly.[9] At independence Macedonia found itself in a precarious situation as Skopje feared spillover from wars elsewhere in the former Yugoslavia and the territorial ambitions

6 Of course, support for keeping Macedonia within Yugoslavia was conditioned on Slovenia, Croatia, and Bosnia-Herzegovina's continued participation in the union. Once these three republics seceded, Macedonia's inclusion into a Serb-dominated rump state was opposed by both major political parties and a referendum on independence was held in September 1991 following declarations of independence in Slovenia and Croatia.

7 Gligorov's appointment as president attested to the strength of personalities over parties in 1990. Also, the VMRO-DPMNE party leader was only 24 years old and lacked political experience at the time of his party's triumph.

8 Following Slovenia and Croatia's 1991 declarations of independence, Gligorov abandoned efforts to establish a Yugoslav confederation and authorized a referendum on Macedonian independence (Perry 1997: 234).

9 Macedonia's referendum on independence included a clause which would permit Macedonia's inclusion in a future Yugoslav state (Poulton 2000: 177). The referendum was boycotted by the major ethnic Albanian political parties in protest of the perceived lack of

of neighboring states (Ackermann 1999: 71; Rossos 2006: 110-113). Skopje's vulnerability was exacerbated by the fact that Macedonia lacked both an armed forces and meaningful weaponry to confront potential adversaries.[10] Given the lack of a domestic armed forces and fearing encroachment by neighboring states, Skopje turned to the United Nations for security and requested the deployment of a UN preventative mission to act as a deterrent.[11] In effect, Skopje outsourced its own state security to an external actor. UNPREDEP was exceptionally robust due to the fact UNPREDEP included troop contributions from the United States along with European Union member states,[12] and therefore acted as a powerful deterrent by signaling a willingness on the part of the US to prevent a spillover of violence into Macedonia from the north (Ackermann 1999: 117). During its existence UNPREDEP not only deterred Belgrade from spreading violent conflict south into Macedonia, but also provided security to a state that failed to gain diplomatic recognition from its immediate neighbors Greece and the Federal Republic of Yugoslavia until 1995. UNPREDEP also assumed border control functions along the Macedonian-Albanian border and established monitoring positions along both the Serbian and Albanian borders (Ackermann 1999: 119).[13] The internationalization of Macedonian state security during the 1990s left a profound legacy upon the Macedonian defense establishment as Macedonia simultaneously created its armed forces and integrated its defense structures into international security institutions such as NATO's Partnership for Peace (PfP).[14]

---

minority rights accorded to Macedonian Albanians (Pettifer 1992: 480-481, Poulton 2000: 177).

10 Macedonia was effectively disarmed by the retreating Yugoslav National Army, which withdrew under an agreement concluded between Gligorov and Belgrade (Ackermann 1999: 71-72).

11 Ackermann notes Skopje eventually came to perceive UNPREDEP as a substitute for a domestic armed forces (1999: 84).

12 See Appendix IV for a comprehensive list of states which contributed troops to the UNPREDEP mission.

13 UNPREDEP's success in preventing violent conflict in Macedonia during the 1990s did not prevent China's veto of the UNPREDEP mission at the UNSC in 1999. China's veto of an extension of the UNPREDEP mission was an act of retaliation for Skopje's diplomatic recognition of Taiwan in January 1999. Although the termination of UNPREDEP's mandate two years before the outbreak of violent conflict in Macedonia contributed to increasing regional insecurity, it should be noted that following NATO intervention in Kosovo and the establishment of KFOR, NATO maintained a support presence in Macedonia known as KFOR-REAR. KFOR-REAR was responsible for maintaining a communications zone (COMMZ) in KFOR's rear area which encompassed Macedonia, Greece, Albania, and Bulgaria.

14 The Macedonian parliament passed a resolution supporting Macedonia's membership in the NATO alliance on the November 23, 1993 and joined NATO's Partnership for Peace program in 1995 (Republic of Macedonia Ministry of Defense 2007b). For more on the perceived linkage between integration into international security institutions and state security see (Republic of Macedonia Ministry of Defense 2007a).

Nevertheless, the international military presence in Macedonia did not engage in addressing the grievances of Macedonia's substantial ethnic Albanian minority, which throughout the 1990s increasingly perceived their community to be marginalized within the emerging Macedonian nation state (Poulton 2000: 184-201). Despite the participation of ethnic Albanian Party for Democratic Prosperity in a coalition government with the SSM until 1998,[15] numerous grievances, such as the Macedonian constitution's distinction between majority ethnic Macedonians and ethnic minorities and the lack of linguistic rights for Albanian speakers, eventually culminated in a radical segment of the Albanian political community forming a paramilitary armed forces known as the National Liberation Army (NLA).[16]

### *The 2001 Conflict and Ohrid: A Limited War*

At the time conflict broke out in the territory of the Republic of Macedonia in March 2001, the nationalist VMRO-DPMNE had been in government for four years.[17] Despite the VMRO-DPMNE having formed a coalition government with an ethnic Albanian political party, the Democratic Party of Albanians, relations between ethnic Albanians and ethnic Macedonians rapidly deteriorated following NATO's 1999 intervention in Kosovo. NATO's intervention exacerbated ethnic cleavages as the 1999 war was highly unpopular amongst ethnic Macedonians, while widely supported by Macedonian Albanians (International Crisis Group 2001a: 19). Although causes of the 2001 conflict are not within the scope of this study, ethnic tensions did escalate significantly following the Kosovo war; however, the flow of refugees across the Kosovo-Macedonian border itself did not lead to an outbreak of violence as most Kosovar Albanians returned to Kosovo following NATO's Operation Allied Force. Instead, in the aftermath of the Kosovo war, there was a growing fear amongst ethnic Macedonians that Macedonia's Albanian community would wage a separatist campaign modeled on the Kosovo Liberation Army's campaign in Kosovo. The formation of a Macedonian Albanian paramilitary organization, the NLA, appeared to confirm these fears. However, unlike the Kosovo Liberation Army, the NLA had more limited objectives,[18] which were achieved through the OFA in August 2001.

15 After 1998, the VMRO-DPMNE formed a coalition government with the Democratic Party of Albanians.

16 For a detailed exploration of the "Albanian question" in Macedonian politics during the 1990s see (Poulton 2000: 184-201).

17 After the 2001 conflict, the Social Democratic Union of Macedonia was returned to government in parliamentary elections held in 2002.

18 Among NLA demands were access to greater economic opportunities, social benefits, Albanian language university education and changes to the Macedonian constitution (International Crisis Group 2001a: 5).

During the 2001 conflict, the response of the Macedonian armed forces to the NLA led rebellion was significantly more restrained than military operations elsewhere in the former Yugoslavia. Therefore, the number of international war crimes investigations initiated against parties of the 2001 conflict never exceeded the single digits. The Macedonian armed forces' response to the ethnic Albanian rebellion were closely monitored by the United States and European Union member states, which explicitly warned Skopje to adhere to a "proportional use of force" against armed Albanian insurgent groups (Ordanovski 2004: 18). Given NATO's in-country presence, the US' and EU's warnings not to use excessive force could explain the restraint of the Macedonian Army during the 2001 conflict. Moreover, the NLA quickly proved itself to be an effective fighting force, and Ordanovski cited rumors that the NLA received assistance from MPRI, a US military contractor (2004: 18). At a crucial engagement with Macedonian government forces at Aracinovo the NLA demonstrated an ability to challenge the Macedonian Army:

> Aracinovo demonstrated that the NLA also had in its ranks a number of experienced, well-trained fighters armed with sophisticated weapons. In some cases, the NLA was better trained and armed than Macedonian security forces, and posed a serious challenge. If it could not be defeated militarily, some reasoned, then avenues of dialogue would have to be opened (Ordanovski 2004: 19).

It was following the failure of Macedonian security forces to defeat the NLA at Aracinovo that momentum for a negotiated settlement emerged as a military victory against the NLA appeared less likely. Overall, in terms of both scale and duration, the conflict in Macedonia never came close to paralleling the significantly more intense conflicts elsewhere in the former Yugoslavia, making groups such as veterans and victims associations, which mobilized against the Tribunal in Croatia, less influential in post-conflict Macedonia. In regard to casualties, only eight civilian deaths could be attributed to attacks mounted by the NLA (Ordanovski 2004: 17). Moreover, Macedonian government forces only suffered 38 combat deaths and 220 wounded (Ordanovski 2004: 17).[19]

The negotiated settlement that ended the 2001 conflict left a profound legacy upon post-Ohrid Macedonia. Segments of the ethnic Albanian community maintained a capability to threaten the survival of the Macedonian state should the Macedonian government abandon the OFA:

> The ethnic Albanians have the political and underground paramilitary capability to destabilize the state at any time, but it is currently not in their interests to do so … (Pettifer 2006: 5).

Thus, a radical shift in policy on the part of Skopje that would result in a break from the pro-EU/NATO consensus in favor of pan-Slavic nationalist policies, such

19 At this point, accurate statistics for deaths on the side of the NLA are unavailable.

as the alternative foreign policy presented by the Serbian Radical Party in Serbia,[20] would entail a destabilization of Macedonia's domestic political order and threaten the survival of the Macedonian state. Moreover, not only would ethnic Albanians leave the political process, but Skopje would jeopardize its strategic relationships with Ohrid's guarantors, NATO, the US and EU member states. Therefore, despite significant populist nationalist mobilization against the OFA on the part of ethnic Macedonians, all of Macedonia's major political parties, including the VMRO-DPMNE, committed themselves to the implementation of the framework agreement.

*The Ohrid Framework Agreement*

The OFA constituted a re-founding of the Macedonian state and included significant alterations to the Macedonian Constitution in order to redefine Macedonia as a civic state. The OFA also directly addressed NLA grievances by affirming the status of Albanian as an official state language, and including a legislative program aimed at empowering local governments (Brunnbauer 2002: 4-7). Significantly, the framework agreement did not partition Macedonia into ethnically defined entities, as the Dayton agreement did for Bosnia-Herzegovina, but rather it attempted to integrate ethnic Albanians into a decentralized Macedonian state. Article 1.2 of the OFA specifically rejected ethnicity based territorial partition:

> Macedonia's sovereignty and territorial integrity, and the unitary character of the state are inviolable and must be preserved. There are no territorial solutions to ethnic issues (Ohrid Framework Agreement 2001).

The maintenance of a unitary state permitted ethnic Albanian political parties to continue to participate in governing coalitions with ethnic Macedonian parties at the state and local levels. Even during the 2001 conflict Macedonia's four major parliamentary parties, two of which were ethnic Albanian, formed a national unity government in order to confront the NLA. In addition to this parliamentary demonstration of inter-ethnic unity, all post-OFA Macedonian governments included major ethnic Albanian political parties within governing coalitions despite the recent legacy of violent conflict. In 2002, a party formed by the NLA's leader Ali Ahmeti was invited into a coalition government with the Socialist Party of Macedonia, which had defeated the VMRO-DPMNE in parliamentary elections. Although the NLA did not participate in negations at Ohrid, Ahmeti formed a political party, the Democratic Union for Integration (*Bashkimi Demokratik për Integrim*, BDI), following the acceptance of the OFA by the NLA. The entrance of the BDI, which was formed by the NLA leadership, into the governing coalition illustrates the extent of post-Ohrid Macedonia's transformation, and it was post-

20 See Chapter 3.

Ohrid Macedonia which would be confronted with the task of cooperating with the ICTY.

*Ohrid and External Actors*

The OFA committed signatories to substantial engagement with international actors through appeals for assistance from the international community, individual states, or international organizations; however, there was no transfer of sovereign control to external actors as assistance was limited to training, assistance, implementation, and monitoring:

> The parties invite the international community to facilitate, monitor, and assist in the implementation of the provisions of the Framework Agreement and its Annexes, and requests such efforts be coordinated by the EU in cooperation with the Stabilization and Association Council (Ohrid Framework Agreement 2001).

Policing and the rule of law were specifically targeted for substantial external assistance. Article 5.3 invited the OSCE, the European Union and the United States to provide training and assistance for the Macedonian police (Ohrid Framework Agreement 2001), while Article 5.4 invited the international community to assist in increasing minority participation within the judiciary:

> The parties invite the international community to assist in the training of lawyers, judges and prosecutors from members of communities not in the majority in Macedonia in order to be able to increase their representation in the judicial system (Ohrid Framework Agreement 2001).

As will be demonstrated below, the engagement of international actors in post-Ohrid Macedonia legitimized the new post-Ohrid order. The European Union was also designated the role of Special Coordinator for a wide range of capacity building activities, which were framed in the context of Macedonia's EU accession process.

*Nationalist Mobilization in Post-Ohrid Macedonia*

While compliance with ICTY arrest and surrender orders remained largely a peripheral question in Macedonian politics, Macedonian nationalists did mobilize against the OFA almost immediately after the agreement had been signed in 2001. However, no major political party transformed nationalist opposition to the OFA into political action that would have threatened the implementation of the 2001 framework agreement. As noted previously, even the nationalist VMRO-DPMNE committed itself to the implementation of the OFA (Gruevski 2004, 2007). The commitment to the OFA on the part of the VMRO-DPMNE was largely the outcome of a perception that implementation of the agreement was vital to Macedonian state survival (Maleski 2003). Any failure to adhere to OFA, on the part of Skopje, would lead to a return to conflict and the potential partition of the Macedonian state along ethnic lines. Nonetheless, there were significant grievances against the OFA expressed by Macedonian nationalists. The primary grievance tended to focus around the allegation that the framework agreement threatened the survival of the Macedonian nation state through constitutional amendments, which emphasized Macedonia's new identity as a civic state (Brunnbauer 2002: 7). Yet, Macedonia's former ambassador to the United Nations, Denko Maleski, emphasized that rather than threaten the survival of Macedonia, the OFA was "in the interest of ethnic Macedonians, because, with its implementation, Macedonia, as a state, is given the chance to survive" (2003). Given the linkage between adherence to the OFA and state survival, mobilization against agreement only served to delay rather than threaten its implementation. Furthermore, because NATO, the European Commission, and the European Council articulated a clear linkage between implementation of the OFA and the advancement of Macedonia's NATO and EU accession processes, public opposition to the OFA was to a large extent muted as domestic public opinion strongly supported Macedonia's membership into two international organizations. In addition, both NATO and the EU established ICTY conditionality for aspirant states in the Western Balkans as a prerequisite to membership negotiations in 2003. Importantly, in neither of the two preceding case studies was the establishment of conditionality alone effective in bringing about first order compliance.

*Nationalist Mobilization and the ICTY*

The indictment of former interior minister Ljube Boškoski and paramilitary commander Johan Tarčulovski in March 2005 was met by little public reaction in Macedonia (Petruševa 2005a) and stands in sharp contrast to the mass demonstrations that followed the indictments of Ante Gotovina and Janko Bobetko in Croatia (Peskin and Boduszyński 2003: 1117-1142). The relative absence of social protest against the ICTY does not, however, mean there was not significant questioning of the Tribunal among ethnic Macedonians. For example, the ICTY's decision not to indict members of the NLA for war crimes led to claims of bias on the part of the Tribunal being expressed by Macedonian Prime Minister Vlado Bučkovski (Petruševa 2005a). Yet, the questioning of ICTY indictments did not translate into state obstruction of Tribunal investigations and attempts to secure custody of indicted persons. The relative absence of institutional obstruction can be explained by the fact that the targeting of a civilian minister of interior and the head of paramilitary unit, the Lions, meant that unlike in Croatia and Serbia where the high commands of both the Serbian and Croatian armed forces perceived themselves as threatened by the ICTY (Edmunds 2003: 6-7), in Macedonia the ICTY did not pose a threat to a wide range of military and civilian elites. Therefore, the external pull for compliance did not encounter powerful institutional resistance within state security services.[21] Because the security services did not mobilize against the Tribunal, the civilian elite were granted increased autonomy for cooperation with the ICTY.[22]

Absent institutional resistance to cooperation from the military, a marginal movement did emerge, which attempted to mobilize nationalist support for Ljube Boškoski through an organization known as the *Associations of Citizens for the Support of Ljube Boškoski*, which maintained a website providing news updates from developments in the Boškoski trial in The Hague.[23] In parallel to organizations formed to support persons indicted by the ICTY in both Croatia and Serbia, there was an attempt to cast the indictments against Boškoski and Tarčulovski as indictments against the Macedonian state. The Association claims, "...the primary aim of the Association is to defend the honor of the Republic of Macedonia put at the pillar of shame" (Boškoski 2007). Attempts to frame the ICTY's investigation against Boškoski as an indictment of the Macedonian state were echoed by an independent deputy in the Macedonian parliament who argued, "If Macedonia is a real state it must stop these foreigners carrying out these exhumations without any permit" (Jovanovski 2002).

The failure of anti-ICTY organizations such as the Association for the Support of Ljube Boškoski to mobilize support is underlined by the fact that Boškoski's own political party, the VMRO-DPMNE, failed to mention cooperation with the ICTY in its 2006 party program (*Program of VMRO-DPMNE* 2006). The omission of the ICTY in the VMRO-DPMNE is striking given the fact that two of the party's former leading members had been indicted by the Tribunal during the previous year. The VMRO-DPMNE decision not to support Boškoski can be partially explained by the fact Boškoski's own political extremism led to his marginalization within the party even before his indictment by the ICTY. In fact, after the VMRO-DPME was removed from government following parliamentary elections held in 2002, Boškoski was prevented from contesting presidential elections held in 2004, when Macedonia's Electoral Commission barred his candidacy in elections on the grounds Boškoski had not continuously resided in Macedonia for 15 years (Petruševa 2005b). Shortly after the electoral commission's decision, Boškoski was indicted by the Macedonian judiciary on charges of murdering seven immigrants

21 In both Croatia and Serbia, the armed forces developed close ties with the Tuđman and Milošević regimes, and armed forces elites were threatened by domestic political change (Edmunds 2003: 1).

22 Serbian Prime Minister Zoran Đinđić was assassinated by members of an elite paramilitary force, "the Red Berets" in response for cooperation with the ICTY. Moreover, in the case of Serbia, political party leaders along with heads of state and government were indicted by the ICTY, while with regard to Croatia ICTY indictments were issued against the former military elite.

23 The site can be found at: http://www.ljubeboskoski.com.mk/ and is available in both English and Macedonian.

from South Asia and fled to Croatia.[24] Instead of expressing support for the former minister of interior – wanted on charges brought by both the domestic judiciary and later the ICTY – the VMRO-DPMNE again emphasized the pursuit of EU and NATO membership as the party's two major foreign policy goals. In the words of the VMRO-DPMNE party program, "The goal of the foreign policy of the Republic of Macedonia is to integrate national security into the global security system of the EU and NATO" (*Program of VMRO-DPMNE* 2006).

### *The Boškoski and Tarčulovski Transfers*

Although Macedonia promptly arrested and transferred Johan Tarčulovski to ICTY custody, Macedonia benefited from the fact the most high profile Macedonian subject of an ICTY indictment, Ljube Boškoski, was a dual Macedonian-Croatian citizen, who at the time of his indictment was already imprisoned in Croatia on criminal charges pertaining to the murder of transient migrants from South Asia. Croatian authorities were, therefore, left with the responsibility of transferring Boškoski to Tribunal custody. Thus, Tarčulovski became the only subject of an ICTY arrest and surrender order addressed to the Macedonian state. Following the arrest and transfer of Tarčulovski to ICTY custody, the Tribunal noted:

> The authorities of the Former Yugoslav Republic of Macedonia deserve credit for the prompt arrest and transfer to The Hague on 16 March 2005 of one accused (J. Tarčulovski). In the reporting period there were no problems in cooperating with the Government (Report of the International Tribunal 2005: 37).

Macedonia stands out among the cases studies as the only state to receive consistent plaudits for cooperation in the ICTY's annual reports (Report of the International Tribunal 2002: 40, Report of the International Tribunal 2003: 54, Report of the International Tribunal 2004: 70, Report of the International Tribunal 2005: 37, Report of the International Tribunal 2006: 21).[25] The close political cooperation between the Macedonian state and the ICTY was further illustrated in 2006 when after meeting with ICTY Chief Prosecutor Carla Del Ponte, Macedonian Prime Minister Nikola Gruevski pledged to maintain close cooperation with the ICTY

---

24 Allegedly, on the orders of Boškoski, seven illegal immigrants in transit from South Asia to Western Europe were lured from Greece to Macedonia and executed near Skopje. Weapons and documents were then planted on their bodies in order to give the appearance Boškoski's security forces had foiled a terrorist plot that included a planned attack on the US Embassy in Skopje. The *Wall Street Journal* later reported the event to be an attempt to "manufacture" a terrorist threat (Cooper 2002).

25 Prior to 2002 no assessment of Macedonian cooperation in available due to the fact ICTY investigations of war crimes committed on the territory of Macedonia only commenced in late 2001.

to both facilitate trials in The Hague and to prepare the Macedonian judiciary for investigations referred back to the domestic courts (Makfax 2006).

## International Justice and Civil Society

In Chapters 2 and 3 we observed mass populist mobilization against the ICTY in both Croatia and Serbia in response to the transmission of Tribunal arrest and surrender orders to state governments. Moreover, it was also noted that transnational advocacy networks and the ICTY failed to generate domestic social protest in support of the enforcement of ICTY arrest and surrender orders. Here, an exploration of the construction of international justice presents us with a more complex task than encountered in Chapters 2 and 3 as cooperation with the ICTY never reached the political salience that was observed in the previous two case studies. With regard to the ICTY, the absence of in-country investigations until 2001 meant that for the first eight years of operation the Tribunal lacked an in-country presence.

### *The ICTY and Transnational Advocacy Groups*

Given the lack of interaction between the ICTY and Macedonia, public opinion received only minimal exposure to ICTY trial processes. Additionally, the ICTY's interaction with Macedonian NGOs was significantly less intense than in regard to Croatia, Bosnia-Herzegovina and Serbia. The ICTY did not maintain a permanent in-country presence that was capable of liaising with domestic civil society and the domestic media. However, in comparison to Belgrade, where the ICTY maintains staff capable of presenting the Tribunal's opinions in the domestic media,[26] cooperation with the ICTY never became a salient political question within Macedonian politics.

Civil society development in Macedonia was promoted by various international actors throughout the 1990s. The United Nations took an active role in diffusing inter-ethnic tensions through the cultivation of inter-ethnic dialogue in what Ackermann described as a civilian counterpart to the military mission, UNPREDEP (1999: 103). Despite attempts to foster a human rights NGO community, international human rights NGOs did not mobilize a significant justice constituency to demand international criminal prosecutions. Although Ackermann noted "The Republic of Macedonia is host to an impressive number of non-governmental organizations, both international and indigenous..." (Ackermann 1999: 149), one common feature of NGOs across the case studies is that foreign sources of funding made it possible for NGOs to operate without attracting grassroots support from local populations (Grodeland 2006: 227). In addition, indigenous Macedonian NGOs

26 In Belgrade Alexandra Milenov of the ICTY field office makes frequent statements to the local media and has appeared on local television.

which did attract domestic support tended to be divided along exclusively ethnic lines (Ackermann 1999: 151). Thus, it is not surprising NGOs failed to mobilize Macedonian public opinion in order to demand the prosecution individuals responsible for serious violations of international humanitarian law.

### *Civil Society: Victims, Veterans and NGOs*

In Chapters 2 and 3 it was noted that anti-Tribunal activist organizations often emerged from groups directly affected by conflict, such as war veterans' organizations. Because the intensity and duration of conflicts in Croatia, Serbia and particularly Bosnia-Herzegovina, which will be dealt with in Chapter 5, powerful veterans' and victims' organizations emerged in these states. HVIDR-a mobilized Croatian war veterans through anti-ICTY demonstrations held in Croatia, while in Bosnia-Herzegovina, the Mothers of Srebrenica, engaged in domestic and international advocacy for the prosecution of those responsible for committing atrocities during the war in Bosnia. Nothing similar to the above organizations ever emerged in Macedonia due to the limited nature of the conflict. As previously mentioned, on the Macedonian side, war crimes indictments targeted only a single paramilitary unit, the Lions, formed by the Macedonian Interior Minister Ljube Boškoski, and not the officer corps of the Macedonian Army. Edmunds notes in both Croatia and Serbia, cooperation with the ICTY became synonymous with attempts to transform powerful military establishments which maintained close ties with senior officials of the authoritarian *ancien regimes* (2003). Recall, in Serbia elements of the security services assassinated Zoran Đinđić in an attempt to end state cooperation with the ICTY, while in Croatia military elites pressured the government not to cooperate with the Tribunal through HVIDR-a (S. Fisher 2003: 74-92). In contrast to the previous two case studies, Macedonian cooperation with the ICTY did not incur high domestic costs. The limited number of indictments issued against Macedonian citizens permitted the war crimes debate to be individualized to a much greater extent than in any of the other case studies where heads of state and government were either implicated or directly indicted for participation in joint criminal enterprises (see for example *Prosecutor v. Ante Gotovina, Ivan Čermak and Mladen Markač* 2007, *Prosecutor v. Slobodan Milošević* 1999, 2001). Moreover, because Boškoski significantly discredited himself through his alleged involvement in the murders of transient migrants from South Asia and fled Macedonia to Croatia following the initiation of an investigation to his crimes and Tarčulovski's direct involvement in the Ljuboten massacres, very few organizations were willing to openly support the two ICTY indictees.

## The International Politics of Compliance

A legal obligation for Macedonia to comply with an ICTY arrest and surrender order only emerged in 2005; however, ICTY investigations in Macedonia began in 2001 following the Ljoboten massacre, which was first brought to light by *Human Rights Watch* (Brunnbauer 2002, Human Rights Watch 2001, Jovanovski 2001). During Macedonia's interaction with the ICTY, Macedonia was subjected to international pressure to fully implement the OFA which was agreed to in August 2001. Although there was an initial reluctance to implement legislation called for in the OFA, six years after Ohrid, most of the reforms called for by the framework agreement had been implemented (Balkan Investigative Reporting Network 2007). Cooperation with ICTY investigations into war crimes committed by Macedonian forces was a key demand of both European Union member states and NATO for Macedonian accession into the respective organizations. In the case of the EU, progress on EU accession and cooperation with the ICTY were explicitly linked for the states of the Western Balkans at Thessaloniki (European Council 2003), while NATO made a similar linkage at Istanbul (Istanbul Summit Communiqué 2004). Yet, despite these linkages, coercive threats to delay ratification of a Stability and Association Agreement (SAA) or to cancel the commencement of EU accession negotiations never materialized as throughout the six years of Macedonian interaction with the ICTY because Macedonia was never found to be in non-compliance with Article 29 obligations.

Macedonian compliance with the arrest and surrender order issued against Johan Tarčulovski occurred shortly after the Tarčulovski indictment was transmitted to the Macedonian Ministry of Interior. In explaining Tarčulovski's transfer rationalists could point to Macedonia's relative weakness *vis à vis* potential third party enforcement agents. Particular attention would also be paid to the fact Macedonia's interaction with the ICTY occurred parallel to Macedonia's EU and NATO accession processes. Failure to comply with an ICTY order could have been perceived as carrying significant costs upon the fragile Macedonian state. However, before exploring compliance in the context of Macedonia's pursuit of EU and NATO accession, it is first important to establish the regional context in which the independent Macedonian state emerged.

### *Regional Insecurity*

As previously mentioned, at independence Macedonia perceived itself to be surrounded by hostile neighbors. Among the neighboring states which presented a threat to the survival of the newly independent Macedonian state was Greece. After Macedonia's declaration of independence, Skopje found itself locked in a dispute with its southern neighbor regarding the constitutional name of the newly independent state. Essentially, the dispute between Athens and Skopje emerged from the use of the geographic term Macedonia. Athens claimed the term Macedonia to be part of Greek national heritage and objected to the use of the term Macedonia by its northern neighbor. Greece also feared its new northern neighbor harbored territorial ambitions against its northern region, also known as Macedonia. Under the Macedonian constitution, Macedonia was to be known as the "Republic of Macedonia"; however due to Greek objection to use of the term Macedonia, Skopje was only able to gain international recognition under title which it used to enter the United Nations,[27] the Former Yugoslav Republic of Macedonia (FYROM). Despite the fact neither Skopje nor Athens made territorial claims upon each other, the name dispute was responsible for significant tensions between the two states during the 1990s and remains unresolved. Danforth's description of Greek sentiment on the question illustrates how the term Macedonia was viewed in Greece:

> … because ancient and modern Greece are bound in an unbroken line of racial and cultural continuity, it is only Greeks who have the right to identify themselves as Macedonians, not the Slavs of southern Yugoslavia, who settled in Macedonia in the sixth century AD and who called themselves "Bulgarians" until 1944. Greeks, therefore, generally refer to Macedonians as "Skopians," a practice which would be comparable to calling Greeks "Athenians" (1993: 4).

Greece's response to Macedonian independence was intensely hostile. Greece waged a successful campaign to block EU recognition of Macedonian independence, and Greece also imposed an economic blockade that deprived Macedonia access to the region's only major international port at Thessaloniki. Skopje, therefore, had good reason to fear Greek intentions as the long-term survival of an independent Macedonian state ran counter to what Pettifer alleged to be Greece's primary foreign policy objective for its northern neighbor: the reversal of Macedonian independence and its subsequent inclusion into a Serb-dominated Yugoslav federation:

> The Greek approach has been to use whatever leverage it can within the EU to prevent recognition of a state called "Macedonia" and attempt to base diplomatic initiatives on the assumption that some sort of new Yugoslav federation may well emerge that will include Macedonia as a component part. In essence, this differs little from the previous policy of backing Serbia to the hilt, and there is a general correspondence between Athens and the main currents of thinking in Belgrade (Pettifer 1992: 482).

Greek hostility to Macedonia initially resulted in the blocking of Macedonian EU recognition (Libal 1997: 84), even though Macedonia, along with Slovenia, was one of only two former Yugoslav republics to meet the EU's criteria for recognition

27 In 1993 UNSC Resolution 817 admitted Macedonia as a member state of the UN under the condition that it uses a designated provisional name: the Former Yugoslav Republic of Macedonia.

set forth by the Badinter Commission (Perry 1997: 234). In 1994, Greece imposed a second economic embargo on Macedonia that lasted 18 months. The embargo was only brought to an end by a settlement sponsored by US assistant secretary of state Richard Holbrooke. The Holbrooke agreement required Macedonia to change its national flag and give assurances that Skopje would not pursue claims upon Greek territory (Perry 1997: 270). During the 2001 conflict, Greece continued to press for a resolution of the name dispute, while also contributing to EU efforts to negotiate a peace settlement (International Crisis Group 2001a: 18-19).[28]

*The United States, NATO and Compliance*

Although the United States only recognized the Republic of Macedonia as an independent state in February 1994,[29] US participation in UNPREDEP signaled the United States' willingness to ensure stability in the newly independent republic.[30] Meanwhile, Skopje actively cultivated a close relationship with the US during the early 1990s (2000: 58). Illustrative of the close relationship between Skopje and Washington was that, unlike Croatia and Serbia, Macedonia promptly adopted an Article 98 agreement[31] with the United States and offered support for the US-led war in Iraq. Boduszyński and Balalovska pointed to a combination of coercive threats and inducements in their explanation of Macedonia's ratification of an Article 98 agreement. Revealingly, however, they note there was little internal debate amongst Macedonian elites as the US had come to be perceived as a guarantor of Macedonian and regional security (2004: 18-30). Thus, despite EU insistence that ratification of an Article 98 agreement with the US would not be consistent with EU expectations for aspirant states, Boduszyński and Balalovska argue the failure of the EU to provide an alternative to US security assistance led Skopje to ratify the agreement as the US was perceived to be the guarantor of regional stability, and not the EU (2004: 22). Furthermore, in addition to the coercive threat of blocking Macedonia's hopes for NATO accession through a denial of access to US military assistance, the US added the inducement of recognizing Macedonia

---

28 During May 2001, Greece appeared confident that Macedonia would agree to a compromise solution that would result in the Republic of Macedonia being recognized as the Republic of Upper Macedonia; however, the wide ranging constitutional changes proposed to resolve the conflict with the NLA made any concessions on the name issue untenable for Skopje (International Crisis Group 2001a: 18-19).

29 Although the US recognized Macedonia on February 8, 1994, full diplomatic relations were not established until September 13, 1995.

30 Perry suggests the lack of US diplomatic recognition was the result of an influential US Greek lobby (1997: 271).

31 The United States sought guarantees, in the form of Article 98 agreements, from state parties to the Statute of Rome that US citizens would not be transferred to the International Criminal Court. Macedonia signed the Statute of Rome in 1998 and ratified the treaty in 2002.

by its constitutional name, as opposed to FYROM (Boduzyński and Balalovska 2004: 21).[32]

It is not possible to overstate the perceived linkage between state security and the pursuit of NATO membership among Macedonian policymakers (see Boduszyński and Balalovska 2004: 22). The perception of NATO as an anchor to regional security was reinforced by the fact that within a month of the Ohrid agreement, Macedonian president Boris Trajkovski requested that NATO establish a longer term in-country peacekeeping presence to follow Operation Essential Harvest. In response to Trajkovski's request NATO initiated Operation Amber Fox. It is also significant to note that concurrent to requests for NATO to maintain an in-state security presence, Macedonia made the pursuit of full NATO membership a central foreign policy objective. While EU conditionality has been addressed in previous chapters, here it will be noted that NATO membership also entailed the fulfillment of a broad range of criteria set by the Alliance, which went beyond the narrow issue areas of defense and security. In a visit to Skopje in 2002, US permanent representative to the North Atlantic Council Nicholas Burns outlined democracy, economic reforms, a commitment to rule of law, combating corruption, and the trafficking in narcotics and people as benchmarks by which Macedonia's NATO candidacy would be assessed. Moreover, Burns committed the US to assisting Macedonia reform and restructure its military (2002).

### *The United States and Ljube Boškoski*

After the OFA was concluded in 2001, Ljube Boškoski and his paramilitary unit, the *Lions*, were increasingly perceived by the United States as a threat to the fragile peace that had emerged. US Executive Order 13304 was issued in response to the perceived threat to the OFA posed by nationalist politicians and permitted, "[persons] to have actively obstructed, or pose a significant risk of actively obstructing, the Ohrid Framework Agreement of 2001…" to be added to a list of *Specially Designated Nationals and Blocked Persons* deemed to either pose a threat to regional security or be under indictment by the ICTY (Federal Register 2003: 32316). Boškoski became the first Macedonian citizen added to the United States' register of individuals deemed by the US government as threats to regional stability (Specially Designated Nationals List 2007).[33] The designation of Boškoski as a "designated national" resulted in significant sanctions directed specifically against Boškoski. These sanctions included a travel ban to the United States, a freezing of assets, and the imposition of a prohibition upon US citizens from funding Boškoski (Petruševa 2005b). The targeting of Boškoski by the United

32 In 2004, the United States State Department began to refer to Macedonia as the Republic of Macedonia in place of the name under which Macedonia was admitted to the UN, the Former Yugoslav Republic of Macedonia (Crook 2005: 254).

33 Ljube Boškoski's name is misspelled on the US Office of Foreign Assets Control list of specially designated individuals and appears as Ljube Boškovski.

States facilitated his political marginalization in Skopje because Boškoski was increasingly identified within Macedonia as a threat to US-Macedonian relations, which as noted above, were perceived as vital to ensuring Macedonian state security in the framework of both defense assistance and support for Macedonian NATO membership.

*Compliance and the European Union*

In 2001 Macedonia signed a Stability and Association Agreement (SAA) with the European Union; however, the outbreak of violence in the summer of 2001 brought a pause to Macedonia's EU accession process. It was also in 2001 that the EU became involved in a broad range of governance and security functions within Macedonia. In fact, the EU was even credited with facilitating the OFA (Risteska 2007: 10). Moreover, not only was the EU designated a special coordinator for capacity building activities called for in the OFA, the EU also undertook a number of missions in Macedonia which included its first military mission, *Concordia*.[34] Yet, despite the EU undertaking a broad range of activities within Macedonia, Skopje continued to perceive NATO as the primary guarantor or regional security (Boduszyński and Balalovska 2004: 22).

Nonetheless, the European Union played an important role in facilitating the implementation of the OFA through post-conflict reconstruction and the provision of financial assistance. From 2000 until 2006 Macedonia received €298.2 million from the EU through the Community Assistance for Reconstruction Development and Stability (CARDS) program (European Commission 2007). Moreover, Macedonia saw a 500 percent increase in EU financial assistance in 2001, the year SAA was signed (European Commission 2007), and the EU also provided assistance for drafting Macedonia's 2002 budget in order to identify costs associated with the implementation of Ohrid. As a result of these estimates an international donor's conference held in Brussels during 2002 raised €300 million in pledged assistance (European Commission Conflict Prevention 2003: 1-8). In addition to financial assistance, the European Union established a Rapid Reaction Mechanism during the 2001 conflict in Macedonia, which carried out various reconstruction activities including the facilitation of refugee returns, the restoration of war affected regions, de-mining assistance, training of local journalists, advising the Ministries of Interior and Justice on restructuring, and drafting legislation on local government as called for in Ohrid (European Commission Conflict Prevention 2003: 1).

Dependence on European Union financial and reconstruction assistance alone cannot explain Macedonian cooperation with the ICTY, as both post-Tuđman Croatia and post-Milošević Serbia received significant amounts of financial assistance from the EU. In fact, while financial assistance to Macedonia through CARDS totaled €298.2 million from 2000-2006, Croatia received €523.8 million

34 Concordia was tasked with monitoring the security environment and facilitating post-conflict confidence building (Risteska 2007: 11).

in CARDS and IPA (Instrument for Pre-Accession Assistance) financial assistance from the EU during this same period of time (European Commission 2007).[35] Meanwhile Serbia and Montenegro, including Kosovo, received €2,559.8 million from 2000-2006 (European Commission 2007). Of course, both Croatia and Serbia were often found to be in non-compliance with their respective obligations toward the Tribunal.

*Explaining Compliance: Macedonia, Ohrid, NATO, and the EU*

Rapid compliance on the part of the Macedonian government to the arrest and surrender order issued for Tarčulovski combined with five years of consistent cooperation with Tribunal investigations was consistent with Macedonia's post-independence foreign policy, which favored integration into international institutions and organizations as a means of guaranteeing state survival. In the words of the Macedonian Ministry of Defense:

> Beside building of its own defence system, [the] Republic of Macedonia has decided to build its strategy upon the collective security and defence systems membership since being a part of the European security mechanism is the only way to achieve greater efficiency and higher combat readiness as well as protection of the sovereignty and the territorial integrity of the country (Republic of Macedonia Ministry of Defense 2007a).

Macedonian cooperation with the ICTY, which was mandated by both NATO and the EU, was consistent with Macedonia's pursuit of Euro-Atlantic integration. However, Croatia provides an example of a state which both sought membership in the EU and NATO and failed to comply with ICTY orders in 2001 and again in 2002. Macedonian cooperation with the Tribunal contrasts with the previous case studies where compliance was often preceded by periods of non-compliance as local elites gauged the costs associated with failing to execute ICTY orders. Cooperation on the part of Skopje, on the other hand, was automatic as even the Tribunal praised Skopje's assistance in a wide range of areas.

In fact, a crisis between Macedonia, the EU and the US was not precipitated by the ICTY's indictments of Macedonian citizens, but instead was the outcome of a conflict between the EU and US over Macedonia's ratification of an Article 98 agreement. The US' successful campaign to secure an Article 98 agreement with Macedonia, despite explicit warnings from the EU that aspirant states should not sign such agreements raises questions about the independent impact of EU enlargement conditionality upon Skopje. The Article 98 debate presents an important insight into perceptions of the EU and NATO, and allows us an opportunity to attempt to disentangle various external pressures for compliance.

35 In 2005, Croatia was moved from CARDS to IPA when Croatia became an EU candidate state.

Boduszyński and Balakovska note that Skopje lacked trust in the EU as a result of the EU having raised expectations of fast track membership in return for Macedonia agreeing to accept large numbers of refugees and host NATO troops during the 1999 Kosovo war (2004: 21-22). In fact, it was pointed out that there was "deep disappointment when the promises were left unfulfilled" (Boduszyński and Balalovska 2004: 21-22). Additionally, despite being the first Western Balkans state to sign a SAA with the EU, Macedonia's accession process has lagged behind that of Croatia, which began accession negotiations in October 2005.

Interestingly, with regard to Croatia, where NATO and the US also demanded compliance with ICTY orders, a causal linkage was established between EU conditionality and compliance which explained the policy shift in Zagreb. And, despite significant pressure from the US, Croatia did not ratify an Article 98 agreement and therefore lost access to US military assistance. Nevertheless, it is important to emphasize that ratification of an Article 98 agreement with the US occurred after a specific threat of sanctions was transmitted from Washington to Skopje. In the case of the Tarčulovski arrest, no such threat was necessary, and compliance on the part of Skopje occurred within hours of the issuing of an arrest and surrender order.

## Conclusions

Macedonia's interaction with the ICTY began much later than that of Croatia and Serbia and involved the arrest and surrender of only a single individual, yet nonetheless, the Macedonian government assisted the Tribunal in its investigative work and promptly executed an ICTY arrest and surrender order during the period under examination. Macedonia's half decade of cooperation with the ICTY stands in sharp contrast to the previous two case studies where episodes of non-compliance were observed. Macedonian compliance was the outcome of a decade long engagement with international actors and the embedding of the Macedonian state in international organizations through the OFA.

Dependence upon external actors for state survival and security, particularly after the 2001 OFA, meant non-compliance with an ICTY arrest and surrender order had the potential to subject Macedonia to significant material costs. However, that cannot in itself explain compliance as Macedonia never waited for third party states to articulate the costs of non-compliance in the days and months following the Tarčulovski indictment. Instead, Skopje simply complied with a standing international legal obligation. Thus, coercive threats and economic inducements, which characterized attempts to secure compliance in Croatia and Serbia, were not required to bring about compliance as Skopje promptly executed an ICTY arrest and surrender order without waiting to measure the response of external actors to non-compliance. Furthermore, domestically, Macedonian cooperation with the ICTY did not entail significant costs upon local elites as the limited number of indictments and lack of intensity and duration of violent conflict meant there was no significant public mobilization against the Tribunal on the part of the security services, veterans' organizations or victims' groups. That is not to say, however, there was not criticism of the ICTY for having issued indictments against Macedonian ministry of interior officials, while not indicting members of the NLA. Nevertheless, public opinion was never engaged with the ICTY to the extent observed in Croatia and Serbia granting the Macedonian government significantly greater autonomy in constructing policy toward the ICTY. Absent significant domestic opposition to compliance and given Macedonia's decade long interaction with international actors ranging from the UN and OSCE to NATO and the EU, Skopje's compliance with the Tarčulovski arrest and surrender order was consistent with an established pattern of Macedonian compliance with international legal obligations. Thus, Macedonia is the only state case study where first order compliance was forthcoming.

# PART II
# Compliance Beyond the State

# Chapter 5
# Bosnia-Herzegovina: Compliance under Diffuse Sovereignty

## Introduction

Although previous case studies took into consideration the interaction between the ICTY and states, a discussion of Bosnia-Herzegovina (BiH)[1] will introduce the question of compliance with ICTY orders in the context of a state under international military and civilian administration. The most extensive post-conflict state building project since the Second World War was undertaken in post-war BiH (Chandler 2005: 307), and the ICTY's role in BiH cannot be viewed in isolation from this project. Because engagement with the ICTY occurred during an externally imposed process of post-war state building, this chapter will explore the question of compliance in the absence of a traditional Westphalian state and, as a result, will require an analytical framework which moves beyond dominant theories of IR that continue to rely on the state as an ontological given.[2] Rather than being viewed as a state, BiH should be seen as an illustrative empirical example approaching Krasner's concept of shared sovereignty (2004: 108). BiH remains formally sovereign as an international legal subject, yet at the same time has had its ability to act autonomously curtailed by external actors. Thus, even though Krasner suggests BiH is under a form of transitional administration (2004: 101-103),[3] Krasner's observation, "Foreigners have been running many of the ministries in Bosnia" (2004: 115) underlines the extent to state-centric approaches to IR are ill equipped to address the question of compliance in post-Dayton BiH.

---

1 The state of Bosnia-Herzegovina came into existence through the Dayton Peace Agreement of November 1995 ending the international legal existence of the previously recognized "Republic of Bosnia and Herzegovina" (Gow 1997: 288).

2 By dominant theories of IR, realism and its neorealist variants can be included alongside neoliberal institutionalist theories. Also of interest is the fact international legal obligations remain largely state-centric creating a situation whereby although the ICTY brings to trial individuals, legal obligations to cooperate with the Tribunal were assigned to states.

3 Krasner does not take into account that there has not been a substantial transfer of powers from international to domestic ownership in the decade following Dayton. Instead, there has only been a transfer of powers from the Peace Implementation Council (PIC), which was established in December 1995 to oversee Dayton and included 55 member states and organizations, to the European Union (Chandler 2006: 18). For a complete list of PIC membership see Appendix VI.

Despite the limitations on sovereignty imposed by the 1995 General Framework Agreement for Peace in Bosnia and Herzegovina, subsequently referred to as the Dayton Peace Agreement (DPA), when referencing BiH, the term *state* will be used to describe BiH's international legal identity.[4] The use of the term *state* should not be read in terms of Westphalian conceptions of sovereignty which imply sovereign control over a given territory because although BiH maintained the legal identity of a state, Sarajevo surrendered its autonomy to act within its own borders to external actors. Thus, traditional interpretations of the nexus between sovereignty and international law enforcement, such as the following put forth by Morgenthau, cannot be applied to post-Dayton BiH:

> … the sovereignty of the nation as the intended object of a law-enforcing action manifests itself in what is called the "impenetrability" of the nation. This is another way of saying that on a given territory only one nation can have sovereignty – supreme authority – and that no other state has the right to perform governmental acts on its territory without consent (1978: 317).

The assumption that only a single actor should exercise sovereignty over a given territory, while more applicable to the previous case studies, serves only to obscure understandings of compliance in the Bosnian context. In BiH tasks related to local governance fell under the authority of the Office of the High Representative (OHR). The OHR was invested with wide ranging powers which included the ability to prohibit individuals or political parties from participation in domestic political life, the power to impose legislation by decree, and ban local media perceived as hostile to the spirit of the DPA (Chandler 2006: 27).[5] Furthermore, external actors such as the European Court of Human Rights and the IMF were delegated the authority to appoint non-BiH citizens to key positions within the Bosnian judiciary and Central Bank, thereby introducing an international component to the state (Gow 1997: 293). Given the above sampling of powers delegated to external actors through the DPA, Morgenthau would assume BiH is a state that has lost sovereignty, and perhaps is no longer a state at all:

> Sovereignty is the supreme legal authority of the nation to give and enforce the law within a certain territory and, in consequence, independence from the authority of any other nation and equality with it under international law. Hence, the nation loses its sovereignty when it is placed under the authority of another nation, so that it is the latter that exercises supreme authority to give and enforce the laws within the former's territory (1978: 321).

4 See Krasner's definition of legal sovereignty (Krasner 1999: 14-20).

5 A more detailed discussion of the OHR's mandate in BiH will follow shortly. For more on the post-Dayton Bosnian state see (Bojičić-Dželilović 2003).

However, Morgenthau's observation is itself problematic, because the alternative presented is that of being placed under the authority of another state and not the delegation of sovereignty to international organizations. As will be demonstrated in this chapter, BiH did not come under the authority of another state, but rather became integrated into a complex network of international organizations and states, which assumed executive, legislative, and even law enforcement powers.[6]

While the above illustrates why it is difficult to explore compliance through the lens of *state* compliance, especially when sovereignty on a given territory is shared between domestic and external actors, the fact that international organizations such as the OHR and NATO played instrumental roles in bringing about the arrest and transfer of ICTY fugitives in BiH further underlines the limitations of state-centered theories of compliance as the very act of compliance was not generally carried out by the state under examination. For example, a majority of individuals arrested and transferred to Tribunal custody from the territory of BiH were apprehended by NATO rather than appendages of the Bosnian state.[7] Of course, in a 1996 incident, which would later prove to be an exception to the rule, BiH became the first state in the former Yugoslavia to execute ICTY arrest warrants (G.J. Bass 2002: 237).[8] Despite an increasing reliance by the ICTY upon multinational peacekeeping or police forces to enforce arrest and surrender orders, existing compliance literature, with the significant exception of Zhou (2006) and Kerr (Kerr 2004: 154-169), has almost exclusively focused on state compliance with international legal obligations rather than compliance on the part of multinational peacekeeping forces.

The relative absence of compliance literature on partially sovereign territories represents a significant gap in the literature as BiH's partial sovereignty is far from *sui generis*. Afghanistan, Cambodia, East Timor, Iraq and Kosovo are all territories which, to varying degrees, have also had their sovereignty curtailed by external actors (Chandler 2006: 20).[9] Moreover, Zhou points out that there is an increasing acceptance of the assumption that following genocide or other serious violations of International Humanitarian Law, local authorities will be left either unable or unwilling to bring to trial perpetrators (Zhou 2006: 203) making the role

6 For a comprehensive list of states and international organizations which presided over the international presence in BiH see Appendix VI.

7 Between 1997 and 2004 NATO transferred 27 individuals to ICTY custody. Three individuals under ICTY indictment were killed by NATO personnel during arrest operations. The Bosnian Serb republic transferred only a single individual, Zdravko Tolimir, to the ICTY, while the Federation of Bosnia-Herzegovina transferred two individuals to ICTY custody in 1996.

8 Although exceptional, this incident should not be underplayed as the Federation of Bosnia-Herzegovina took the unprecedented step of arresting Bosnian Muslims for war crimes against Bosnian Serbs at a time when both Croatia and Serbia were failing to comply with ICTY arrest and surrender orders.

9 In the case of Kosovo, which will be addressed in Chapter 6, the province was transformed into an international protectorate under UN Resolution 1244, while concurrently remaining within the Republic of Serbia.

of international peacekeeping forces, where present, crucial to IHL enforcement. Given the inability of theories of state compliance to explain international law enforcement, or the lack thereof, within shared or partially sovereign entities, this chapter will explore compliance not just on the part of domestic actors but also international actors with a presence in BiH. However, first a historic-institutional context will be provided which will both explore the DPA and international and domestic institutions of governance created at Dayton. Second, there will be an exploration of compliance on the part of domestic (local) actors, which will be followed by an exploration of the construction of international justice within BiH. Then, there will be a discussion of compliance on the part of international actors.

## Contextualizing Compliance in Post-Dayton Bosnia-Herzegovina

The DPA, which established the framework for the post-war international administration of BiH, contained only ten points and was supplemented by 11 annexes (Gow 1997: 286). The DPA brought an end to the war in BiH and was agreed upon on November 12, 1995 by representatives of BiH, Croatia and the Federal Republic of Yugoslavia (Kaufman 2004: 132-134). For the relevant period under examination (1995-2006), BiH was a state under international administration legalized through the 1995 peace agreement. The powers ceded to external actors by the warring parties were robust. Allin even observed, "At Dayton, the Bosnian parties effectively submitted themselves to military occupation" (2002: 83). Yet, while post-Dayton BiH cannot be described as exercising Westphalian sovereignty over its own territory, the DPA paradoxically reaffirmed BiH's status as a state under international law:

> The Republic of Bosnia and Herzegovina, the official name of which shall henceforth be "Bosnia and Herzegovina," *shall continue its legal existence under international law as a state*, with its internal structure modified as provided herein and with its present internationally recognized borders. It shall remain a Member State of the United Nations and may as Bosnia and Herzegovina maintain or apply for membership in organizations within the United Nations system and other international organizations (Annex 4, Article 1).[10]

The DPA also laid the foundation for an international presence which effectively decoupled the linkage of the state and sovereign control over a given territory. Chandler provides perhaps the most succinct description of post-Dayton Bosnia:

> BiH highlights the contradictions of having the existence of a formally sovereign state with regularly contested elections at state, entity and local levels and, alongside this, the existence of a parallel administration headed by unaccountable

10 Emphasis added by author.

> international appointees with the power to draw up and impose legislation and sack elected officials (2005: 314).

It will be illustrated that it was the powers of the parallel international administration which would prove instrumental to ensuring the transfer of persons indicted by the ICTY to Tribunal custody.

Despite BiH's autonomy deficit, the fact the DPA preserved the international legal personality of the Bosnian state meant Sarajevo remained the legal subject of an obligation to cooperate with the ICTY. This obligation was reaffirmed in the DPA, which committed the three signatory parties to cooperate fully with the Tribunal. Although BiH assumed a legal obligation to comply with Tribunal orders, it must be emphasized state-level institutions were unable to fulfill an obligation to cooperate with the ICTY. BiH's state-level autonomy to act was constrained by external actors, such as the OHR and NATO, and internally state-level autonomy was further limited by the creation of powerful sub-state entities, the Bosnian Serb *Republika Srpska* (RS) and the Muslim-Croat Federation of BiH (FBiH). BiH's division into two sub-state entities permitted the RS to maintain an independent law enforcement capability and judicial system, which led to a significant divergence in levels of ICTY cooperation between the two entities.

*BiH under International Administration*

Any description of the international civilian presence in BiH must begin with the Office of the High Representative (OHR). The OHR was established through Annex 10 of the DPA to provide international civilian oversight for domestic governance, and it was presided over by a High Representative, who was tasked with coordinating civilian implementation of the DPA, coordinating activities with the NATO mission in BiH, and maintaining contacts with international actors (Gow 2006: 54). The High Representative was nominated by the Steering Board of the Peace Implementation Council and nominations were then subject to endorsement by the United Nations Security Council.[11] Since 1996 there have been seven High Representatives.[12] In addition, the appointment of Lord Paddy Ashdown as High Representative in March 2002 coincided with the position of High Representative

11 Members of the PIC Steering Board include: Canada, France, Germany, Italy, Japan, Russia, United Kingdom, United States, the Presidency of the European Union, the European Commission, and the Organization of the Islamic Conference, represented by Turkey (*OHR General Information* 2007).

12 BiH's first High Representative was Carl Bildt (December 1995-June 1997) who had previously served as the EU's peace mediator for the Former Yugoslavia. Subsequent High Representatives were: Carlos Westendorp (June 1997-July 1999), Wolfgang Petritsch (August 1999-May 2002), Paddy Ashdown (May 2002-January 2006), Christian Schwartz-Schilling (February 2006-June 2007), Miroslav Lajcak (July 2007-March 2009), Valentin Inzko (March 2009-present).

assuming the additional role of EU Special Representative to BiH (EUSR). The appointment of a EUSR was intended to permit the EU to inherit the wide ranging powers which the OHR had by then accumulated (Chandler 2006: 32).[13]

The double hatting of the position of High Representative as both the head of the OHR and the EUSR combined with the double hatting of lower administrative positions and the creation of positions exclusively under the authority of the EUSR, was part of a wider process designed to bring about an increasing EU-ization of post-Dayton BiH. The European Commission Delegation to BiH has become one of the Commission's largest out-of-EU delegations numbering over 100 staff and including offices in both Sarajevo and Banja Luka (European Commission Delegation to Bosnia and Herzegovina 2007a). Moreover, the European Commission established a broad range of objectives for its Delegation to BiH which include consolidation of the peace process and fostering inter-entity cooperation (European Commission Delegation to Bosnia and Herzegovina 2007c). Since 2002, the European Union has increasingly assumed a leading role in BiH. This shift is contextualized as part of BiH's EU accession process:

> As BiH moves from the era of Dayton onto the road to Brussels, the EU itself has assumed a leading position in BiH's international engagement – not to the exclusion of other partners, but through a naturally evolving relationship based on BiH's aspiration to obtain EU membership (European Commission Delegation to Bosnia and Herzegovina 2007b).

However, while the EU-ization of BiH's international administration began in 2002 with the appointment of Paddy Ashdown as both the High Representative and EUSR, for much of the period of time examined in this case study, the OHR remained at the apex of the international presence in BiH.[14]

*Powers of the OHR*

The High Representative was invested with significant powers which included the final authority to interpret civilian provisions of the DPA (Gow 2006: 54). The OHR's powers were amplified at a Peace Implementation Council (PIC) meeting in Bonn during 1997 to include the ability to remove from office any individual who violates legal commitments to which the belligerent parties committed themselves at Dayton, impose legislation by decree, and amplified the OHR's ability to censor the domestic media. These powers subsequently became known as the Bonn

---

13 In addition to a EUSR for BiH, the EU has appointed EUSRs for Afghanistan, Central Asia, the Former Yugoslav Republic of Macedonia, the Great Lakes region, the Middle East, Moldova, the South Caucasus, and Sudan. In addition, at the time of writing planning was underway for the appointment of a EUSR for Kosovo (European Council Secretariat 2007).

14 This, of course, does not include NATO's military presence, which operated under a separate command structure independent from the OHR.

Powers. Despite an effort to reduce the frequency the Bonn Powers were used by the OHR,[15] the Bonn Powers have continued to be employed a decade after the DPA to both implement legislation by *fiat* and remove individuals from public office. The authority to remove individuals from public office has been exercised against the highest officials of the Bosnian state. For example, Carlos Westendorp relied on the Bonn Powers to remove nationalist Bosnian Serb politician Nikola Poplasen following his electoral triumph over the more moderate Biljana Plavšić in 1998 (Gow 2006: 60), and Paddy Ashdown relied on the Bonn Powers to dismiss the Bosnian Croat member of the BiH presidency, Dragan Čović, following Čović's indictment on corruption charges (Ashdown 2005). More recently, in July 2007, the Bonn Powers were exercised when High Representative Miroslav Lajcak imposed legislation to reform Bosnia's prison system. Lajcak also removed a number of officials suspected of either assisting ICTY fugitives or suspected of involvement in war crimes from RS police forces (Clifford 2007).

Not only could the OHR remove recalcitrant politicians and civil service from office, but the OHR also exercised the authority to censor media coverage that was perceived as a threat to the Dayton peace process.[16] NATO forces in BiH have acted to seize transmission towers from broadcast media for what NATO described as inflammatory news coverage and have also facilitated the transmission of media deemed by the alliance to be non-inflammatory (W. Clark 1998). Furthermore, local television broadcasters were also required to provide coverage of trials at the ICTY as a condition of maintaining their broadcasting licenses.[17]

### *Internationalization of the Bosnian State*

In addition to the OHR's robust powers, the DPA stipulated key positions within the Bosnian government could not be held by citizens of BiH or its neighboring states (Gow 1997: 293). While the OHR existed as a parallel international administration

---

15 Former political advisor to the OHR, Siw Skjold Lexau, notes that from 2002 onwards there was an attempt to use the Bonn Powers to stimulate reform rather than as a negative sanction. Skjold Lexau uses the example of the OHR choosing to amend locally drafted equal rights legislation rather than imposing legislation by decree (Skjold Lexau 2004: 5). However, with Miroslav Lajcak's appointment as High Representative in 2007 and the subsequent dismissal of entity-level personnel in the Bosnian Serb republic and the imposition of legislation pertaining to prison security, it does appear that negative sanctions remain an import tool of the OHR.

16 The OHR was formally delegated the authority to censor Bosnian media by the Peace Implementation Council at a meeting in Sintra, Portugal in May 1997. In July 1997 Bosnian Serb television, SRT, was taken off the air after broadcasting a news report which compared international peacekeeping forces in BiH to the Nazi SS (Deluce 2000-2001).

17 As of 2007, there are three public broadcasters in BiH, one broadcaster for each entity (RTFBiH – Federation of Bosnia and Herzegovina and RTRS – Republika Srpska) and a state-wide broadcaster (BHRT) and three major commercial broadcasters, OBN, TV Pink BiH, and Mreza Plus (Haraszti 2007).

to the state, which maintained the ability to intervene in the domestic governance of BiH, the Bosnian state itself acquired an increasingly international hue as judicial and economic governance positions were delegated to non-BiH citizens. These positions included the Human Rights Ombudsman, appointed by the OSCE, the governor of BiH's Central Bank, appointed by the IMF, and nine representatives on the Constitutional Court, appointed by the European Court of Human Rights (Gow 1997: 293).

### *The Rules of Road: The ICTY as Bosnia's War Crimes High Court?*

Not only were international actors granted substantial authority over domestic political life, but the ICTY was also integrated into the domestic judiciary to a much greater extent than in any previous case study. In previous case studies the Tribunal Statute granted the ICTY primacy over war crimes proceedings. Primacy meant the Tribunal could order domestic courts to defer a case to the Tribunal; however, the Tribunal had no authority to prevent domestic courts from bringing war crimes charges against individuals on their own accord. With regard to BiH, the Tribunal's powers went beyond primacy as the 1996 Rome Agreement, informally known as the Rules of the Road agreement, placed domestic courts under a legal obligation to refer all war crimes cases to the Tribunal before domestic proceedings could commence. In fact, the Rome Agreement stated that persons other than those already indicted by the ICTY could be detained only "...pursuant to a previously issued order, warrant or indictment that had been reviewed and deemed consistent with international legal standards by the Tribunal" (Report of the International Tribunal 1999: 35). Thus, whereas in both Croatia and Serbia domestic courts could independently initiate war crimes proceedings the Bosnian judiciary could not bring war crimes charges against individuals without first submitting indictments to supra-national judicial review.

The Rules of the Road agreement was established in order to prevent domestic judiciaries and police forces from inflaming inter-ethnic tensions through war crimes prosecutions and arrests. This was a serious concern at the end of 1995 because local judiciaries tended to be staffed by members of the ethnic majority community and war crimes trial processes were deemed so unfair that war crimes prosecutions could serve to prevent members of an ethnic community from traveling to a region where they were in a minority as this could result in arbitrary arrest and detention (OSCE 2005: 4). Furthermore, convictions on war crimes charges in the domestic judiciary prior to the Rules of Road were highly flawed. Take for example Sretko Damjanović who was sentenced to death in 1993 by the District Military Court in Sarajevo, a sentence later commuted to 20 years imprisonment following BiH's abolishment of the death penalty. In 1997 the Human Rights Chamber of BiH ruled the District Military Court, which convicted Damjanović, "lacked a sufficient appearance of independence" and overturned the conviction (OSCE 2005: 4).[18] In order to prevent abuses of the judiciary, the ICTY established A, B, and C classifications for BiH war crimes cases. Only when a case was assessed to be category A could the domestic judiciary commence proceedings against an accused.

The Rules of the Road placed a significant burden on the Tribunal as the review of domestic cases was not adequately funded by international donors. This resulted in the accumulation of a significant backlog of cases (Report of the International Tribunal 1999: 35). Because the Rules of the Road program was funded through voluntary contributions (Report of the International Tribunal 1997: 24), the ICTY was reliant upon donations from organizations such as the Coalition for International Justice and the American Bar Association's Central and East European Law Initiative to fund reviews during 1998 (Report of the International Tribunal 1999: 35). The Rules of the Road expired in October 2004. The ICTY's completion strategy committed the Tribunal to begin preparing for its closure, and therefore the Rules of the Road program was discontinued. However, as the Rules of the Road exclusively dealt with domestic war crimes prosecutions, there must be a distinction between the domestic judiciary's submission of cases to the ICTY for judicial review and the wider question of state compliance with orders stemming from ICTY indictments.

### *States within a State? The Creation of a Dual Entity State*

Before turning to an examination of the politics of compliance with ICTY orders, it is of utmost importance to stress that in addition to establishing a mandate for a robust international civilian and military presence, the DPA created a two-entitied state with two separate legal systems, law enforcement agencies, and even two separate armed forces. This led Gow to observe that post-Dayton BiH was a state which had been effectively partitioned (2006: 50-51).[19] The DPA not only constrained BiH autonomy to act from above in the form of the OHR, but also from below in the form of powerful entity-level governments. In contrast to the entity level governments, the powers reserved for state-level were effectively limited to responsibility over foreign policy, certain aspects of economic policy, inter-entity communication, and criminal law enforcement (Gow 1997: 289). In regard to foreign policy, however, there were provisions which, subject to the approval of the Parliamentary Assembly, permitted entity-level governments to enter into agreements with states or international bodies (Gow 1997: 289). Additionally, the close relationship between the Republic of Croatia and the Bosnian Croat community in the FBiH led to the transfers of indicted Bosnian Croats being

18 It was later revealed two of the individuals Damjanović had been convicted of murdering were in fact alive (Garms and Peschke 2006: 264-265).

19 While two entities were established through Dayton, the *Republika Srpska* and the Federation of Bosnia-Herzegovina, during the 1990s, there was a third Bosnian Croat *de facto* entity within the Federation.

brought about by Zagreb rather than Sarajevo as throughout the 1990s Zagreb exercised considerable control over Bosnian Croat political life.[20]

While the OHR exercised authority in both entities, the Federation of Bosnia-Herzegovina and the Republika Srpska, the two entity governments were held together by relatively weak state institutions. Bergling notes:

> The entities … are best described as *de facto* mini-states within a very loose and uneasy confederation. Notably, there is no enforcement mechanism capable of compelling them to implement state-level decisions. Further, as the state institutions depend on the entities for funding, these institutions are only as strong as the entities permit. As there are strong constituencies, particularly in the RS and the Croatian dominated cantons of the Federation, that do not wish the joint structures to function, the institutions of state are often manipulated or even held hostage in a political game of give and take (2001: 494).

Subsequent to Bergling's observation, there has been an attempt by the OHR/EUSR to strengthen state level institutions through the creation of a state level VAT tax and the police and defense reforms; however, overall the entity level governments have continued to hold significant powers *vis à vis* state institutions.

Although BiH's two entities compiled very different records when it came to cooperation with the Tribunal, paradoxically we are confronted with a single international legal personality both complying and failing to comply with its obligations toward the ICTY. Divergent levels of cooperation between entities became an almost constant feature of the BiH compliance landscape and will be described in greater detail below. The dual entity structure of BiH led the Tribunal to issue two separate assessments of cooperation, for the Federation of Bosnia-Herzegovina and for the *Republika Srpska*. Furthermore, *within* BiH indictments issued by courts within the FBiH could not be enforced in the RS or vice versa (International Crisis Group 2000: 9). The difficulty in exploring state compliance in a dual entity state under international administration provides an opportunity to move beyond the question of state compliance with ICTY orders and address the question of compliance on the part of sub-state actors.

## The Domestic Politics of Compliance

Louise Arbour noted the greatest challenge facing the ICTY in its early years was the question of arrests of indicted individuals (2004: 397). While Chapter 2 demonstrated the coercive linkage of external assistance on the part of the United States proved effective in bringing about Croatia's transfer of Bosnian Croats to Tribunal custody in 1997, the failure to apprehend fugitives on the territory of BiH, in particular the *Republika Srpska*, and Serbia cast a pall over the ICTY. As

20 See the subsequent discussion of Croatian and Bosnian Croat compliance.

of February 1998, the ratio of indictments to individuals in custody remained 78: 25 (Allison 1998). Bringing about compliance with ICTY orders in BiH required interaction with sub-state entities and international actors, in addition to the state-level institutions of BiH. In order to disentangle the politics of compliance, first entity level compliance will be explored and second there will be an exploration of compliance on the part of international actors in BiH.

### *Entity-Level Compliance*

The following discussion of entity-level compliance will look at local compliance with international legal obligations imposed upon the state of BiH. Because of BiH's division into two distinct entities, such an exploration is unavoidable; however, the necessity of sub-state enforcement of international legal obligations itself is not unique to BiH. For example, Henkin observed that the United States' Headquarters Agreement with the United Nations required the ratification of specific legislation in the state of New York and the adoption of local police regulations to accommodate this agreement (1968: 57). Yet, unlike federal states such as the US, no enforcement mechanisms were established for BiH's state level government. Entity-level governments could effectively ignore state level decisions (Bergling 2001: 493). It is the absence of an enforcement mechanism that separates BiH from other federal states because while mechanisms exist to bring about compliance with international legal obligations within federal state entities such as the United States, Sarajevo was unable to effectively counter non-compliance on the part of an entity-level government.

Despite a perceived inability on the part of local actors to effectively execute ICTY arrest orders (Figà-Talamanca 1996: 173), cooperation with the ICTY was initially left to entity-level governments and local police forces resulting in the FBiH accumulating a good record of cooperation, while the *Republika Srpska* for the most part failed to cooperate with the Tribunal. As will be discussed shortly, in the months immediately following the DPA, the FBiH initially proved too aggressive in its pursuit of war criminals garnering criticism from IFOR and praise from the ICTY. In addition to divergent levels of cooperation between the two entities, perceptions of the ICTY varied greatly between the RS and FBiH as well. Residents of the RS perceived the ICTY as disproportionately targeting ethnic Serbs in its investigations and indictments, while the Tribunal was viewed considerably more favorably in the FBiH.[21]

### *Republika Srpska*

The RS consistently opposed cooperation with the ICTY and like Serbia was often singled out for non-compliance with its obligations toward the Tribunal (Report of the International Tribunal 1999: 28-29). RS opposition to cooperation with the

21 For more on perceptions of the ICTY as anti-Serb see Saxon 2005: 556-567.

Tribunal must, however, be placed in the context of RS obstruction to cooperation with the OHR, the creation of central state institutions, refugee returns, and the restoration of property rights (Kerr 2005: 327). The RS consistently obstructed not just the ICTY but also the strengthening of Bosnian state institutions. Even in regard to Dayton, the RS only reluctantly agreed to its inclusion within a Bosnian state.[22] RS political leaders also continued to threaten a referendum on independence from BiH, leaving the state-level government fragile at best (Vogel 2006).

The RS' rejection of an obligation to cooperate with the Tribunal was reaffirmed during 1996 when the RS' first post-Karadžić president, Biljana Plavšić, claimed ICTY indictments were not considered legitimate by RS authorities (Sharp 1997-1998: 120).[23] Plavšić's rejection of legal obligations to cooperate with the Tribunal was more than just rhetorical as the RS not only failed to transfer individuals to ICTY custody, but also failed to remove indicted persons from public office. Non-compliance with ICTY arrest orders combined with an almost complete lack of war crimes prosecutions in the domestic judiciary during the first eight years following the DPA (Garms and Peschke 2006: 274), transformed the RS, along with Serbia, into a safe haven for individuals suspected of war crimes. In the Tribunal's 1999 annual report to the UNSC it was noted:

> … the Republika Srpska has continued its policy of refusing to execute arrest warrants against indictees believed to be residing on its territory. Of the 36 publicly indicted persons at liberty at the end of the reporting period … approximately 25 are in the Republika Srpska (Report of the International Tribunal 1999: 28-29).

Non-compliance on the part of the RS persisted until June 2007, when Zdravko Tolimir was arrested by RS police near the entity's border with Serbia. Tolimir's arrest marked the first time RS police executed an ICTY arrest warrant. However, this event coincided with a renewed rhetorical commitment on the part of Belgrade to transfer remaining ICTY indictees to The Hague in exchange for the unfreezing of Serbian Stability and Association Agreement negotiations (N. MacDonald and Dombey 2007). Moreover, as Tolimir was arrested crossing from Serbia into the RS, there was speculation Tolimir was delivered to RS police for transfer to the ICTY by Serbian authorities (Sadović 2007).

### *RS Domestic Politics of Compliance*

Despite entity level non-compliance, Matias Hellman, of the ICTY Registry in Sarajevo, pointed out that because most of the crimes prosecuted by the ICTY

22 Note the RS leadership was excluded from Dayton and Milošević negotiated on behalf of the RS.

23 This argument of course ignores the fact the parties committed themselves to continued cooperation with the ICTY in the Dayton Peace Agreement.

occurred on the territory of the RS against non-Serb populations, non-Serb victims groups from the RS strongly support the Tribunal.[24] But, given the domination of RS entity level government by ethnic Serb political parties, this support was not reflected in government policy. Even when Biljana Plavšić broke with Radovan Karadžić and established a more moderate tone in RS internal politics, cooperation with the ICTY was not forthcoming on the part of local governments within the RS.[25] During the 1997 Plavšić-Karadžić conflict, the RS was internally divided between central and western regions under the control of Plavšić and eastern regions, which remained loyal to Karadžić. It should be noted it was during this conflict that NATO forces began to execute ICTY arrest warrants against Karadžić supporters, in a move that was seen to decisively strengthen Plavšić's faction (Gow 2006: 59-60).

In the RS, the Tribunal is perceived considerably more negatively than the FBiH. Polling data from 2002 suggests the ICTY is trusted by only 4 percent of the population (Kerr 2005: 325), making the population of the RS the most Tribunal-skeptic in the entire former Yugoslavia. It is the deep unpopularity of cooperation with the ICTY, which made any attempt at cooperation with the Tribunal on the part of elected RS officials untenable over the long term (Gow 2006: 60). Illustrative of the unpopularity of cooperation with the ICTY was the fact that the RS' parliament was only able to secure passage of a law on cooperation with the ICTY by a single vote.[26] However, obstruction of the DPA, while popular amongst the electorate was also untenable over the long term due to the threat of sanction by the OHR. For example, following Plavšić's defeat to hard-line nationalist Nikola Poplasen in 1998, Poplasen was promptly dismissed from his post by High Representative Carlos Westendorp (Gow 2006: 60).[27] Over all, while coercion on the part of the OHR through the use of the Bonn Powers strengthened moderates within the RS, the persistent lack of cooperation with the ICTY within the entity continued until 2007.

---

24 Personal interview with Matias Hellman of the ICTY Field Office in Sarajevo, 16 January 2007.

25 Biljana Plavšić received substantial assistance from international actors in her successful ousting of Radovan Karadžić. In 1997, the US released targeted loans to regions of the RS under the control of Plavšić (CNN 1997).

26 The RS' 2001 Law on Cooperation with the ICTY contained numerous caveats, such as granting the RS the right to not enforce ICTY arrest warrants should they be deemed a threat to the interests of the RS. A representative of the RS' Bosnian Muslim community within the RS parliament even suggested the 2001 law would be more appropriately titled the law on 'obstruction of cooperation' with the ICTY (International Crisis Group 2001b: 24).

27 It should also be noted that Radovan Karadžić's wartime Serbian Democratic Party (*Srpska demokratska stranka*, SDS) remained the largest single parliamentary party in the RS Assembly following elections from 1996-2006 when moderate nationalist Milorad Dodik's Union of Independent Social Democrats (*Savez nezavisnih socijaldemokrata*, SNSD) won an absolute majority of Assembly seats.

*Federation of Bosnia and Herzegovina*

The FBiH was the creation of the 1994 Washington Agreement which ended the Croat-Muslim conflict and brought the two ethnic communities together into a single entity, and the FBiH's existence as an entity was reaffirmed by the DPA. The FBiH was subdivided into 10 cantons, which themselves enjoy a significant level of autonomy (Bergling 2001: 496). The FBiH proved more supportive of the Tribunal's mission as the ICTY was perceived as acting to bring to trial individuals responsible for massacres carried out against Bosnian Muslim civilian populations in places such as Srebrenica.[28] In fact, while the ICTY was perceived negatively elsewhere in the former Yugoslavia, it is in the FBiH where the Tribunal was most favorably viewed. The ICTY enjoyed the trust of 51 percent of those polled in 2002 (Kerr 2005: 325).

Moreover, the very establishment of the Tribunal in 1993 was perceived as a triumph for the besieged Bosnian state (Saxon 2005: 563). In 1995 Sarajevo requested the inclusion of stringent arrest and surrender procedures in the DPA. These measures included a clear obligation upon each party to the agreement to arrest, detain, and transfer ICTY indictees. Furthermore Sarajevo requested the imposition of sanctions on parties that failed to cooperate with the Tribunal, a constitutional provision requiring cooperation with the Tribunal on the part of sub-state entities, a vetting process to remove war criminals from positions of influence, and a prohibition on suspected war criminals from holding elected office or public positions (Williams and Scharf 2002: 163-164). The response to the Bosnian delegations' proposals from Contact Group representatives present at Dayton demonstrated the extent to which European governments sought to marginalize the ICTY in post-war BiH. As Keith Doubt pointed out, "…the more the Bosnian delegation insists on justice, the less the Bosnian delegation is viewed as being interested in peace" (Doubt 1997: 125).[29] Williams and Scharf noted Britain and France rejected any automatic re-imposition of sanctions on recalcitrant parties and Contact Group military representatives rejected the inclusion of any binding obligation to arrest war criminals or even assign staff to identify individuals responsible for war crimes (2002: 165). In the end, Bosnia's requests to strengthen the role of the Tribunal in post-Dayton BiH were summarily rejected at Dayton (Sharp 1997-1998: 120, Williams and Scharf 2002: 162-164). The Bosnian delegation was rebuffed out of a fear that the aggressive pursuit of indicted persons would threaten the peace or, even worse, prove to be a deal breaker for the Serbian delegation at Dayton (Gow 2006: 50, Kerr 2005: 320). In fact, IFOR would make it clear in 1996 that the international peacekeeping force would not tolerate the aggressive pursuit of war criminals by either the FBiH or the ICTY.

---

28 One significant qualification is that Bosnian Croats within the FBiH at times attempted to obstruct cooperation with the ICTY.

29 Also quoted by Williams and Scharf 2002: 163.

An early desire to enforce ICTY arrest warrants on the part of Sarajevo may be partially explained by the fact that a preponderance of ICTY indictments issued during the 1990s targeted ethnic Serbs. However, Sarajevo's zeal for prosecutions extended beyond those publicly indicted by the ICTY and within three months of Dayton, Sarajevo would demonstrate a willingness to arrest high ranking Bosnian Serbs, even without IFOR's assistance. In fact, when two senior Bosnian Serbs, Đorđe Đukić and Aleksa Krsmanović, made a wrong turn into the FBiH in January 1996, they were arrested by FBiH authorities and war crimes proceedings were initiated. Given that the ICTY lacked a single high ranking suspect in custody, The Hague issued its own arrest warrants and requested Đukić and Krsmanović's transfer to ICTY custody (G.J. Bass 2002: 251). Rather than express support for the ICTY and the FBiH's efforts to bring to trial two senior Bosnian Serb officers, IFOR expressed outrage that Sarajevo and the ICTY worked in concert to force the Đukić and Krsmanović transfers. RS authorities were also enraged and retaliated by breaking off relations with IFOR for a period of two to three weeks (G.J. Bass 2002: 251).[30] Richard Holbrooke expressed his disapproval of the actions of the ICTY in his memoirs:

> [US Secretary of State] Christopher and I were greatly disturbed by this incident [*the Đukić and Krsmanović transfers to ICTY custody*]. The seizure of the two men, neither of whom were ever indicted, had disrupted the implementation process and set a bad precedent for the future. We were determined to try to prevent any repetition of such an incident before it became a pattern (1999: 346).

A month later, in February 1996, the Rules of the Road agreement was put in place, thus putting an end to any more surprise arrests of Bosnian Serbs on the part of the FBiH and unexpected transfer requests from The Hague.

When the ICTY indicted lower ranking Bosnian Muslims for war crimes perpetrated against Bosnian Serbs in March 1996, Sarajevo promptly executed the ICTY's arrest warrants and transferred the individuals in question to The Hague (G.J. Bass 2002: 257). BiH thus became the first state in the former Yugoslavia to execute an ICTY arrest warrant. Although once indictments were issued against senior Army of BiH officers, there was a hesitance on the part of international peacekeeping forces to rely upon local authorities to carry out an arrest. For example, when it came to the arrest of wartime Bosnian Muslim general, Naser Orić, the arrest was carried out by NATO as opposed to FBiH police (Foreign and Commonwealth Office 2003: 167).

### *Croatia and Bosnian Croat Compliance*

Bosnian Croats indicted by the ICTY were often surrendered to the Tribunal via authorities in Zagreb as the Croatian government exercised *de facto* control over

30 G.J. Bass noted there were even fears the Bosnian Serbs would take US soldiers hostage in retaliation for the arrest of Bosnian Serb war crimes suspects (2002: 250-251).

Bosnian Croat territory within the FBiH. Furthermore, political decisions affecting the Bosnian Croat community, such as the selection of the Croatian Democratic Union's Bosnian branch leadership, were often reached in Zagreb. An example of the direct control Zagreb exercised over Bosnian Croats was Croatian president Franjo Tuđman's dismissal of Bosnian Croat president Mate Boban (Granić 2005: 92-93). In fact, the direct control Zagreb established over the Croatian Democratic Union BiH branch during the 1992-1995 war continued after the end of hostilities and only ended following the Croatian Democratic Union's defeat in Croatian parliamentary and presidential elections in 2000. However, because Zagreb brought about the transfer of high profile Bosnian Croats, such as Vinko Martinović and Mladen Natelilić, as opposed to institutions of the Federation of Bosnia and Herzegovina or even NATO, these transfers were dealt with in Chapter 2.[31] But, it should be noted that despite Zagreb's role in the transfer of Bosnian Croats to ICTY custody, Bosnian Croat veterans' organizations have used ICTY indictments and judgments against Bosnian Croats as part of a wider campaign against Federation institutions (Bojičić-Dželilović 2004: 12).[32]

## International Justice and Civil Society under Diffuse Sovereignty

The wartime Bosnian Muslim-led government in Sarajevo was the ICTY's strongest advocate among the states of the former Yugoslavia. Even at Dayton, it was the Bosnian delegation alone that pushed for a stronger commitment to cooperate with the Tribunal to be built into the peace agreement. Meanwhile, Bosnian Muslim victims groups demanded the prosecution of individuals responsible for serious violations of IHL and acts of genocide both within Bosnia-Herzegovina and at The Hague. Matias Hellman of the ICTY Registry in Sarajevo observed that the Tribunal draws support from Bosnian Muslim victims groups within both of Bosnia-Herzegovina's two entities.[33] The ICTY drew considerable support from Srebrenica victims' organizations, which mobilized within months of the July 1995 massacre. Despite disappointment expressed by Bosnian Muslim victims' associations regarding the brevity of sentences handed down by ICTY trial chambers, Bosnian victims' groups have both lobbied for the expansion of

31 An exception to this would be the arrest of Anto Furundžija and Vlakto Kupreškić in December 1997 by NATO (Report of the International Tribunal 1998: 30).

32 Bojičić-Dželilović notes that Bosnian Croat veterans groups use occasions when indictments are issued, an arrest or transfer has taken place or when a judgment is rendered to demand the creation of a separate Croat entity within BiH (2004: 12). Additionally, at times Bosnian Croat opposition to inclusion in the FBiH has come close to violence, particularly in 2001 when the Croatian Democratic Union under Ante Jelavić attempted to dissolve the Federation and create a Bosnian Croat entity.

33 Personal interview with Matias Helmann of the ICTY Field Office in Sarajevo, January 16, 2007.

prosecutions and have petitioned to keep the ICTY open past its planned 2010 closure date (Nettelfield 2006: 113).

Despite the domestic impetus for war crimes prosecutions among the Bosnian Muslim community, demands for war crimes prosecutions among Bosnian Croats and Bosnian Serbs are substantially weaker. With regard to Bosnian Croat and Bosnian Serb communities, powerful veterans' organizations emerged that act to pressure local elites into voicing opposition to war crimes proceedings. The Bosnian Croat branch of the Croatian veterans' organization, HVIDR-a HVO, organized social protest events, such as the blocking of roads, in response to the arrests of Bosnian Croat veterans.[34] But, unlike in Croatia and Serbia, compliance and non-compliance decisions were not exclusively in the hands of local elites, and therefore mobilization against compliance acts on the part of local elites has been muted.[35] Therefore, when exploring causality behind compliance decisions we must turn to external actors.

## Compliance and International Organizations

The DPA was aimed at both bringing an end to a devastating conflict, which had by 1995 resulted in the almost complete destruction of BiH as a state, and establishing a framework for post-conflict governance which included both a military and civilian component. While the powers of the OHR were outlined in an exploration of BiH's international civilian administration, the military and security component of the international presence, which maintained a capability to execute ICTY arrest orders remains to be discussed. Because the OHR did not exercise authority over NATO peacekeeping forces, compliance on the part of NATO must be examined before returning to a discussion of compliance on the part of the OHR.

### *NATO: IFOR, SFOR and EUFOR*[36]

Although Annex 6 of the DPA bound signatories[37] to a legal obligation to cooperate with the ICTY, the RS failed to honor ICTY arrest orders (Western 2004: 235).

34 In September 2000 protests were held in response to the arrest of Bosnian Croat veterans by international peacekeeping forces and local police (Croatian Radio Television 2000).

35 Compliance acts were carried out exclusively by NATO forces in the RS until Tolimir's arrest at the RS-Republic of Serbia border in 2007.

36 IFOR (Implementation Force) was NATO's first mission in BiH and transitioned into SFOR (Stabilization Force) in 1997. Following NATO's decision to draw to a close its SFOR mission in 2004, the European Union led EUFOR assumed control of the international security presence in BiH.

37 Signatories include the Republic of Croatia, the Federal Republic of Yugoslavia and the warring parties of BiH.

Moreover, in 1996 there was no international authority in BiH willing to undertake arrest operations. The peace enforcement mandate assigned to the international military presence, through Annex I-A of Dayton, meant the initial deployment of peacekeeping forces to BiH was primarily tasked with separation of belligerent parties and the establishment of the Inter-entity Boundary Line (IEBL) (Schear 1996: 92). Meanwhile, law enforcement functions were left to entity level governments and local police forces, which were monitored by a United Nations led Police Task Force (IPTF); however, shortly after the IFOR presence was established, it quickly became apparent that were arrests of war crimes suspects in the *Republika Srpska* to occur, they would have to be carried out by NATO. Despite an initial aversion to law enforcement tasks, NATO eventually accumulated an impressive record when it came to the arrest and transfer of persons indicted by the ICTY. Zhou reflected on the significance of an international military organization engaging in what was an essentially law enforcement function, "…NATO is the only organization in modern history that has been directly involved on a significant scale in the apprehension of persons indicted by an international criminal tribunal" (2006: 204). In fact, the importance of the relationship between the ICTY and international organizations, such as NATO, was highlighted by the Tribunal itself in 1999, "productive working relationships with [international] organizations in the former Yugoslavia continue to be critical to the success of the Prosecutor's mandate" (Report of the International Tribunal 1999: 35). Yet, before turning to an exploration of NATO's active law enforcement role, it is first necessary to explore why NATO initially failed to carry out arrests during 1996.

### *IFOR's Failure to Arrest ICTY Suspects*

The immediate objectives for IFOR established in Annex I-A of the Dayton Agreement included the establishment of a durable ceasefire, lasting security, and arms control measures (DPA, Annex I-A, Article I(2), 1995). Any references to the execution of arrest orders were noticeably absent because at the time the arrest of high profile Bosnian Serbs was feared to raise the prospect of a return to violence thus constituted a significant risk to IFOR (Gow 2006: 50, Kerr 2005: 320). Instead, Annex I-A called specifically upon "the parties" or local signatories to the DPA[38] to comply with ICTY orders (DPA, Annex I-A, Article IX, 1995), while it remained silent on whether or not the multi-national peacekeeping force was obliged to comply with ICTY orders (Figà-Talamanca 1996: 172).[39] The failure to specifically commit international peacekeeping forces to arrest individuals under ICTY indictment effectively ensured NATO forces would not undertake arrest

38 Three parties signed the Dayton agreement: the Republic of Croatia, the Federal Republic of Yugoslavia, and the Republic of Bosnia and Herzegovina.

39 Recall, at Dayton representatives from the international community opposed any obligation imposed upon the peacekeeping force to arrest war crimes suspects.

and transfer missions in support of the Tribunal. A former British commander of Multinational Division South-West, General Mike Jackson, recalled:

> The Dayton Agreement had been well thought through, with enough detail to make it all work, a tribute to the work of Richard Holbrooke and his team. Dayton laid out an end-state to which all the parties had agreed, with a clear mechanism for getting from start to finish. This clarity would prove invaluable in the weeks and months to follow. Dayton also stipulated strict timelines: what had to be done by D+30, D+60, D+90. *For us, the Dayton Agreement became kind of a "bible" to which I would refer whenever any kind of dispute arose. I carried a copy of Dayton around with me everywhere* (2007: 201).[40]

Unfortunately for the ICTY, securing the arrest of war crimes suspects was not part of Dayton's strict timelines. The lack of clarity regarding war crimes suspects brought about an almost complete obfuscation of any responsibility to arrest ICTY indictees on the part of multinational peacekeeping forces. In fact, even when an indicted war criminal walked into a NATO base in July 1997, peacekeepers proved unable to secure custody of the accused:

> In July last year, Bralo walked into the Dutch SFOR base in Vitez in order to "inquire" whether he was indicted. Confused Dutch soldiers checked the public list of those accused, and having established that he was not on it, they told him to go in peace. Several hours later, they remembered to check the list of those wanted on the sealed indictments, but it was already too late: "Cicko" had vanished without a trace (Tribunal Update 1998).

Further complicating efforts to bring about the transfer of ICTY indictees to Tribunal custody was the fact local police forces retained law enforcement responsibilities and were only monitored by the IPTF, which had, "a vague mandate and no timetable" (Sharp 1997-1998: 118). Significantly, the IPTF mandate did not include the authority to make arrests (G.J. Bass 2002: 240). Sharp noted the IPTF left local police forces, which often consisted of former paramilitaries, effectively unreformed and unmonitored:

> During 1996 the armies of the former warring factions were under the tight control of 60,000 NATO-led troops, but the police were being monitored by less than 2,000 unarmed IPTF personnel. This would not have been so serious if the local police had been trained in law enforcement and public service. Most Bosnian police, however, were former paramilitaries who switched uniforms but retained their weapons and remained answerable to local warlords (1997/1998: 118).

40 Emphasis added by author.

In light of the failure on the part of IFOR to arrest a single war crimes suspect during 1996, and the prohibition imposed upon the IPTF from making arrests, indicted war criminals in the *Republika Srpska* confidently assumed an increasingly high profile in domestic political life, and Radovan Karadžić's behind the scenes influence in the RS began to threaten the very implementation of the DPA (G.J. Bass 2002: 249-250).

NATO's failure to engage in law enforcement activities during the first year of its presence in BiH led to serious criticisms of the alliance's role in BiH and accusations NATO fueled a postwar breakdown of law and order (International Crisis Group 2000: 70-71, Sharp 1997/1998: 118). However, it must be noted describing NATO as a monolithic actor is itself problematic as certain NATO member states such as the United Kingdom and Canada would later prove more willing to commit forces to high risk task such as the apprehension of war criminals and providing security for refugee returns, while the US remained preoccupied with force protection (Western 2004: 236). Moreover, France was even accused of having foiled an attempt by NATO to apprehend Karadžić. As a result of the above national variations pertaining to the willingness of NATO member states to pursue individuals indicted by the ICTY, certain regions within BiH developed a reputation for being safe havens for persons alleged to have committed war crimes. The Brussels based *International Crisis Group* reported in November 2000:

> Many of the alleged and as yet unindicted war criminals in Bosnia appear to reside in either the French or US sectors. The perception that, at least until quite recently, French and US forces have been reluctant to act against those suspected of war crimes – reflected in the relatively small numbers of arrests in the French and US sectors – has fostered an image of these areas as a safe haven (International Crisis Group 2000: 70).

This perception that French and US armed forces were reluctant to pursue the arrest of suspected war criminals also stemmed from an alleged incident where a French officer warned Karadžić of an impending arrest operation (Castle 2002).

The question as to whether or not the ICTY could issue legally binding orders upon international organizations such as NATO has been the subject of significant debate. Zhou points out, "…it has been suggested that while individual states participating in IFOR could be required to execute an ICTY arrest warrant specifically addressed to them, the obligation would not extend upon NATO itself…" (2006: 215).[41] Kerr also takes note of this line of argumentation:

> Even though States contributing forces to the multinational force were all bound by an individual obligation to cooperate, States were bound to carry out their obligations under international law within their own territory, and not in the

41 The ICTY has issued arrest orders directly to states with a military presence in BiH such as France, the United States and the United Kingdom (Figà-Talamanca 1996: 173).

> territory of other States. *The NATO force was not the sovereign authority in the territory of Bosnia, so it was not obliged to cooperate on that basis* (2004: 154).[42]

Therefore, because Dayton preserved BiH as a state under international law, international forces in post-Dayton BiH did not exercise *de jure* sovereign authority and therefore could not be legally bound to enforce ICTY orders. Under NATO's interpretation of Article 29, the obligation to comply with Tribunal orders applied almost solely to the Bosnian state. However, under existing ICTY case law, an unambiguous obligation has been established for intergovernmental organizations to cooperate with the ICTY:

> A purposive construction of the Statute yields the conclusion that such an order should be as applicable to collective enterprises of States as it is to individual States; Article 29 should, therefore, be read as conferring on the International Tribunal a power to require an international organization or its component organ such as SFOR to cooperate with it in the achievement of its fundamental objective of prosecuting persons responsible for serious violations of international humanitarian law, by providing the several modes of assistance set out therein (Decision on Motion for Judicial Assistance 2000).[43]

While the extent to which NATO may have been legally bound to actively pursue the arrests of persons indicted by the Tribunal remains challenged, NATO did not perceive itself as being under a legal obligation to assist the ICTY secure custody of accused persons on the territory of BiH.

### *Transition to Law Enforcement*

When NATO entered BiH, the alliance narrowly defined the conditions under which peacekeeping forces could arrest an individual under indictment by the ICTY endorsing, the "apprehension of individuals indicted by the ICTY only when encountered in the course of IFOR/SFOR's duties" (Zhou 2006: 214). Yet, this clarification left open the prospect NATO commanders would intentionally avoid areas where ICTY fugitives were known to reside (Sharp 1997/1998: 121). Moreover, IFOR commanders were not authorized to engage in the search for individuals indicted by the ICTY. Had IFOR been a state, it would have been in

42 Emphasis added by author.

43 See also the *Decision on Defence Motion for Access to EUMM Archives*, the Prosecutor v. Enver Hadzihasanovic and Amir Kubura, December 13, 2003 and the *Order for the Production of Documents by the European Community Monitoring Mission and Its Member States*, the Prosecutor v. Dario Kordic and Marko Cerkez, August 4, 2000.

non-compliance with obligations to enforce Tribunal arrest and surrender orders.[44] However, even though multinational peacekeeping forces did not actively pursue the arrest of persons indicted by the Tribunal during IFOR's first year in BiH,[45] this changed dramatically in 1997. In 1999, it was even noted, "SFOR has provided exceptional support and attempted four apprehensions of indicted accused, of which three were successful and one resulted in the death of the accused" (Report of the International Tribunal 1999: 35).

NATO's undertaking of arrest operations in 1997 was not a reflection of an acceptance of a legal obligation to assist the ICTY, but rather coincided with a change in how the ICTY issued indictments. In 1997, Chief Prosecutor Louise Arbour began to issue "secret indictments" against individuals NATO routinely had contact with so that the arrest and transfer of ICTY indictees would fall within the international peacekeeping force's own narrowly defined mandate. Bass noted, "Arbour called the bluff the Pentagon had written into Dayton" (2002: 265-266). ICTY Deputy Chief Prosecutor Graham Blewitt recalled Arbour's secret indictments created:

> … an almighty ruckus in NATO and elsewhere. There was a lot of resistance and pressure to get us to back off. Because they were saying it was just unfair that these people were not given the opportunity to flee … So we didn't back off at all. We just said we'll go public and expose you for the fraud you are (G.J. Bass 2002: 266).

Unlike publicly indicted individuals, who were aware of the need to avoid contact with international peacekeeping forces, individuals under secret indictment had no such advance warning.

The first operation on the part of the multinational military force in BiH to arrest an individual indicted by the ICTY occurred on July 10, 1997 (Gow 2006: 59, International Crisis Group 1997: 3) and this event proved to be a watershed moment when it came to the enforcement of arrest orders by NATO forces in BiH. The radical shift from a strict peace enforcement role limited to maintenance of the IEBL to the pursuit of individuals indicted by the ICTY warrants an explanation, and it has been argued that NATO's change in policy was the outcome of three key events that coincided with the ICTY's shift from issuing public indictments to secretly indicting individuals believed to reside in BiH. Three additional factors which have been argued to have facilitated NATO's undertaking of arrest operations included US President Clinton's 1996 re-election, the subsequent promotion of former US Ambassador to the UN Madeleine Albright to the office of Secretary of State, and the election of a Labour government in the United Kingdom, which

44 Under ICTY Rules and Procedures the Tribunal claims to hold the authority to impose binding orders upon international peacekeeping forces.

45 Sharp notes that during 1996 even when indicted persons were encountered by IFOR, no arrests were made (1997/1998: 121).

saw Robin Cook, a vocal supporter of the ICTY, assume the post of UK foreign minister (G.J. Bass 2002: 262-271, Sharp 1997/1998: 133-134). Because a vast majority of arrests from 1997-2000 occurred in the British sector, Multi-National Division Southwest (International Crisis Group 2000: 71), there is considerable evidence to support the assertion that arrests post-1997 were the result of a British change of policy *vis à vis* the arrest of persons indicted by the ICTY. Regardless of the immediate cause, it is clear that there was a change in perception on the part of key NATO member states. However, despite NATO's shift to a more aggressive policy concerning the arrest of ICTY indicted persons in BiH, arrests themselves were carried out by international as opposed to local forces and the question of whether or not NATO could be obliged to enforce an arrest orders remained to be answered. In fact, as late as 2000, NATO continued to insist that the arrest of ICTY fugitives was not part of its peace enforcement mandate in BiH although by that time NATO had carried out a number of arrests (International Crisis Group 2000: 70).

More recently, following the transition from SFOR to EUFOR, the EU-led security presence increasingly depends on local authorities to execute arrests. Although EUFOR's website notes that providing support to the ICTY is among the mission's key supporting tasks (EUFOR 2007a), EUFOR's mandate when it comes to the arrest of persons indicted by the ICTY is restricted to the ability to arrest an accused should EUFOR become aware of an accused's location, which bears similarity to the restrictive mandate initially adopted by NATO in 1996. In fact, in an internal EUFOR document provided to the author it was noted:

> EUFOR has authority to detain [persons under ICTY indictment], and would not hesitate to do so if it had reliable information on which to act. *Nevertheless, the main responsibility for their detention and arrest lies with BIH authorities.* One condition for concluding the Stabilization and Association Agreement with the EU is BIH's full cooperation with the ICTY (EUFOR 2007b).

However, as EUFOR's replacement of SFOR followed the apprehension of all but one senior ICTY indictee believed to be on the territory of BiH, EUFOR's willingness to assist the ICTY enforce arrest warrants has not to this point been tested.[46]

### *Compliance and the OHR*

Although the OHR was invested with a broad range of powers, the OHR was not in a position to execute arrest warrants and relied on the multi-national military presence to support cooperation with the ICTY. However, the OHR had

---

46 The fact EUFOR has assisted local police forces in the enforcement of arrest warrants issued by the Special War Crimes Chamber in Sarajevo suggests, EUFOR would arrest ICTY fugitives should their locations become known to the peacekeeping force.

at its disposal a wide range of powers which could prevent persons indicted by the ICTY from serving in or receiving assistance from entity level governments. Yet, these powers were not exercised during 1996 as the OHR initially did not robustly pursue war crimes suspects at a time when the RS political leadership included individuals publicly indicted by the ICTY. As late as November 2000, the OHR along with the OSCE, United Nations Mission in BiH (UNMBiH), UNHCR and SFOR were criticized for meeting regularly with individuals alleged to have committed war crimes (International Crisis Group 2000: 68). Moreover, many individuals suspected of war crimes were permitted to remain in office even after the powers of the OHR were amplified to include the ability to unilaterally remove individuals from office.

When exploring the question of compliance with ICTY orders it is important to emphasize the OHR lacked authority over the NATO presence in BiH and could not issue binding orders on peacekeeping forces under NATO command. The OHR could, however, take action against local actors suspected of supporting war crimes fugitives. But, because the OHR was dependent upon NATO to provide security, the robustness of the OHR's support of the Tribunal could only shadow that of NATO. The OHR could not take action against the RS without NATO support. As a result, during 1996 there was no action taken to facilitate the arrest of Radovan Karadzic and Ratko Mladić and instead NATO reassured war crimes suspects in the RS that the IFOR mandate did not include the execution of arrest warrants (W. Bass 1998: 107). Karadžić was even permitted to remain president of the RS during the first months of the OHR mission.

When the OHR did begin to take action against individuals suspected of harboring persons indicted by the ICTY, following NATO's shift in policy in 1997, the OHR was able to make it difficult for persons indicted by the Tribunal to openly participate in politics. Also, action by the OHR against civilian support networks for persons indicted by the ICTY has been cited by the Tribunal as playing an important role in bringing about the arrests of war crimes fugitives. By removing individuals from positions within entity level security services, the OHR was able to prevent local governments from obstructing international efforts to apprehend war crimes fugitives. An example of such action occurred in July 2007 when the ICTY requested Miroslav Lajcak remove from office RS police-training director Dragomir Andan because Andan was suspected of supporting ICTY fugitives evade capture (Clifford 2007). Lacjak promptly complied with the ICTY request.

### *International Criminal Law Enforcement as Capacity Building*

When exploring compliance in BiH it is important to distinguish between non-compliance as a result of political obstruction and non-compliance as symptomatic of a lack of capacity. Chayes and Chayes noted that non-compliance with international legal obligations can often be the result of a lack of capacity on the part of target states (1995: 13-15). Moreover, the international presence in Bosnia-Herzegovina often described its activities as capacity building in order to assist the Bosnian state in its transition to a more traditional sovereign state actor (Jeffrey 2006: 203-227).[47] While previous case studies emphasized traditional enforcement models for compliance – coercion, inducement, and legitimacy – such models prove difficult to apply to BiH as the boundaries between the state and external actors have been blurred. As demonstrated above, compliance with ICTY orders was brought about by international and not domestic actors, making an examination of state action on the part of BiH epiphenomenal to the question of compliance. For example, the arrests of ICTY indictees within the RS, where the entity level government rejected its obligations to cooperate with the Tribunal, were carried out by international forces and not local governments, and therefore, it must be emphasized compliance acts did not reflect the preferences of local actors. On the other hand, reliance upon international forces to carry out an arrest is not necessarily a reflection of a rejection of legal obligations or on the part of local authorities. Even in the FBiH, where there existed broader support for the ICTY than in the RS, the arrest of former Bosnian Army general Naser Orić was executed by NATO instead of FBiH security forces. The failure of local authorities to carry out an arrest cannot always be interpreted as an act of deliberate non-compliance as Figà-Talamanca points out even the ICTY recognized the manifest inability of BiH to independently comply with arrest orders (1996: 173).

In a context where local governments can find themselves in non-compliance due to a lack of capacity to conduct an arrest, an additional mechanism through which compliance can be viewed is compliance through capacity building, especially when examining compliance in the FBiH. In post-conflict states, judicial institutions and law enforcement bodies are often either non-existent or unable to hold fair proceedings. In the case BiH, the OSCE noted the almost complete destruction of judicial institutions:

> Domestic courts in BiH, civilian and military, did indeed proceed to try war crimes cases during and immediately after the conflict. However, the loss of skilled members of the legal profession and the judiciary, as well as the physical destruction and lack of proper equipment or facilities significantly hampered the ability of the courts to administer justice properly or efficiently … The loss of many pre-war judges resulted in the judiciary and prosecutor's offices, in different parts of the country, being dominated by the majority ethnicity. New, inexperienced judges and prosecutors were appointed on ethnic and political grounds (OSCE 2005: 4).

Widespread problems regarding the prosecution of war crimes cases at the entity level combined with the expiration of the Rules of the Road program led to the 2005 establishment of an internationalized War Crimes Chamber, the War Crimes Chamber of Bosnia and Herzegovina (OSCE 2005: 10). While the proceedings

47 The European Commission delegation in BiH also frames its activities as capacity building (European Commission Delegation to Bosnia and Herzegovina 2007d).

before the internationalized War Crimes Chamber are not within the scope of this study, the inclusion of a temporary international component serves as an example of ongoing efforts to capacity build on the part of external actors. Additionally, like the ICTY, the War Crimes Chamber has also relied on international forces to execute arrest warrants.[48] However, as the ICTY completion strategy commits the Tribunal to closing in 2010 and as the War Crimes Chamber transitions from an internationalized court to an exclusively domestic court, there is an expectation that domestic actors will assume ownership of war crimes trial processes.

## Conclusions

This chapter has explored the politics of compliance in a partially sovereign state and has demonstrated a narrow theoretical focus on state compliance can provide for at best a distorted picture of the politics of compliance. As noted in the introduction, shared sovereign entities are becoming increasingly common and both states and international organizations have found themselves increasingly engaged in post-conflict state building projects with robust legal mandates that curtail the autonomy of local actors. BiH is one such state building project. BiH's contradictory legal identity as both a UN member state and a state under international civilian and military administration, highlights a gap within contemporary conceptions of international law which continue to view states as the almost exclusive subject of international legal obligations (Cassese 2005: 3). NATO and EUFOR's denial of a legal obligation to execute ICTY arrest orders serves to underline the extent to which the relationship between international tribunals and multi-national peacekeeping forces needs to be further defined.

While domestic support for the ICTY varied substantially between and within BiH's two entities, international support for the work of the Tribunal gradually increased as NATO moved from a strict adherence to a peace enforcement mandate to the acceptance of law enforcement responsibilities, although not obligations. This shift from an initial willingness to tolerate the continued presence of indicted war criminals to conducting arrest operations was an outcome of the growing acceptance among NATO member states, in particular the US and UK, that the removal of war crimes indictees from BiH would be conducive to the implementation of the DPA. For example, Kovačević's transfer to ICTY custody in 1997 strengthened Bosnian Serbs moderates at the expense of Radovan Karadžić, who himself eventually withdrew from Bosnian Serb politics. Post-1997 instead of generating a fear of Bosnian Serb retaliatory violence, arrests were increasingly perceived as providing for increased security while war crimes suspects were increasingly perceived as

48 Continued incidents of torture being used by local police forces in post-war Bosnia to extract confessions and the abuse of arrest warrants as a pre-text for torture (Garms and Peschke 2006: 263) raises serious questions about whether local police forces should, even when capable, be utilized to execute warrants in war crimes cases.

a threat to security (Gow 2006: 58-60). Yet, the causation of this shift from non-compliance to compliance was not initiated by the Bosnian state or its two entities, but was rather the outcome of a transformation among NATO member states. In fact, when it comes to exploring the arrest of ICTY indictees, local governments were often completely excluded from the decision-making process. Moreover, the shift from compliance did not coincide with an acceptance of a legal obligation to cooperate with the ICTY under Article 29 of the Tribunal Statute, but rather was the outcome of the recognition of pragmatic gains which could be achieved through the marginalization of individuals under ICTY indictment. Thus, the arrest and transfer of ICTY accused in July 1997 was not dictated by perceptions of appropriate action, but rather it was the logic of expected consequences which guided NATO member states into undertaking arrest and transfer operations.

# Chapter 6
# The United Nations Interim Administration Mission in Kosovo: International Justice in an International Protectorate

## Introduction

On June 10, 1999 the United Nations Security Council adopted Resolution 1244 establishing the United Nations Interim Administration Mission in Kosovo (UNMIK) to govern Serbia's southern province in the aftermath of NATO's 78 day air campaign against the Federal Republic of Yugoslavia (*Savezna republika Jugoslavija*, SRJ). Resolution 1244 called for the creation of "…an international civilian presence in Kosovo in order to provide an interim administration for Kosovo under which the people of Kosovo can enjoy substantial autonomy within the Federal Republic of Yugoslavia…," (1999: 3) and transformed Kosovo into the only case study that pertains to a territory which lacks international legal recognition as a state.[1] Krasner notes:

> When NATO forces occupied Kosovo in 1999 they ignored conventional rules of Westphalian/Vattelian and domestic sovereignty. The major powers did not attempt to establish Kosovo as an independent state, nor did they seek to make it part of a larger Albania. Rather they seized effective control of the territory while still recognizing it as part of Yugoslavia (2001: 244).

Kosovo, therefore, confronts the student of compliance with a territory which remained *de jure* part of the SRJ but under the sovereign control of UNMIK. The assumption that states are the subjects of international legal obligations constitutes an *a priori* assumption behind rationalist theories of compliance grounded in neorealism and neoliberal institutionalism. After all, neorealists construct compliance as a reflection of the distribution of state power, while neo-liberal institutionalists construct compliance as a reflection of state interest. Remove the state as the subject of international legal obligations and the explanatory power of existing rationalist approaches to IR evaporates. The absence of a state actor makes Kosovo fundamentally different from the preceding Bosnian case study.

1 This was the case during the period under time in this chapter, and should not be interpreted as making any claim regarding Kosovo's international legal status post-declaration of independence.

Whereas the Bosnian state retained its independent international legal identity, along with corresponding legal obligations, UNMIK was tasked with governing a territory that remained legally within the SRJ.[2] UNMIK was the sole sovereign authority in Kosovo.[3] Throughout the period of time covered in this case study (1999-2006) UNMIK presided over the international civilian presence in Kosovo and drafted a framework for self-government for the province, which culminated in the 2001 Constitutional Framework for Self-Government. UNMIK was also obliged to cooperate with the International Criminal Tribunal for the former Yugoslavia (ICTY) as Resolution 1244 explicitly demanded cooperation from the international presence in Kosovo (1999: 4).

When the ICTY Statute was drafted in 1993 the prospect that the Tribunal would be confronted with enforcing orders upon an international protectorate, as opposed to a state, was not considered given the reluctance at the time of international actors to countenance the use of force in the former Yugoslavia to seize territory; hence, the restrictive and state-centric wording of Article 29 of the Tribunal Statute.[4] As demonstrated in Chapter 5, the establishment of an international civilian administration in Bosnia-Herzegovina, alongside a robust international military presence, raised significant questions regarding the extent to which the Tribunal Statute could be considered binding upon external actors such as NATO and the OHR given Bosnia-Herzegovina remained the legal subject of an obligation to cooperate with the Tribunal.

In Kosovo, UNMIK and the NATO-led KFOR mission could not deny their obligations to carry out Tribunal orders. At the time of Resolution 1244's drafting, Security Council member states recognized that the legal subject of Tribunal obligations would have to be clarified. Therefore, Article 14 of Resolution 1244 went beyond Dayton's obligations, which were imposed exclusively upon the local parties to the 1995 peace agreement, and demanded cooperation with the ICTY on the part of the "international security presence" in Kosovo (Resolution 1244 1999: 4). Having established an obligation to cooperate with the ICTY, it should be expected that UNMIK would demonstrate a greater degree of cooperation with the Tribunal than that which was observed in the previous case studies. After all, UNMIK was neither a state nor a party to the 1998-1999 conflict. Moreover, like the ICTY, UNMIK was a Chapter VII creation of the UNSC. Unfortunately, UNMIK

2 The SRJ (later the State Union of Serbia and Montenegro) consisted of two constitute republics, the Republic of Serbia and the Republic of Montenegro. Kosovo was an autonomous province within the former and thus remained within Serbia once the Republic of Serbia declared independence in 2006 following Montenegro's secession from the State Union of Serbia and Montenegro.

3 It must be emphasized that despite remaining within the sovereign shell of the SRJ, UNMIK had no obligation towards Belgrade (Brand 2001: 463).

4 It should also be noted that at the time the Tribunal Statute was drafted the ICTY was, according to former US Assistant Secretary of State Richard Holbrooke, "widely viewed as little more than a public relations device" (1999: 190).

proved reluctant to assist the ICTY, and in 2006 the ICTY reported UNMIK's non-cooperation to the UNSC (Report of the International Tribunal 2006: 666). Despite the enforcement of arrest and surrender orders, UNMIK failed to assist the Tribunal in a wide range of functions from providing assistance to Tribunal personnel in Kosovo to providing adequate witness protection.[5]

While non-compliance on the part of states can be viewed through existing mainstream theories of IR, non-compliance on the part of an international administration or peacekeeping forces requires theories of compliance to grapple with the question of international legal obligations imposed upon non-traditional international legal entities which exercise sovereign authority over a given territory. In order to explore the interaction between UNMIK and the ICTY, the historic and institutional context of compliance will first be established. This will include both an exploration of UNMIK and Kosovo's institutions of self-government. Second, the domestic politics of compliance will be discussed with a special emphasis on Fatmir Limaj and Ramush Haradinaj's[6] surrenders to ICTY custody in 2003 and 2005 respectively. Finally, the international politics of compliance will be addressed. It will be noted the overriding concern of the states which created UNMIK did not include cooperation with the ICTY (Williams and Scharf 2002: 208); however, given Priština's struggle for recognition as an independent state, cooperation with the ICTY was perceived as a means of demonstrating local institutions of self-government were responsible members of the international community (Dedushaj 2007: 10). As a result, Kosovo's institutions of self-government embraced human rights norm affirmation as part of a public diplomacy campaign to demonstrate Kosovo's ability to meet human rights standards for membership into the international community of states.

## Contextualizing Compliance

NATO's Operation Allied Force was brought to an end shortly after Martti Ahtisaari and Viktor Chernomyrdin secured SRJ president Slobodan Milošević's acceptance of an international security presence in Kosovo on June 2, 1999.[7] A

---

5 Personal interview with Alexandra Milenov of the ICTY Field Office in Belgrade, January 23, 2007.

6 Fatmir Limaj and Ramush Haradinaj were both senior commanders within the Kosovo Liberation Army who went on to play an active role in politics in post-conflict Kosovo preceding their indictments by the ICTY.

7 Viktor Chernomyrdin was Russia's envoy tasked with bringing an end to the conflict between NATO and the SRJ and acted as a contact between Milošević and US State Department officials throughout Operation Allied Force. Martti Ahtisaari was chosen by Chernomyrdin to accompany him on his final trip to Belgrade during NATO's air campaign so as to include someone "with stature in Europe but no connections to NATO" (McGeary 1999).

week after the Ahtisaari-Chernomyrdin talks in Belgrade, NATO and the Yugoslav Army agreed to a Military-Technical Agreement, which established a timetable for the withdrawal of Serb forces from Kosovo (Jackson 2007: 248-254). Although the SRJ is often described as having capitulated to NATO (Hosmer 2001: 123-128, Lambeth 2001: 82), Herring notes that the terms of Resolution 1244 were more favorable to Belgrade than those offered preceding Operation Allied Force at Rambouillet (2001: 232). Importantly for Belgrade, whereas Rambouillet granted NATO access rights to the SRJ in its entirety, Resolution 1244 was much more restrictive and granted the international security presence access only to Kosovo (H. Clark 2000: 183, Herring 2001: 232). Also, Rambouillet's rigid three year time frame for a final status agreement, which was envisioned to grant Kosovo recognition as an independent state, was not included in Resolution 1244 (H. Clark 2000: 183). Moreover, Belgrade continued to attempt to negotiate concessions from NATO following the Ahtisaari-Chernomyrdin agreement. For example, during negotiations for the Military-Technical Agreement, Belgrade insisted the military mission in Kosovo should be placed under UN and not NATO command (Jackson 2007: 251). While NATO did assume command of the KFOR security mission, Resolution 1244 stipulated the international security presence was to be under UN auspices (H. Clark 2000: 183, Herring 2001: 232).[8]

### *Establishing UNMIK*

In June 1999 external actors were once again confronted with the task of establishing an international civilian administration in the former Yugoslavia. Matheson described the international civilian presence created for Kosovo as "unprecedented in scope and complexity" (2001: 79). Indeed, the administration that emerged in Kosovo was considerably more robust than in Bosnia-Herzegovina. UNMIK was initially granted full legislative and executive powers over the province (Carlowitz 2004: 307) and even after it devolved certain powers to self-governing authorities established through the 2001 Constitutional Framework for Provisional Self-Government in Kosovo, UNMIK retained reserved powers over law and order, judicial appointments, minority rights, customs, monetary policy, external relations, property rights, and supervision of the Kosovo Protection Corps (KPC) (UNMIK 2007: 4-5).[9]

Before the creation of Kosovo's self-governing institutions in 2001, UNMIK assumed a vast array of powers over a territory that lacked functioning governing

8 It must be emphasized that this does not mean UNMIK exercises any form of command and control over KFOR.

9 The KPC was created by UNMIK as a successor organization of the Kosovo Liberation Army. The KPC was not an armed forces and acted to provide employment to disbanded Kosovo Liberation Army personnel.

structures.[10] In fact, as Yugoslav Army and Ministry of Interior troops departed Kosovo in June 1999, most elements of the existing judicial order from police to judges and prosecutors fled because at the time almost all members of Kosovo's police forces and judiciary were ethnic Serbs (Jackson 2007: 291). Therefore, the task facing Sergio de Mello, temporarily appointed the United Nations Secretary General's Special Representative (SGSR) to Kosovo, was daunting and required the immediate imposition of an international police force and judiciary to counter campaigns of arbitrary violence and retribution (Jackson 2007: 290). Unfortunately, UNMIK was unable to quickly recruit police forces. The result was a triumphant Kosovo Liberation Army (*Ushtria Çlimtare e Kosovës*, UÇK), which had fought the ground war in Kosovo during NATO's air campaign, was able to "walk into town halls and take possession" of local governments (Hopkinson 2006: 170) allowing the UÇK to establish itself as the dominant ruling body within the province (Demjaha 2000: 37, Hopkinson 2006: 170, Jackson 2007: 285). Furthermore, the inability of UNMIK to rapidly recruit police forces compounded the negative effects of UÇK "self-establishing" local authorities, and Kosovo was left un-policed for the first several weeks of UNMIK's mandate (Hopkinson 2006: 170).[11]

In a development that further complicated efforts to establish UNMIK, Hopkinson notes that the United Nations was unprepared for the return of Kosovo's refugees, who returned to the province before UNMIK was able to establish itself (2006: 170). Although the UNHCR had drawn up detailed plans for an orderly return of Kosovar refugees from Macedonia and Albania, once the conflict ended refugees failed to wait for the UNHCR to put into place its plans and returned to the province *en masse* (Jackson 2007: 287). The head of British forces in Macedonia, General Mike Jackson used less than flattering terms to describe the effect the massive flow of refugees had on the deployment of KFOR to the province. Jackson recalled, "The bloody idiots were blocking our route into Kosovo" (2007: 264).

### *Challengers to UNMIK*

In 1999 UNMIK was confronted with three immediate potential challengers to its authority. Two challengers emerged from the Kosovar Albanian community, while the latter consisted of Kosovo Serbs. With regard to the two Kosovar Albanian challengers, the first was the UÇK, which claimed the "right of conquest" and the second was Kosovo's pre-war parliament and government under Ibrahim Rugova (Hopkinson 2006: 171). The UÇK initially represented a significant obstacle

---

10 This does not include *ad hoc* self-governing authorities established by the UÇK, which exercised justice in a violent and arbitrary manner. These self-governing authorities will be described in greater detail below.

11 It was during this period of time violent reprisals were carried out against Kosovo Serbs. As of October 1999, the UNHCR estimated 130,000 Kosovo Serbs had fled the province (Herring 2000: 233).

to KFOR's attempts to establish control over security in the province because of reluctance on the part of the UÇK to disarm. In fact, it was only with great difficulty that the UÇK was convinced to re-brand itself as the KPC (Jackson 2007: 294-301). As a result of the UÇK's acceptance of its new KPC status, the former Kosovar army was transformed into a "quasi-police force," which was granted legal status by UNMIK. Oddly, for a quasi-police force, the KPC was prohibited from participation in any law enforcement activities (Kola 2003: 370).[12]

With regard to the second challenger, Kosovo's pre-war ethnic Albanian governing structures had coalesced into a parallel state following Serbia's revocation of Kosovo's autonomy in 1989 and were later described by Clark as a "state-in-embryo" (H. Clark 2000: 177). Kosovo's parallel state, which effectively governed ethnic Albanian communities in the province from 1989-1999, was led by Ibrahim Rugova's Democratic League of Kosovo (*Lidhja Demokratike e Kosovës*, LDK). The LDK's parallel structures could have served as the basis for a post-war government had UNMIK not dissolved all pre-existing institutions of government. However, this may not have been desirable as Clark noted that one of the characteristics of Kosovo's parallel governing structures was a tendency to imitate the negative features of pre-existing single party state bodies. In fact, despite being reliant on voluntary participation, Kosovo's pre-war parallel government was described as follows:

> While the structures were brought into existence and crucially depended on voluntary activity, at the same time they had a traditional hierarchy: command structures and other features of the old one-party style mixed with pre-communist authority patterns (H. Clark 2000: 177).

Devic noted when Rugova established the LDK-led parallel government in 1989, Rugova modeled the ruling party on the province's branch of the Yugoslav League of Communists (2006: 260). Thus, parallel governing structures were not only intrinsically linked to the party but were also inclusive of unions and civil society (Devic 2006: 260, Kosovar Institute for Policy Research and Development 2005: 5-6). But, rather than inhibit the growth of NGOs, Devic notes many of Kosovo's indigenous NGOs emerged in the period following the establishment of Kosovo's parallel government and preceding NATO's Operation Allied Force. Kosovo's post-1989 NGO community included the Mother Teresa Society, the Council for the Defense of Human Rights and Freedoms, and the Kosovo Helsinki Council (Devic 2006: 260).

Due to the upheaval of the 1999 conflict Rugova's government was left displaced. Rugova's displacement opened up an opportunity for the UÇK to assume control of the province in the weeks after the NATO air campaign through its aforementioned "self-establishing" local authorities; however, UÇK rule was short lived. A December 1999 agreement between UNMIK and leaders of Kosovo's

12 Instead, the KPC was to provide assistance during natural disasters.

parallel governing structures required local leaders to relinquish all pre-UNMIK claims to authority and dismantle all non-UNMIK sanctioned governing structures (Brand 2001: 468). In a development which would further reduce the influence of the UÇK, Rugova's LDK triumphed over a party formed by the UÇK's political leader Hasim Thaçi, the Democratic Party of Kosovo (*Partia Demokratike e Kosovës*, PDK), in Kosovo's first postwar elections held in 2001.

While the LDK returned to power in 2001, there remained significant tension between UNMIK and Kosovo's ethnic Albanian political parties given the latter's desire to assume greater control over governance. There existed a programmatic consensus among ethnic Albanian parties in support of Kosovo's independence from the Republic of Serbia, a position which was supported by SGSR Joachim Rücker.[13] Because UNMIK has largely been perceived as facilitating a process, which will bring about Kosovo's independence rather than serving as an obstacle to independence, anti-UNMIK sentiment has remained muted during the period of time under examination in this case study.

On the part of Kosovo's Serb minority, who for the most part were driven north of the Ibar River or left isolated in enclaves in southern Kosovo (Hehir 2006: 203), there was an almost complete non-recognition of UNMIK's authority and instead Belgrade assisted Kosovo Serb enclaves in establishing their own parallel administration (Yannis 2004: 73). Although Kosovo Serb non-recognition of UNMIK was not consequential to compliance episodes under examination here, as no ethnic Serbs under ICTY indictment resided in postwar Kosovo, the appeals of Kosovo Serbs to Belgrade's continued legal sovereignty over Kosovo was illustrative of the difficulties encountered by UNMIK in imposing an international administration upon Kosovo. Belgrade symbolically asserted control over the province by protesting almost every piece of legislation ratified by UNMIK as violations of SRJ sovereignty (Yannis 2004: 70). Moreover, violence against Kosovo Serbs remained routine throughout the period of time under examination in this case study (Hehir 2006: 203-204). It took a great deal of cajoling on the part of UNMIK to secure Kosovo Serb participation in Kosovo's first post-conflict elections in 2001; however, in 2004, Kosovo Serbs boycotted Kosovo's second post-conflict elections (Hehir 2006: 207). In addition, Kosovo Serbs continued to exercise their right to vote in Republic of Serbia elections.

### *UNMIK Consultative Bodies*

UNMIK recognized the need to engage local actors in order to prevent the exacerbation of local grievances when it established temporary Joint Interim Administrative Structures (JIAS) in February 2000 (see Figure 6.1). Although the JIAS was established in order to replace "all previous parallel structures for revenue collection and provision of public services," there was an attempt to include major

13 Rücker argues absent a rapid move toward independence the potential for anti-UNMIK mobilization within the province would increase (United Nations 2006).

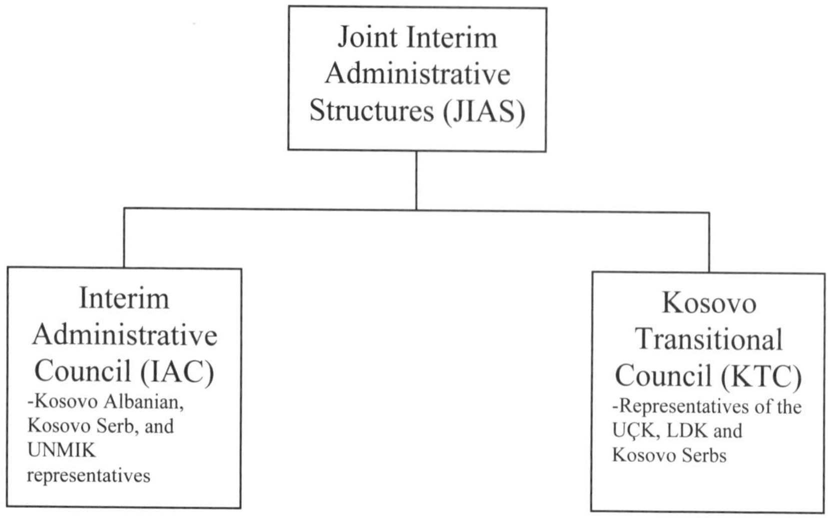


**Figure 6.1 UNMIK consultative bodies under JIAS (2000-2001)**

Kosovar political parties into *ad hoc* consultative bodies (UNMIK 2000). The first of these bodies was the eight member Interim Administrative Council (IAC), which included Kosovar Albanians who were present at Rambouillet, a representative of Kosovo's Serb minority,[14] and representatives from UNMIK. The IAC could only make policy recommendations and could not independently legislate. The second consultative body, the Kosovo Transitional Council, was described by UNMIK as being "the highest-level consultative body" of the JIAS (UNMIK 2000) and included representatives of Kosovo's three major political players, the UÇK, the LDK and Kosovo Serbs (Kola 2003: 371).

Like the IAC, the 35 member KTC held no executive or legislative powers, but members were regularly briefed by KFOR representatives on the security situation in the province, and the SRSG was committed to "taking into account" KTC recommendations when formulating policy. Both the IAC and KTC were dissolved along with the JIAS following the enactment of the Constitutional Framework for Interim Self-Government.

*Institutional Structure of UNMIK*

The wide range of powers assumed by UNMIK necessitated a considerable delegation of responsibilities. As in Bosnia-Herzegovina, a number of international

14 The ethnic Serb representative was not a full member of the Interim Administrative Council, and maintained observer status. Other observers included a representative of Kosovo's civil society and a UNMIK representative for humanitarian affairs (UNMIK 2000).

**Table 6.1 UNMIK's four pillars**

| | Pillar I | Pillar II | Pillar III | Pillar IV |
|---|---|---|---|---|
| *Issue Areas* | Police and Justice | Civil Administration | Democratization and Institution Building | Reconstruction and Economic Development |
| *Institution Delegated Responsibility* | United Nations | United Nations | Organization for Security and Cooperation in Europe | European Union |

organizations were integrated into the international civilian administration; however, unlike Bosnia-Herzegovina, where the international administration was placed under the Peace Implementation Council, in Kosovo the United Nations Security Council headed the international civilian presence. In order to clarify responsibilities, four areas of governance were delineated. These four areas of governance, known as UNMIK's four pillars, were delineated as follows: 1) police and justice, 2) civil administration, 3) democratization and institution building and 4) reconstruction and economic development.

In addition to establishing a four pillared system of governance, UNMIK was presided over by a Special Representative of the Secretary General (SRSG), who was granted significantly greater powers than the High Representative in Bosnia-Herzegovina. UNMIK's first SRSG to serve a full term was Bernard Kouchner of France, who replaced temporary SRSG Sergio de Mello.[15] The powers granted to the SRSG included:

- The power to dissolve parliament and call for new elections
- Final authority over appointment of judicial officials
- Control over law enforcement
- The power to veto the budget
- Conduct Kosovo's foreign relations
  (*Constitutional Framework* 2001)

Furthermore, the following positions were subject to appointment exclusively by the SRSG:

- Economic and Fiscal Council
- Governing Board of the Banking and Payments Authority of Kosovo
- Chief Executive of the Customs Service and Tax Inspectorate
- Auditor General
  (*Constitutional Framework* 2001)

15 For a full list of SRSGs see Appendix VIII.

Legislation was considered binding once signed by the SRSG. The SRSG even had the authority to impose retroactive legislation (Brand 2001: 470). The first piece of legislation promulgated by UNMIK confirmed the SRSG's investment with all legislative and executive powers, while also noting that the laws of the SRJ would continue to apply in the province insofar as they did not conflict with UNMIK's mandate or specific regulations enacted by UNMIK (Matheson 2001: 80).

UNMIK's exclusive hold over all executive and legislative functions was to only be a temporary measure because under Resolution 1244, UNMIK was expected to devolve limited governing responsibilities to local bodies once such institutions came into existence (1999: 4). Moreover, UNMIK's broad range of powers was a reflection of the fact that unlike the Dayton Peace Agreement, which essentially legitimized pre-existing governing bodies,[16] UNMIK was tasked with establishing governing bodies instead of legitimizing pre-existing governing structures.

*Kosovo's Provisional Institutions of Self Government*

In keeping with Resolution 1244, which committed UNMIK to transferring administrative responsibilities to institutions of self-government (1999: 4), UNMIK enacted Regulation 2001/9 in May 2001, which brought into force the "Constitutional Framework on Interim Self-Government," hereafter referenced as the Constitutional Framework. The Constitutional Framework established Kosovo's first postwar institutions of self-government and replaced the *ad hoc* consultative councils established by UNMIK in 1999. Kosovo's institutions of self-government included a parliamentary assembly, an office of president, a government, and courts (Constitutional Framework 2001: 9). The Constitutional Framework reserved significant powers for the SRSG, which included those powers previously outlined, while also devolving a number of tasks to the newly created self-governing bodies.[17] In the event of an overlapping of competencies between UNMIK and self-governing bodies, the SRSG reserved final authority to interpret the Constitutional Framework.

The main legislative body created by the Constitutional Framework was the Assembly, which was composed of 120 members. 100 seats were elected through proportional representation and the remaining 20 seats were reserved for ethnic minorities. Significantly, Article 9.1.6(d) and (e) of the Constitutional Framework made specific reference to the ICTY. The Constitutional Framework stated any individual "serving a sentence imposed by the International Criminal Tribunal for the Former Yugoslavia or under indictment by the Tribunal and has failed to comply with an order to appear before the Tribunal; or deprived of legal capacity

16 Dayton recognized the pre-existing war time entities of the *Republika Srpska* and the Federation of Bosnia-Herzegovina and imposed an overarching OHR along with state-level institutions.

17 See Appendix IX.

by a final court decision" could not stand in Assembly elections (Constitutional Framework 2001: 20). Notably, an individual who was indicted by the Tribunal, but voluntarily appeared before the court could be permitted to stand in elections. This loophole permitted UNMIK to allow Ramush Haradinaj to head his party's lists during Kosovo's 2007 elections, despite protest from the ICTY.

Although the Constitutional Framework established self-governing bodies, the powers of Kosovo's self-governing institutions were significantly limited by UNMIK. The Assembly was granted the authority to form a government, to adopt laws,[18] and to elect a president (Constitutional Framework 2001: 22-23). The president lacked the authority to dissolve the Assembly or call for elections and could only request the SRSG take such action (Constitutional Framework 2001: 26). The president was to be the nominal head of state for the province and had the authority to propose a prime minister, in consultation with political parties in Assembly (Constitutional Framework 2001: 26). The president could also work in close consultation with the SRSG when taking action "in the field of external relations."[19]

## The Politics of Compliance in an International Protectorate

Domestic politics in Kosovo were defined by a contest between UNMIK and institutions of local government, in which local institutions demanded increasing rights to self-government (Hopkinson 2006: 173). Although external relations, including Kosovo's relationship with the ICTY, remained a reserved competency even after the 2001 Constitutional Framework, Kosovo's self-governing bodies nonetheless attempted to engage in foreign policymaking. Because the 2001 Constitutional Framework did not create a foreign ministry, Kosovo's informal foreign policymaking centered around the Office of International Cooperation and Regional Dialogue (OICRD), which was an office within the Office of the Prime Minister. However, as Peci notes, the OICRD failed to function as a credible alternative to a foreign ministry (2007: 8). Moreover, the creation of a foreign office within the Office of the Prime Minister created a considerable degree of confusion as the 2001 Constitutional Framework delegated a consultative role to the Office of the President as oppose to the head of Kosovo's parliamentary government. The ensuing demands from the Office of the Presidency to be granted similar competencies, which were rejected by UNMIK, led to paralysis and bureaucratic

18 Of course legislation could only be adopted on issues that fell within the Assembly's delegated responsibilities. See Appendix IX.

19 As matters of external relations were reserved for the SRSG, the president could not take independent action on questions of external relations without the approval of the SRSG. UNMIK maintained the sole authority to conduct external relations. However, UNMIK did grant the Kosovo Assembly a consultative role in the ratification of bilateral or multilateral agreements (Peci 2007: 6).

infighting between the Presidency and Office of Prime Minister. In fact, in 2007, despite having been invited to open representative offices in Washington and Brussels, these positions were left vacant due to the aforementioned conflict (Peci 2007: 28-29). Nevertheless, Kosovo's institutions of self-government engaged in a public diplomacy campaign to secure external support for a final status agreement that would recognize Kosovo's independence. This campaign will be addressed in greater detail in a discussion of the international politics of compliance.

Ownership of legal obligations to cooperate with the ICTY was part of the aforementioned contest between UNMIK and Kosovo's self-governing institutions. Mirroring laws on cooperation with the ICTY adopted in Croatia and Macedonia, the Kosovo Assembly passed a law on cooperation with the ICTY in 2003, which effectively established a dual obligation upon local authorities and UNMIK to cooperate with the ICTY (UNMIK 2003). Despite the initiative shown on the part of the Assembly to assume ownership of obligations to cooperate with the Tribunal, Kosovo's self-governing institutions lacked a legal mandate to independently respond to ICTY requests and orders.[20]

*UNMIK and Compliance*

UNMIK's record on cooperation has been mixed. The Tribunal noted in its 2006 annual report to the Security Council, "...the Prosecutor had serious concerns regarding the lack of full cooperation provided by the United Nations Interim Administration Mission in Kosovo" (Report of the International Tribunal 2006: 666). Unlike in the Tribunal's detailed criticisms of non-compliance in Croatia and Serbia, the ICTY's report failed to specifically identify acts of non-compliance on the part of UNMIK and limited its discussion of cooperation on the part of Kosovo to two sentences. However, an ICTY official identified serious concerns with regard to UNMIK assistance provided to Tribunal officials in Kosovo.[21] Moreover, there are two episodes where the ICTY transmitted arrest and surrender orders to UNMIK and KFOR that demonstrated a hesitance on the part of the international presence to execute arrests in support of the Tribunal. These two episodes, the first in 2003 and the second in 2005, will be discussed in greater detail below.

---

20 In an interview with UNMIK spokesperson Alexandar Ivanko, it was emphasized that legal obligations toward the ICTY were assumed exclusively by UNMIK and the international security presence under KFOR. Personal interview, November 8, 2007.

21 Personal interview with Alexandra Milenov of the ICTY Field Office in Belgrade, January 23, 2007. UNMIK spokesperson Alexander Ivanko responded to the above allegations by noting that UNMIK has only been criticized by the Office of the Prosecutor and has never been found to be not cooperating by the Tribunal's Trial Chambers. However, it must be noted that compliance assessments are made by the Office of the Prosecutor and not the Trial Chambers. Personal interview with UNMIK spokesperson Alexander Ivanko, November 8, 2007.

*UNMIK and the Limaj Incident*

The ICTY's indictments of Haradin Balaj, Fatmir Limaj, Isak Misliu and Agim Murtezi marked the first time KFOR and UNMIK received sealed indictments from the Tribunal. Although Balaj, Misliu and Murtezi were detained within weeks of UNMIK and KFOR's receipt of the ICTY's indictments, the fact Limaj, the most senior of the four indictees and head of the PDK's parliamentary delegation, was permitted to leave Kosovo for Slovenia two weeks after his indictment caused ICTY Chief Prosecutor Carla Del Ponte to publicly criticize Kosovo's international administration. Moreover, UNMIK's attempts to avoid Limaj's arrest through its encouragement of a voluntary surrender were rejected by the Tribunal, which demanded Slovenian authorities prevent the accused's return to Kosovo.

UNMIK's 2003 non-compliance act proved the most spectacular public display of contempt for the ICTY on the part of the UN mission in Kosovo. While at this point it remains difficult to deconstruct the decision-making process behind this act, the Kosovo daily, *Koha Ditore*, provided a sketch of events leading up to Limaj's eventual arrest in Slovenia. On January 27, 2003 KFOR commander Fabio Mini was alleged to have received the ICTY's indictments and met with UNMIK chief administrator Michael Steiner, who granted KFOR operational authority to carry out the arrests as ordered by the Tribunal. Two weeks later Fatmir Limaj left Kosovo unchallenged by UNMIK border security officials. Only after Limaj's departure were the lower ranking indictees, Balaj, Misliu and Murtezi, arrested. With Limaj in Slovenia, ICTY Chief Prosecutor Carla Del Ponte publicly accused KFOR of having failed to arrest Limaj. Despite assurances from UNMIK that Limaj would voluntarily surrender to the Tribunal at the end of his Slovenian ski vacation, Del Ponte requested Slovene police prevent Limaj from returning to Kosovo and immediately arrest and transfer the accused to ICTY custody (UNMIK 2003). In the aftermath of the Limaj incident, Del Ponte told the BBC, "It escapes all understanding … that Fatmir Limaj could be allowed to leave Kosovo with such ease." Del Ponte went on to note Limaj, "…simply booked the flight ticket like an ordinary citizen … It was that simple. And it is outrageous" (BBC News 2003). The following year Del Ponte publicly accused UNMIK of failing to cooperate with the Tribunal's ongoing investigations against UÇK officials (BBC News 2004). Two years later UNMIK and KFOR would once again receive ICTY arrest orders, and Kosovo's sitting prime minister would be among those indicted by the Tribunal.

*UNMIK and Haradinaj*

Two years after the Limaj incident, the ICTY once again transmitted an indictment against a senior member of Kosovo's self-governing institutions. The indictment of Kosovo's Prime Minister, Ramush Haradinaj, was feared to have the potential to destabilize UNMIK's fragile political order in the province. While UNMIK was singled out for criticism by the ICTY, it is important to note that the indictment of Ramush Haradinaj also met with significant popular opposition within the province. Moreover, as illustrated in the preceding discussion of challengers to UNMIK, UNMIK was dependent upon the continued support of the local population to carry out its administrative mandate. Although UNMIK was not democratically accountable to Kosovar public opinion, UNMIK did take into account Haradinaj's popularity when confronted by the ICTY's indictment of the former UÇK commander. Preceding Haradinaj's indictment, threats of violence against UNMIK were transmitted through the local media, which ominously warned "nobody has surrendered all the weapons from war-time" (Nosov 2005: 523). In addition, the head of a UÇK veterans' association even described UNMIK as "neo-colonial" and compared the international administration to Serbian rule (Hehir 2006: 205). The Kosovar media also reinforced the popular perception of the UÇK as a liberating army that could not have committed war crimes (Nosov 2005: 523), and local print media launched personal attacks against witnesses who had testified against UÇK leaders on trial before the Tribunal. A 2005 report published by the *Youth Initiative for Human Rights* presented an example of one such attack citing the following headline, "the Prosecutor is using a drug addict against Limaj" (Nosov 2005: 606). Following the indictment of Ramush Haradinaj, the Kosovar media widely proclaimed Haradinaj as a "hero" (Nosov 2005: 609-610) and even local NGOs protested the indictment (Nosov 2005: 610).

The perception of Haradinaj as having been unjustly indicted was reinforced by statements made in support of Haradinaj by foreign leaders such as former UK Foreign Secretary Robin Cook (Cook 2005). US Representative Eliot Engel of the House Subcommittee on Europe also issued a press release that emphasized Haradinaj's "indictment is not proof of guilt" (Steinbaum 2005). Furthermore, perhaps the most explicit statements in support of Haradinaj came from UNMIK's SGSR, Søren Jessen-Petersen who developed a close working relationship with the accused and visited Haradinaj's family shortly after his surrender to the ICTY (Nosov 2005: 611). Jessen-Petersen, in an official statement delivered in response to Haradinaj's decision to resign as prime minister and voluntarily surrender himself to ICTY custody, claimed to empathize with "the sense of shock and anger over [the indictment]" (International Crisis Group 2005: 2, UNMIK Press Office 2005). Moreover, Jessen-Petersen expressed regret at Haradinaj's decision to resign:

> I have taken note of Ramush Haradinaj's decision to step down with immediate effect as Prime Minister of Kosovo. I do, of course, respect his decision, but I cannot hide the fact his departure will leave a big gap … Personally, I am saddened to no longer be working with a close partner and friend (UNMIK Press Office 2005).

The SRSG even went on to describe the ICTY's indictment of Haradinaj as painful for UNMIK:

> The decision announced by Mr. Haradinaj to co-operate with the Tribunal, despite his firm conviction of innocence, and although painful for him, his

> family, Kosovo and for his many friends and partners, *including UNMIK*, is at the same time an example of Kosovo's growing political maturity as a responsible member of the international community (UNMIK Press Office 2005).[22]

Absent from Jessen-Petersen's statement was a reference to the ICTY's charges against Haradinaj, which included 37 counts of crimes against humanity, or a reference to the UÇK's wartime victims.

UNMIK's praise of Haradinaj's voluntary surrender and Haradinaj's appeals for calm were credited with ensuring stability was maintained in Kosovo following Haradinaj's transfer to The Hague. The International Crisis Group singled out Haradinaj's voluntary surrender and appeals for calm along with the actions of UNMIK officials for averting violence in the province (International Crisis Group 2005). Haradinaj's appeal for calm following his indictment had the effect of blunting public manifestations of anger toward the Tribunal and UNMIK. Moreover, Haradinaj emphasized that his actions were in Kosovo's interest given any final status outcome which affirmed Kosovo's independence would require the support of the United States and European Union member states (UNMIK 2005). Failure to comply with an ICTY order and the political crisis which would have followed could have undermined progress in reaching a final status agreement favorable to Priština. In response to Haradinaj's appeal the UÇK veterans' organization even cancelled a planned anti-ICTY demonstration.[23]

## International Justice and Civil Society in an International Protectorate

In describing the impact of UNMIK upon the development of a local human rights community, Mertus laments, "...not only has a principled human rights culture failed to emerge, but many of the positive aspects of the previously existing human rights culture have disappeared" (2004: 339). The marginalization of Kosovo's pre-existing human rights culture was attributed to UNMIK's failure to constructively engage local human rights activists who had held prominent positions within Kosovo's human rights NGO community before the 1999 Kosovo War (Mertus 2004: 339).[24] Mertus noted one such activist, Vjosa Dobruna resigned from her UNMIK position in protest of the refusal of UNMIK to permit local input in the drafting of Kosovo's Constitutional Framework (2004: 339). The result was a growing gap between international administrators in UNMIK and their constituents in Kosovo. Daut Dauti, a Kosovar journalist, pointed to

22 Emphasis added by author.

23 NATO also deployed additional troops to Kosovo in anticipation of a violent reaction to the Haradinaj indictment (Reuters 2005).

24 Mertus cites Dobruna as noting that unlike Bosnia- Herzegovina, before the war in Kosovo there was a strong local civil society. However, local NGOs were marginalized once UNMIK assumed control of the province (2004: 340).

an anecdotal example of a UNMIK appeal for Kosovars to return to their jobs in the face of widespread ethnic violence in 2004 as having been met with derision to illustrate the extent to which UNMIK administrators were perceived as being out of touch with the local population (Kostovicova and Bechev 2004). Kosovo's unemployment rate, according to a 2004 UN Human Development Report, was 44.4 percent (UNDP 2004: 19), and therefore many demonstrators had no jobs to which they could return.

### *The Internationalization of Civil Society*

UNMIK's disbanding of Kosovo's parallel government and marginalization of local NGOs sidelined Kosovo's leading indigenous human rights activists in favor of international NGOs which entered the province following NATO's 1999 air campaign. Furthermore, local NGOs that formed after 1999 were encouraged to function as "cheap service providers" for the international administration, rather than engage in substantive human rights activism:[25]

> Internationals reward the local NGOs that were willing to be cheap service providers for international programs and penalize those who fail to obey the international agenda. In this regard, local human rights organizations that monitor the international community for human rights violations are particularly unwelcome (Mertus 2004: 341).

Thus, a considerable percentage of the population came to view the NGO community as acting on behalf of foreign governments rather than acting as a transmission belt between civil society and government (Kosovar Institute for Policy Research and Development 2005: 1, Mertus 2004: 341).[26] In fact, Mehmet Kraja, a writer for Kosovo's leading daily newspaper vocalized this distrust of NGOs when he accused UNMIK of having directed funding towards, "…those channels which seek the destruction of Kosovo's Albanian identity and the creation of so-called civil society…" (Kosovar Institute for Policy Research and Development 2005: 1).[27] Dauti even described the international administration as forming a barrier to locals from entering the political process, which was the domain of "internationals"

---

25 A senior figure with a prominent Belgrade-based NGO expressed concern that human rights groups from the former Yugoslavia that are critical of the practices of internationals are branded as extremists. Personal interview, January 23, 2007.

26 Such an analogy may be inappropriate here as given the highly restricted mandate of institutions of self-government. NGO lobbying of local government institutions on human rights issues (refugee returns, prosecution of war crimes) that largely remain the prerogative of the international administration is not perceived as a means of exercising meaningful influence over policy (Devic 2006: 262).

27 Note strong parallels here with attacks on foreign funded NGOs in the Croatian media (see Chapter 2).

(Kostovicova and Bechev 2004). Absent a linkage between the externally funded NGO community and indigenous civil society, NGOs are unable to carry out the function identified in Sikkink and Keck's boomerang model (1998).

### *Mobilization against the ICTY*

As observed in Croatia, a substantial segment of Kosovo's non-internationalized NGO community did not support cooperation with the ICTY. While UÇK veterans' organizations may be included among these, it should be emphasized opposition to the Haradinaj indictment was widespread within local civil society and not restricted to veterans groups (International Crisis Group 2005: 2-4). However, as pointed out earlier, Kosovar veterans' groups proved receptive to appeals for calm from Haradinaj and therefore did not mount large scale anti-ICTY demonstrations such as those witnessed in Croatia and Serbia. Moreover, even in the event of widespread public mobilization against the ICTY, there was no democratic means for Kosovars to demand non-compliance with ICTY orders on the part of governing authorities. Cooperation with the ICTY fell to UNMIK and not the provisional institutions of self-government. Absent a means for the local provisional self-government to comply, the cooperation the ICTY would receive in Kosovo was determined by international administrators within UNMIK.

## Compliance and International Organizations

Prefacing any discussion of the international politics of compliance, it is important to emphasize three characteristics of Kosovo which highlight the difficulties of tracing compliance causality. First, from 1998-2008 Kosovo did not claim to be a sovereign state, but rather remained legally within the Republic of Serbia. Thus, a strict reading of Article 29 of the Tribunal Statute would suggest Belgrade remained the legal subject of any obligation to transfer persons wanted by the Tribunal from Kosovo to The Hague. Of course, Kosovo operated as a *de facto* sovereign territory under UNMIK's sovereign authority. Second, UNMIK and KFOR, the two institutions with both a capability and obligation to cooperate with the Tribunal were not accountable to local bodies of government established through the Constitutional Framework for Provisional Self-Government in Kosovo. Third, unlike in Bosnia-Herzegovina, where local police forces were not disbanded post-Dayton but rather monitored by the International Police Task Force, in Kosovo, UNMIK established an independent international police force drawn from contributing UN member states. Equipped with an independent police force, UNMIK could directly secure custody of individuals indicted by the ICTY, whereas in Bosnia-Herzegovina the OHR was entirely reliant upon cooperation from NATO, and later EU, led international forces, or the local police. Given the above restraints upon local actors, the international politics of compliance would dictate the level of cooperation between Priština and the ICTY.

*The International Politics of Compliance*

Despite Resolution 1244's imposition of an obligation upon UNMIK and KFOR to cooperate with the ICTY, the Security Council did not establish enforcement mechanisms to counter non-compliance acts. When the Kosovo Albanian delegation arrived at Rambouillet in January 1999, the Kosovars sought to include a robust mandate for the ICTY within a peace agreement for the province. Much like the Bosnian delegation at Dayton, the Kosovars requested that any peace agreement with Belgrade include a compliance regime for ICTY fugitives on the territory of Kosovo *and* the SRJ. Furthermore, given NATO's obfuscation of its responsibilities to assist the Tribunal in Bosnia-Herzegovina, the Kosovar delegation requested the inclusion of a clause which would obligate NATO to enforce Tribunal orders upon the SRJ through "the use of force under the NATO Activation Order" (Williams and Scharf 2002: 197-198). Belgrade, of course, opposed any mention of the ICTY. The Contact Group sided with Belgrade and rejected the Kosovars' proposals, with French and OSCE representatives at Rambouillet going so far as to accuse the Kosovar delegation of attempting to derail the peace process by demanding an ICTY compliance regime that was unacceptable to Belgrade (Williams and Scharf 2002: 200). The result was that Rambouillet included only an obligation to cooperate with the Tribunal, and enforcement mechanisms were discarded (Williams and Scharf 2002: 200-203).

Although the Rambouillet agreement was rejected by Belgrade, Rambouillet did serve as the basis for UNSC Resolution 1244 which established the institutional framework for the postwar international civilian administration.[28] Notably, Resolution 1244, like the Dayton Peace Agreement, failed to put in place a robust sanctions regime to counter non-compliance with Tribunal orders. As Williams and Scharf note:

> … the Security Council missed an opportunity to craft a sanctions regime that would have empowered the Tribunal to compel compliance with its orders and to obtain access to Serbia proper. Again though, such a regime would have had little chance of being adopted given the Russian and French opposition (2002: 208).

Resolution 1244, did however, differ slightly in language from the Dayton accords, which committed the parties, Bosnia-Herzegovina, Croatia, and the SRJ, to cooperation with the Tribunal. Article 14 demanded, "…full cooperation by all concerned, including the international security presence, with the International

28 Herring points out UNSC Resolution 1244 included a commitment to only "take into account" Rambouillet. It is important to emphasize Rambouillet was never implemented (2001: 232). Also see UNSC Resolution 1244 1999: 3.

Tribunal for the Former Yugoslavia" (UNSC Resolution 1244 1999: 4).[29] Nonetheless, no sanctions regime was put in place for non-compliance on the part of the concerned parties. And crucially, for the SRJ, UNSC Resolution 1244 did not include specific language obligating Belgrade to grant Tribunal personnel access to the SRJ outside of Kosovo. Thus, Resolution 1244 had no positive impact on SRJ cooperation with the Tribunal. However, when it came to securing custody of ICTY suspects in Kosovo, UNMIK and KFOR benefited from the fact Kosovo's most high profile war crimes suspect, Ramush Haradinaj, voluntarily surrendered to the ICTY.[30]

### *Explaining Voluntary Cooperation*

Kosovo's self-governing institutions, throughout the period under examination, were engaged in a process of attempting to secure international recognition. Much like Croatia during 1991, Priština saw membership in international institutions as means of affirming recognition as an independent state. Kosovo's institutions for self-government also sought to demonstrate Priština's ability to meet international human rights standards as part of a campaign to demonstrate that Priština's self-governing bodies were prepared to preside over an independent state. In December 2003, the UNSC endorsed a plan drafted by UNMIK called *Standards for Kosovo* which committed Kosovo to demonstrating compliance with international human rights norms, particularly with regard to the protection of ethnic minorities, before a final status agreement could be reached for the province (UNMIK 2007). Two years later, a final status process was initiated as Martti Ahtisaari opened final status talks through the newly created United Nations Office of the Special Envoy of the Secretary General for the Future Status Process for Kosovo in Vienna (Ahtisaari 2005).

The pursuit of a final status agreement that would confirm Kosovo's status as an independent state was perceived as extremely urgent due to the fact Kosovo's ambiguous status under international law prevented Kosovo from participating on an equal footing in international institutions designed to promote regional cooperation in Southeastern Europe such as the European Union's Stability Pact and Stability and Association Process (Yannis 2004: 72). In addition, Kosovo's institutions of self-government were unable to enter into contractual agreements with the EU, such as the Stability and Association Agreement, which formed the foundation of EU accession processes.[31]

---

29 In the preamble to Resolution 1244 the following clause appears, "recalling the jurisdiction of the International Tribunal for the Former Yugoslavia."

30 Haradinaj emphasized, at the time of his surrender, his decision was in the best interest of Kosovo (UNMIK 2005: 3-5).

31 Instead, Kosovo participates in the Stabilization and Association Process Tracking Mechanism, a precursor to the Stability and Association Process.

Absent a foreign ministry, embassies or even a diplomatic corps, Kosovo's institutions of self-government have engaged in an informal foreign policymaking process. In fact, a policy paper financed by the *Kosovo Foundation for Open Society* reminded readers, "Even as a non-sovereign entity, Kosovo has conducted foreign relations in the last two decades" (Peci 2007: 6). Dedushaj pointed out:

> Today with the global information revolution the Government of Kosovo does not need that large network of embassies around the world to get their message heard. They can contact their counterparts abroad by telephone and e-mail. Their message does not need to pass through ambassadors (2007: 11).

Dedushaj noted that the surrender of Haradinaj was a positive public diplomacy exercise for Kosovo that served to counter Serbian claims Kosovo was a lawless failed state, through demonstrating a commitment to adhering to international legal obligations. A domestic political crisis that would have followed Haradinaj's failure to surrender to the ICTY could have threatened to delay if not derail Kosovo's final status process. Interestingly, in response to Belgrade's claims Kosovo's institutions of self-government were unable to ensure the rule of law, Dedushaj contrasted Haradinaj's transfer to ICTY custody with the continued failure of Serbia to surrender the ICTY's most wanted fugitives (2007: 10).

### *Kosovo and the European Union*

While Chapters 2 and 3 dealt with the impact of EU membership conditionality on compliance. The European Union, despite direct involvement in governing Kosovo through Pillar Four of UNMIK, has been unable to utilize conditionality to improve cooperation with the Tribunal on the part of UNMIK. As previously noted, the EU was unable to enter into contractual accession agreements with Priština, and neither UNMIK nor the provisional institutions of self-government could formally request the initiation of an EU accession process for the province. Furthermore, given Serbia's SAA negotiations with the EU, the initiation of a separate accession process for what was under international law a province of Serbia would have been an unprecedented act. Nonetheless, the EU began to lay the foundations for Kosovo's accession by decoupling Serbia's and Kosovo's interactions with the bloc. Beginning in June 2004, the EU began a process that would effectively allow Kosovo to interact with the EU as an independent entity, if not as a state. First, the European Council adopted the European Partnership for Serbia and Montenegro including Kosovo as defined by the UN Security Council Resolution 1244 of June 10, 1999, which issued independent assessments for Kosovo, Serbia, and Montenegro. Then, in 2005 the European Council emphasized, "the Western Balkans including Kosovo" were considered potential future members of the EU; however, the Council explicitly stated its role in preparing the province for EU integration would not prejudice the final status process, which had yet to determine whether or not Kosovo would be recognized as an independent state (European

Council 2005a). Then in 2006, in the clearest single indication yet that Kosovo was being prepared for an EU accession process, the Council called upon UNMIK to draft a separate plan to prepare the province for EU membership (European Council 2006).

Despite the fact the EU engaged UNMIK in a pre-accession process for Kosovo, ICTY conditionality could not be deployed against UNMIK.[32] Moreover, European Union member states never took action to sanction UNMIK for non-cooperation with the ICTY. Whereas the European Commission publicly condemned non-cooperation with the ICTY on the part of Belgrade, Sarajevo, and Zagreb, the European Commission remained silent on non-cooperation on the part of UNMIK. Only, in instances where responsibilities have been devolved from UNMIK to the institutions of self-government has conditionality been utilized by the European Commission. For example, in January 2006, the European Commission included UNMIK's standards process into the European Partnership for Kosovo and the EC requested self-governing authorities establish an Action Plan to oversee the implementation of goals established by UNMIK in its 2004 Kosovo Standards Implementation Plan (UNMIK 2007). The establishment of the Action Plan in 2006 spurred a series of reforms to the organizational structure of Kosovo's self-governing bodies, which included the creation of an Office of European Integration within Kosovo's Office of the Prime Minister. Moreover, following UNMIK's authorization of the creation of a self-governing ministry of the interior and justice, the Action Plan was able to target improving the rule of law in Kosovo (UNMIK 2007).

### *International Administrations and Contested Norms*

UNMIK's reluctance to cooperate with the ICTY and act in a manner consistent with international justice norms should not be viewed in a vacuum as other norms such as ensuring the right of return for ethnic minorities to the province have also fallen victim to a desire to ensure short-term stability in the province. In fact, the UNHCR even advised against the return of Kosovo Serbs, Roma, Ashkaelia, Egyptian, and other minorities as "such returns could contribute to further destabilize the situation in Kosovo" (Blitz 2006: 259). The UNHCR's warning was probably the direct result of KFOR, UNMIK's international police, and local police all having failed to provide security for Kosovo's ethnic minority communities during an outbreak of anti-Serbian violence during 2004 (Human Rights Watch 2004).[33] The failure of the international security presence to protect

32 This is for the obvious reason that UNMIK itself was not seeking membership into the European Union, but rather was engaged in making preparations for EU accession on behalf of a future Kosovan state.

33 Human Rights Watch provided a few illustrative examples of how risk adverse international forces refused to carry out their security mandate. First, French forces refused to leave their base to protect a Serb enclave within just yards of the base leaving the village

ICTY witnesses from violence and intimidation can be provided as an additional example of attempts to minimize risk to international personnel in Kosovo. UNMIK and KFOR compliance decisions, like decisions on whether or not to provide protection to ethnic minorities or encourage refugee returns, were dominated by a weighing of the expected consequences of a given act on the security situation in the province.

As in Bosnia-Herzegovina the preference of international peacekeeping forces was the minimization of risk to their personnel and the maintenance of stability. Intervention in interethnic clashes and the arrest of high profile war crimes suspects were perceived as potentially jeopardizing both of the above. Because of risk aversion on the part of international peacekeeping forces, it can be expected that in order to ensure the enforcement of arrest warrants a clear legal obligation coupled with clear enforcement provisions must be accepted by international peacekeeping forces. However, as seen in Bosnia-Herzegovina, while international peacekeeping forces are willing to assume the authority to carry out arrests, there remains an unwillingness to acknowledge an obligation to do so.

## Conclusions

Theories of compliance with international law have yet to attempt to explain compliance on the part of international administrations or other non-state governing bodies. Unlike the previous four case studies, Chapter 6 addressed the question of compliance in the absence of a state actor or state legal subject. UNMIK, which assumed sovereign control over the territory of Kosovo through UNSC Resolution 1244, was the legal subject of demands for assistance from the ICTY. As both the ICTY and UNMIK were UN organizations created by UNSC *fiat*, the fact that the latter organization failed to assist the former requires explanation. It has been demonstrated that while the ICTY sought to prosecute individuals suspected of serious violations of International Humanitarian Law, UNMIK's primary concern was the maintenance of stability in the province and a minimization of risk to international peacekeeping forces. The ICTY was unable to effectively counter non-cooperation on the part of UNMIK due to the fact that traditional methods of coercion and inducements could not be deployed against an international administration operating under a UNSC mandate. Moreover, because UNMIK and the ICTY were both established under Chapter VII of the UN Charter, the two organizations enjoyed a more horizontal legal relationship. In the previous case studies, where we have examined the ICTY and states, the relationship between the Tribunal and the legal subjects of Tribunal orders was unambiguous.

---

to be burnt to the ground. Second, Ashkeli homes were destroyed within the vicinity of two French bases. Third, German KFOR troops refused to come to the assistance of UNMIK police trapped in Prizen while crowds destroyed all traces of Serbian life in the town (Human Rights Watch 2004: 21).

The horizontal legal relationship that exists between UNMIK and the ICTY limits the ability of *ad hoc* tribunals to enforce their orders and conduct investigations in territories under international civilian or military administration and creates a situation whereby tribunals are dependent upon voluntary assistance provided by international administrations. Absent the ability to issue legally binding orders, compliance outcomes will reflect the extent to which international administrations are prepared to assist the work of international criminal courts.

Kosovo's provisional institutions of self-government, on the other hand, were more receptive to norm affirmation in support of the ICTY and sought to demonstrate compliance with international human rights norms as part of a public diplomacy campaign to build international support for Kosovo's independence. In fact, Haradinaj's decision to voluntarily surrender to the ICTY was framed as legitimizing Kosovo's self-governing institutions. When traditional methods for bringing about compliance, coercion and inducements, are the only tools available to challenge non-compliant behavior, non-compliance on the part of multi-national administrations operating under a UNSC mandate is unlikely to be challenged. States seeking to negotiate or maintain their statuses in international institutions, such as Croatia during the 1990s, are far more susceptible to coercive threats on the part of third party states. With regard to non-state multi-national administrations, alternate compliance methods can be deployed such as public shaming of the non-compliant institution, as seen in the ICTY's 2006 report to the UNSC which highlighted UNMIK's non-compliance. However, in the case of UNMIK public shaming proved ineffective in improving compliance as UNMIK was once again singled out for non-compliance by the ICTY in 2007. Moreover, it is important to emphasize that UNMIK's encouragement of voluntary surrenders in the Limaj and Haradinaj transfers is more reminiscent of the level of cooperation Belgrade's Koštunica-led government provided to the ICTY then what should be expected from a United Nations administration.

Chapter 7

# Conclusions: The Politics of Compliance with Tribunal Orders

## Introduction

Despite the prolific growth in tribunal literature that followed the establishment of the ICTY (1993), the ICTR (1994) and the ICC (1998[2002]), examinations of compliance and non-compliance with tribunal orders remain a lacuna in international justice scholarship. This book set out to explain compliance with international criminal tribunal orders through competing theories of IR and IL which can be broadly dichotomized into rationalist and constructivist approaches to compliance (Table 1.1). While the number of state subjects of international criminal tribunal requests and orders remains relatively small, the ICTY offers an opportunity to test theories of compliance across a diverse spectrum of states and territories under international civilian or military administration which were all subject to the same legal regime, the Statute of the Tribunal. Moreover, with the coming into effect of the Rome Statute in 2002, we can expect an ever increasing number of states to come into contact with an emerging international judiciary making compliance focused research agendas ever more relevant to understandings of international justice.[1]

The failure to integrate the study of compliance into tribunal scholarship can be at least partially explained by the fact existing explorations of post-cold war international criminal tribunals which focus on legal precedent and law creation often fail to take into account that the emerging international judicial infrastructure differs fundamentally from its predecessors at Nuremberg and Tokyo. In fact, as mentioned in Chapter 1, the post-Second World War military tribunals bear little functional resemblance to the post-cold war tribunals as the former were established in the aftermath of the total military defeat of Germany and Japan and therefore did not depend upon or require cooperation from states. Thus, whereas the military tribunals at Nuremberg and Tokyo were integrated into postwar occupation administrations that exercised both *de jure* and *de facto* sovereignty over the defeated powers, the ICTY was a court that lacked a constabulary. When the ICTY issued its first indictments in 1995, which were transmitted to

1 While the International Criminal Court operates under the Rome Statute which differs from the ICTY Statute of the Tribunal, Sudan's referral to the ICC through Resolution 1593 under Chapter VII of the UN Charter has established an enforcement regime identical to that which exists for the ICTY.

Bosnia-Herzegovina [BiH],[2] Croatia, and Serbia [SRJ], the Tribunal could not compel any supranational actor or occupation police force acting in support of the Tribunal to carry out its orders in the face of local non-compliance. Even in Bosnia-Herzegovina and Kosovo, where external actors assumed varying degrees of control over police and security functions, the ICTY could not depend upon the cooperation of international civilian administrations or military peacekeeping missions.

Instead, the international judicial apparatus that emerged in the 1990s rested upon the foundation of the cooperation of external actors. In Chapter 1 it was emphasized that the ICTY was invested with an unprecedented legal mandate to obligate states to cooperate with the Tribunal. Article 29 of the Tribunal Statute created an unambiguous legal obligation upon all UN member states to comply with Tribunal requests and orders. This legal obligation was then clarified by a 2002 ICTY Appeals Chamber decision on Croatia's appeal of the Bobetko indictment. States, according the Appeals Chamber, were under a legal obligation to exercise ministerial functions in support of the Tribunal and were not in a position to question, challenge or reinterpret Tribunal orders (Decision on Challenge by Croatia 2002). The position of states in relation to the Tribunal was ministerial in the sense that states were under an obligation to carry out Tribunal orders without question. Yet despite the Tribunal's robust legal mandate, the ICTY was not imbued with any direct enforcement capabilities. As the Appeals Chamber noted in the *Prosecutor v. Blaškić*, the ICTY could not subpoena states, as failure to respond to a court subpoena would necessitate legal consequences.[3] Taken together the Appeals Chamber's findings in the *Prosecutor v. Bobetko* and the *Prosecutor v. Blaškić*, it becomes apparent that the Tribunal enjoyed a hierarchical legal relationship with states while also lacking any direct means to sanction non-compliance.

Given the above disconnect between the ICTY's legal mandate and the ICTY's ability to independently compel compliance with Tribunal orders, the preceding case studies provided an opportunity to discern the extent to which material incentives and disincentives framed compliance decisions on the part of states. While Chapters 2 and 3 identified third party state coercion and inducements as the intervening variable which brought about state compliance with ICTY orders on the part of Croatia and Serbia, it was noted that in the case of Serbia

2 Radovan Karadžić and Ratko Mladić's indictments, which were certified by the Tribunal in July 1995, preceded the deployment of the NATO-led IFOR mission to BiH in December 1995/January 1996. However, it should be pointed out that the UN-led UNPROFOR mission was in-country at the time and failed to carry out a single arrest and transfer operation in support of the ICTY.

3 Therefore, the ICTY could only subpoena state officials in their private capacity. Also, it should be noted that the ICTY retained the ability to order states to undertake certain activities in support of the Tribunal; however, failing to comply with an order does not grant ICTY Trial Chambers the authority to impose legal consequences on a non-compliant state.

coercion proved significantly less effective than in neighboring Croatia due to a vastly different constellation of local elites. Moreover, Chapter 4 presents an example of a state that voluntarily complied with not just an ICTY arrest order, but also cooperated voluntarily with the Tribunal's in-country investigations. Macedonian state cooperation forms a contrasting backdrop to difficulties the ICTY encountered in securing assistance from international peacekeeping forces in Bosnia-Herzegovina and Kosovo, the subjects of Chapters 5 and 6. Chapters 5 and 6 highlighted the fact that the legal position of the ICTY *vis à vis* the subjects of Tribunal orders is significantly blurred when taking into account multi-national civilian administrations or peacekeeping forces which exercised *de facto* or *de jure* sovereignty over Bosnia-Herzegovina and Kosovo. In both BiH and Kosovo multinational administrations derived their mandates directly from the UNSC under Chapter VII of the United Nations Charter.[4] The result was that while the relationship between the ICTY and states was unambiguously hierarchical, the relationship between the Tribunal and IFOR (later, SFOR then EUFOR), the OHR, UNMIK and KFOR was, to a greater extent, horizontal. Despite an Appeals Chamber decision suggesting the opposite (Decision on Motion for Judicial Assistance 2000), UNMIK and EUFOR explicitly claimed the Tribunal lacked the authority to impose legal obligations upon the above entities through Article 29, which addressed states. Instead, UNMIK, in particular, argued its legal obligations derived solely from UNSC Resolution 1244.[5]

## The Gap between Obligation and Compliance

A common observation evident throughout the case studies, with the possible exception of Chapter 4, is that the mere establishment of legal obligation alone cannot explain compliance with Tribunal orders. Managerial models of compliance (Chayes and Chayes 1995) therefore lack applicability to the case studies discussed here. In fact, from 1993-1996 the Tribunal was confronted with almost complete non-cooperation on the part of the states of the former Yugoslavia. The first accused transferred to Tribunal custody, Duško Tadić, was only delivered to The Hague due to the fact Tadić had already been charged and arrested in Germany.[6] Furthermore, in 1995, despite certifying 36 indictments, not a single accused was transferred to Tribunal custody by local authorities in the former Yugoslavia. Then, in 1997, four years after the UNSC unanimously adopted Resolution 827, the almost complete absence of voluntary state cooperation and the failure of NATO to arrest ICTY

4 NATO derived its mandate in BiH UNSC Resolution 1031, whereas UNMIK and KFOR derived their mandates from UNSC Resolution 1244.

5 This argument was put forward an UNMIK official in personal communications with the author.

6 Duško Tadić went on to become the first defendant to stand trial before the ICTY.

fugitives in BiH led Scharf to suggest the ICTY would require an independent police force to effectively function (1997: 228).

A decade after Scharf's assessment that compelling state cooperation might be an unachievable goal, the ICTY had successfully secured custody of all but four accused under Tribunal indictment. With the assistance of NATO in BiH, the transfer of Bosnian Croats under Tribunal indictment by Zagreb and even Milošević's transfer of Erdemović, during the last three years of the 1990s the ICTY gradually began to secure custody of war crimes indictees. At present, 12 years after the ICTY issued its first indictments, only four ICTY fugitives remain at large[7] and the Tribunal's 2006 annual report to the UNSC emphasized cooperation received from Croatia, Macedonia, and the multi-national presence in BiH (Report of the International Tribunal 2006). In fact, only UNMIK, Serbia and the Bosnian Serb republic were cited for continued non-cooperation with the Tribunal. It is this transformation of preferences from non-compliance to compliance and in some cases the persistence of non-compliance that this book has sought to explain. However, before exploring the ICTY's interactions with international peacekeeping missions and multinational civilian administrations, let us first return to state compliance.

## State Compliance: Croatia, Serbia, and Macedonia

In the cases of Croatia and Serbia coercion and inducements proved effective in bringing about compliance; however, the level of coercion or inducements required to transform state behavior varied greatly between the two states. Because similar material incentives and disincentives produced divergent compliance outcomes, the explanatory power of rationalist theories of IR must be more closely examined. On the other hand, a look at ideational structures illuminated by the rhetorical appeals of states highlights that Croatia and Serbia adopted divergent trajectories of legal argumentation to rationalize non-compliance acts. Croatia never characterized a non-compliance act as an act of total non-recognition of ICTY's jurisdiction, and Croatia never claimed the UNSC lacked the authority to establish the ICTY. Rather non-compliance acts were always attributed to either legal questions regarding a specific indictment, an inability to transfer accused persons due to reasons of ill health, or an inability to locate an accused.[8] Thus, when policymakers in Zagreb shifted from non-compliance to compliance, compliance acts could be more easily rationalized as a fulfillment of international legal obligations.

---

7 Among the four fugitives that remain at-large at the time of writing are two of the ICTY's most high profile indictees, Radovan Karadžić and Ratko Mladić.

8 See for example Croatia's rationalization of non-compliance which framed non-compliance as occurring within the Tribunal Statute (Statement Delivered by the Croatian Delegation 1998).

In Chapter 2 it was illustrated that from 1996, when the first Croat indictee was transferred to ICTY custody, until 2005, when the last Croatian citizen under indictment for serious violations of IHL was transferred to The Hague, compliance acts were framed in the context of fulfillment of legal obligations – even if the compliance act was itself coerced. Moreover, Croatia proved significantly more receptive to cooperation with the ICTY than Serbia although there were periods where Croatian compliance with Tribunal orders was not forthcoming, particularly during the late 1990s and between 2001 and 2003.[9] Because domestic civil society mobilized against the ICTY during the 1990s and early to mid-2000s, the demand for state cooperation with the ICTY was almost exclusively external. Thus, periods of non-compliance were marked by a mobilization of veterans' organizations against specific arrest orders. The result of domestic anti-ICTY mobilization was that absent third party enforcement, the Croatian state was vulnerable to a significant domestic non-compliance pull. In fact, Chapter 2 stated that the absence of a strong domestic justice constituency within the former Yugoslavia, permitted anti-ICTY groups, recalcitrant states, and a hostile media to monopolize the international justice debate within the region.

Even though at first glance an exploration of Croatian interaction with the ICTY, in isolation from the accompanying case studies, seems to confirm rationalist assumptions regarding international law enforcement, when Croatian interaction with the ICTY is contrasted with Serbia, it is important to emphasize Zagreb accepted the norm of international criminal justice and would thus resort to contesting ICTY indictments through legal mechanisms that fell within the Tribunal Statute.[10] While cooperation with the ICTY was domestically unpopular in both Croatia and Serbia, Zagreb's acceptance of the normative and legal framework of the tribunal system meant that coercion and inducements, when applied, proved more effective in altering non-compliant behavior because the Croatian government was not faced with the prospect of violating a countervailing normative framework.[11]

Chapter 3 imparted that norms and ideational structures can act to constrain states in their interactions with international criminal tribunals. However, while Finnemore, Risse, Sikkink and Walling suggest the normative and ideational power of human rights can transform state behavior (Finnemore and Sikkink 1998, Risse

9 Interestingly, this observation was particularly true during from 1994-1998, during a period of time when ICTY indictments targeted almost exclusively Bosnian Croats and Bosnian Serbs leaving elites in Belgrade and Zagreb un-indicted. Thus, divergent levels of compliance during the 1990s cannot be dismissed as the outcome of Serbia being the recipient of indictments which targeted state elites, which only occurred in 1999.

10 Croatia characterized the July 1998 adoption of the Statute of Rome as a "political, legal and moral victory" for international criminal justice and the tribunal system (Statement Delivered by the Croatian Delegation 1998).

11 In a sense, there was considerably less risk of what Putnam described as an "involuntary defection" (1988: 427-460).

2001, Sikkink 1993, Sikkink and Walling 2005), Chapters 2 and 3 suggest that states can act to create and entrench countervailing norms which can constrain a state's ability to cooperate with international criminal tribunals. Our explorations of Croatia and Serbia demonstrated that compliance regimes are more effective when a given rule or law is internalized by states as conforming to domestic norms of appropriate action. In extra-legal terms, R. Fisher's distinction between a non-compliance act which is *malum in se* (bad in itself) and a non-compliance act that is merely *malum prohibitum* (bad because it is prohibited) (1981: 108) can serve to illustrate the power of domestic normative structures.[12] Fisher, Henkin, and Moravcsik all identified a causal relationship between domestic norms and compliance with international legal regimes (R. Fisher 1981: 141-235, Henkin 1968, Moravcsik 1995: 157-189). However, existing liberal theories of IR limit theorizing compliance to a community of liberal democratic states where the rule of law has already been internalized. Take for example the following, "the most important preconditions for the creation of and compliance with the sort of highly refined regime norms found in Europe are strong pre-existing norms, practices and institutions of liberal democracy..." (Moravcsik 1995: 184). Nevertheless, this book demonstrates that because even illiberal states rationalize policy choices through an appeal to legal norms, both internally and externally, an illiberal regime which accepts legally binding human rights obligations can find itself constrained by domestic norm internalization.[13]

Because Serbian public opinion's rejection of the ICTY's claim to exercise jurisdiction over the territory of the SRJ was reinforced by the position of the SRJ judiciary, which considered the transfer of an SRJ citizen to the ICTY to be an unconstitutional act, Belgrade faced significant difficulties in rationalizing compliance with Tribunal orders. When compliance acts occurred they were characterized as *sui generis* events. For example, when Dražen Erdemović, an ethnic Croat member of the Bosnian Serb Army, was transferred to ICTY custody by Belgrade in 1996, Erdemović's lack of SRJ citizenship was said to provide the legal basis for the accused's transfer. The difficulty surrounding the Erdemović transfer, even given the fact Erdemović expressed a personal preference to voluntarily surrender to Tribunal custody, illustrates the extent to which non-compliant behavior had been internalized as legitimate action within the SRJ and the extent to which any form of cooperation with the Tribunal was perceived as illegitimate. The internalization of the norm of state sovereignty, as articulated in the foreign ministry's legal challenge to the ICTY, restricted the scope for

12 Franck makes a similar observation in his study of why states obey the law in the absence of coercion (Franck 1988: 708). Of course, this study is inclusive of why states violate international law in the presence of coercion.

13 As Hafner-Burton and Tsutsui note, mere acceptance of international human rights accords alone is insufficient (2007: 407-425). Rather, here is argued the state in question must have engaged in substantive legal argumentation in support of a given norm.

compliance on the part of Serbia's post-Milošević elites in the aftermath of the collapse of the Milošević regime in October 2000.

The Milošević transfer in 2001 was perhaps the most spectacular display of compliance. However, after Milošević's transfer to the ICTY, Serbia once again failed to comply with ICTY requests and orders as the United States proved less willing to coerce Belgrade into surrendering the remaining ICTY indictees on the territory of the SRJ. Moreover, although Serbian Prime Minister Zoran Điniđić supported Serbian fulfillment of ICTY obligations and the transfer of all individuals under ICTY indictment to The Hague, Điniđić's compliance strategy was never fully implemented and eventually brought about his assassination through an operation led by elements of the state security services (CSCE 2003b: 12).

While the linkage of EU accession to compliance with Article 29 obligations did not initially bring about actual arrests, by 2005 the Serbian government began to increasingly perceive the presence of ICTY fugitives on its territory as a liability and actively encouraged persons indicted for war crimes on the territory of Serbia to "voluntarily surrender" themselves to the Tribunal. However, as mentioned in Chapter 3, these surrenders were characterized as "patriotic" acts and no mention was ever made of the contents of the ICTY indictments against persons accused of war crimes.[14] Furthermore, in instances where voluntary surrenders were not forthcoming such as with regard to Ratko Mladić, the Serbian government failed to promptly take action to bring about an arrest. Andrej Nosov of the Youth Initiative for Human Rights in Belgrade's observation that post-Milošević state cooperation with the ICTY has been exclusively rationalized in functional or material terms as opposed to moral or legal obligation illustrates the extent to which the norm of state sovereignty and non-cooperation with the ICTY has been internalized by Belgrade.[15]

Chapter 4 presented the only instance of a state which has consistently complied with its obligations toward the Tribunal. Although Macedonia was only required to execute a single arrest, Macedonia proved cooperative when it came to cooperation with the Tribunal over a broad range of investigative issues over a period of five years. Macedonia's acceptance of the 2001 Ohrid Framework Agreement, which ended a brief civil conflict, marked a watershed moment in shaping the identity of the Macedonian state as Macedonia accepted its transformation from nation-state into a decentralized multi-ethnic state (Brunnbauer 2002: 4). The extent of Macedonia's post-Ohrid transformation can be illustrated by the fact that in 2002 the head of the political wing of the National Liberation Army, an ethnic Albanian paramilitary force, which led a violent campaign against Macedonian government forces in 2001, entered a coalition government with an ethnic Macedonian political party. Moreover, Ohrid enmeshed the Macedonian state in international institutions

14 Personal Interview with Alexandra Milenov of the ICTY Field Office in Belgrade, January 23, 2007.

15 Personal interview with Andrej Nosov of the Youth Initiative for Human Rights in Belgrade, January 23, 2007.

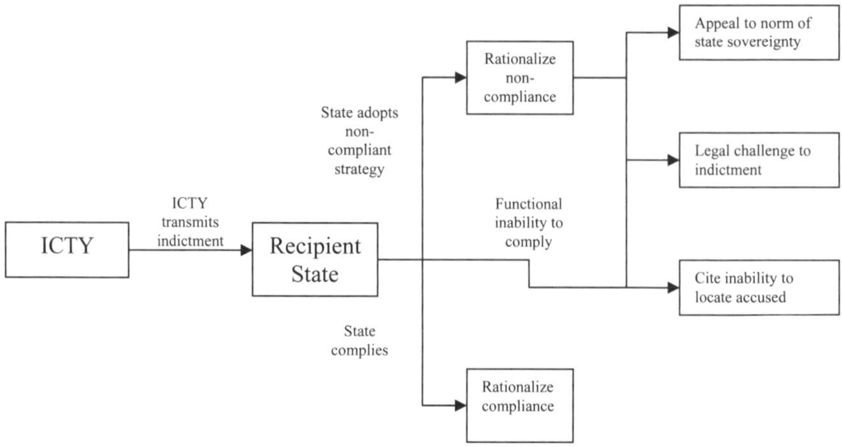


**Figure 7.1 The ICTY and states**

such as the OSCE and the EU, which were invited to oversee and advise domestic governance (Ohrid Framework Agreement 2001). At the time of Tarčulovski's 2005 indictment there was an elite consensus in Skopje which favored not just EU and NATO membership, but a deepening enmeshment of the Macedonian state into international institutions. Apart from an isolated independent MP, who felt Macedonia's cooperation with the ICTY threatened "state sovereignty," all major political parties adopted integrationist foreign policies directly into their party programs. Thus, when the ICTY began its investigations into violations of IHL on the part of Macedonian security forces, cooperation with international institutions was already a deeply entrenched norm. Moreover, due to the lack of intensity and duration of the 2001 conflict, powerful veterans' organizations did not emerge to challenge Macedonian state cooperation with the Tribunal.

An examination of three states to which ICTY arrest and surrender orders were addressed demonstrates multiple policy options for the recipient states. In the event that a state is able to locate an accused, the recipient state can a) comply with the ICTY arrest and surrender order or b) not comply with the ICTY arrest and surrender order. If a state selects the latter option then the state is confronted with the task of rationalizing its non-compliant behavior (see Figure 7.1). Given cooperation with the ICTY is a legal obligation imposed upon all UN member states under Chapter VII of the UN Charter, the burden was upon the non-compliant state to explain non-cooperation with the Tribunal.

In the event a state opts for non-compliance there are multiple rationalizations available through which states can characterize non-compliance acts. As demonstrated in our exploration of Croatia and Serbia, an appeal to a countervailing norm has the effect of locking-in non-compliance while mounting legal challenges to individual indictments or citing an inability to locate an accused allows for the

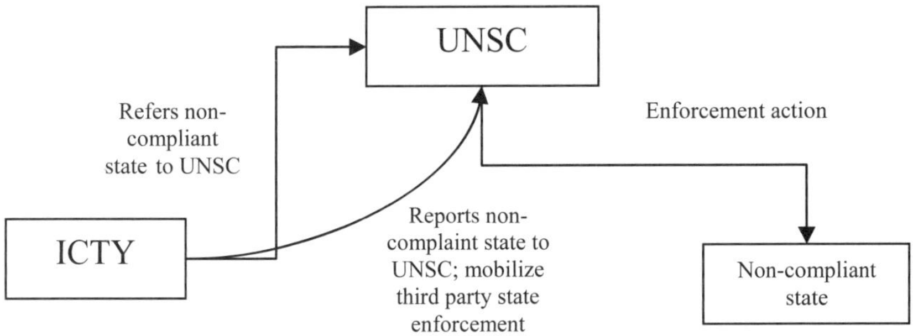


**Figure 7.2 ICTY referral and reporting to UNSC**

non-compliant state to rationalize a compliance act as fulfillment of an accepted legal obligation at a later date.

Given non-compliance has proven a general norm when it comes to initial state reactions to ICTY orders,[16] it is important to understand how non-compliance was confronted by the ICTY. The ICTY was limited in ways it could confront non-compliant behavior on the part of states. First, the Tribunal could adhere to the legal processes set out in the Tribunal Statute, referral of the non-compliant state to the UNSC, or, second, the Tribunal could pursue an extralegal bargaining process through a utilization of third party states. Because the UNSC was not prepared to take enforcement action under Article 41 or 42 of the UN Charter, ICTY reports to the UNSC were not expected to generate enforcement action on the part of the Council, but rather served as a public forum in which non-compliant states could be publicly named. Despite naming and shaming before the UNSC having not been effective in itself transforming non-compliant behavior on the part of recalcitrant states, ICTY reports submitted before the UNSC provided an powerful normative tool with which the Tribunal could galvanize third party state enforcement action outside the Council.

### *State Compliance and Third Party Coercion*

While the establishment of legal obligation nevertheless remains an integral antecedent condition for explaining compliance, we must look elsewhere for causation. As previously noted, in the event a state failed to fulfill its legal obligations toward the ICTY, the Tribunal was invested with only a single mechanism for legally challenging non-compliance: referral of the recalcitrant state to the UNSC (see Figure 7.2). In practice, however, the UNSC never authorized enforcement action against state non-compliance with ICTY Article 29 obligations. Russia and China only reluctantly supported the creation of the ICTY and were not prepared to authorize sanctions against a state for failing to cooperate

16 Macedonia is the only notable exemption to this general observation.

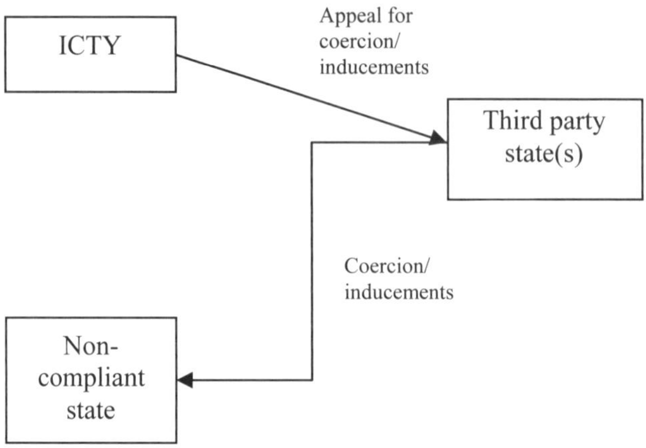


**Figure 7.3 The ICTY and third party states**

with the court. Therefore, despite persistent non-compliance on the part of the SRJ throughout the 1990s, UNSC Resolution 1044, which both deplored Belgrade's non-cooperation with ICTY and demanded improved cooperation on the part of Belgrade, demonstrated the only action the UNSC was prepared to take against non-compliant states was restricted to the rhetorical realm.

In the absence of UNSC enforcement action, the ICTY approached third party states in order to coerce compliance from Croatia and Serbia through the application of sanctions or inducements (see Figure 7.3). It was the utilization of third party state coercion which former Croatian foreign minister Mate Granić labeled as the "coercive model" for securing custody of individuals under Tribunal indictment.

In any discussion of the theoretical implications of the three state case studies it is important to recall international law remains for the most part state centric and Article 29 of the Tribunal Statute reflects this fact. States were unambiguously established as legal subjects of Tribunal obligations. Non-compliant states were therefore confronted with either denying the legality of UNSC imposed obligations to cooperate with the Tribunal through an appeal to countervailing norms or accepting the jurisdiction of the Tribunal. Croatia, Bosnia-Herzegovina, and Macedonia chose the latter option, while Serbia went with the former. Acceptance of a legal obligation alone did not in turn lead to compliant behavior as seen with regard to Croatia because the state retained the ability to challenge indictments through ICTY Trial and Appeals Chambers.[17] Moreover, rejection of a legal obligation toward the Tribunal does not entirely preclude cooperative

17 Although more fragrant violations, such as simply ignoring arrest and surrender orders absent a legal rationale grounded in the Tribunal Statute, are not compatible with an acceptance of ICTY jurisdiction.

behavior as illustrated by the Erdemović transfer from SRJ custody in 1996. Here it is argued that while the legal arguments deployed by states do not establish absolute parameters in which state actions are constrained, states can transform ideational incentive structures through appeals to legal norms. The compliance pull identified by Franck is not an entirely autonomous exogenous force,[18] but rather it is vulnerable to normative deconstruction on the part of state actors (1990).

Despite the above findings which indicate a causal relationship between ideational perceptions of appropriate action and compliance, the ICTY perceived itself as reliant upon third party state coercion and inducements in order to secure compliance with Tribunal orders from recalcitrant states in the former Yugoslavia. The isolation of spectacular coercive threats, such as the US threat to block Serbian access to international financial institutions led Goldsmith and Posner to dismiss the prospect of international criminal courts exercising any normative pull over states:

> The [ICTY] has had modest success in trying war criminals, including Slobodan Milosevic. But, it was not the gravitational pull of the ICTY charter that lured these defendants to The Hague. Rather, it was NATO's (and primarily American) military, diplomatic, and financial might (2005: 116).

In fact, former ICTY spokesperson Florence Hartmann's claim that the ICTY was largely dependent upon and vulnerable to the assistance of the "great powers" (2007) coincides with Goldsmith and Posner's rationalist state and power centric assessment. Hartmann suggested the ICTY had little independent agency and was entirely dependent upon the support of third party states to secure arrests (2007). Perhaps as a result of this state power-centric focus in The Hague, the ICTY invested minimal resources into attempts at engaging in normative persuasion or engagement with regional civil society groups receptive to the ICTY, which permitted the unchallenged emergence of a powerful domestic non-compliance pull in Croatia and Serbia. However, because of Zagreb's acceptance of the normative framework of the tribunal system, the non-compliance pull exerted against Zagreb was significantly weaker than that which confronted post-Milošević elites in Belgrade.

### *State Compliance and the European Union*

One instrument of coercion often appealed to by the ICTY Chief Prosecutor Carla Del Ponte was the threat to obstruct or block the EU accession processes of non-compliant states in the event of non-cooperation with the Tribunal. In October 2007, Del Ponte noted:

---

18 Henkin also identified the existence of a compliance pull; however, Henkin argued this pull toward compliance was based on the prudential desire to "keep the system intact" (1979: 51).

> Without the strong support of the EU and its member States, the implementation of my mandate would be an impossible mission. Permit me to remind you that, since I took office in 1999, we have brought 91 individuals into the custody of the Tribunal. Much of that great success could not have been achieved without the strong, principled and consistent support of the European Union … *The European Union's policy of pre-accession and accession conditionality has thus far proven to be the sole successful tool in the recent past in stimulating States to fully cooperate with the Tribunal and obtaining the arrest of fugitives* (Del Ponte 2007b).

However, the preceding chapters have illustrated that Del Ponte's assessment has overstated the effectiveness of EU pre-accession and accession conditionality. In the case of Croatia, while the linkage of the initiation of EU accession negotiations to cooperation with the Tribunal stimulated the Croatian government's search for the fugitive general Ante Gotovina, a similar linkage failed to produce a compliance outcome in Serbia. Moreover, during the 1990s it was the US, not the EU, which coerced Croatian compliance with ICTY arrest and surrender orders. Prefacing our discussion of EU coercion induced compliance, it should be first pointed out that there does not appear to be any correlation between distance from EU accession and compliance. As of 2007, Croatia, Macedonia, and Serbia were all at different stages of the EU accession process; however, no correlation can be drawn between a state's distance from accession and compliance.[19]

Cooperation with the ICTY itself appears not to have affected the speed of accession processes for the states of the former Yugoslavia as the EU has lacked consistency in applying ICTY conditionality over the period of time covered in the case studies (1993-2008). Moreover, as EU accession and pre-accession agreements are conditioned upon the fulfillment of numerous criteria, compliance with Article 29 obligations cannot in itself secure an acceleration of a state's EU accession.[20] For example, Croatia secured recognition as an EU candidate state before Macedonia despite Croatia being cited by the Tribunal for having failed to fully cooperate with efforts to locate Ante Gotovina. Meanwhile, Bosnia-Herzegovina's EU accession process was frozen due to a failure to strengthen the powers of BiH's central state institutions over entity level governments.

The absence of policy coherence in regard to the obligations of accession states toward the ICTY also greatly impaired the ability of the EU to coerce compliance through the threat of freezing accession processes. Even after March 2005, when the EU cancelled Croatia's accession negotiations, EU member states such as Austria and Hungary unsuccessfully attempted to decouple the linkage between

---

19 Croatia achieved candidate status in 2004 before Macedonia, which achieved candidate status in 2005. In addition, as of March 2008 neither Serbia nor Bosnia-Herzegovina signed a Stability and Association Agreement with the EU.

20 Although non-compliance acts could result in the suspension of an accession process as observed in Chapter 2.

cooperation with the ICTY and Croatia's EU accession process. Similarly, with regard to Serbia, a bloc of primarily Southern and Central European member states argued against linking Serbia's EU accession process to the transfer of ICTY fugitives to Tribunal custody. While Croatia was unsuccessful in securing a decoupling of ICTY obligations and Croatia's EU accession process, Serbia's minister for Human Rights, Rasim Ljajić articulated an expectation that Belgrade's EU accession process could progress absent full cooperation with the ICTY (B92 2007b).

*State Compliance and Norms*

Existing norm-focused studies of compliance with international human rights regimes identify norms as causal phenomena which explain compliances outcomes; however, this book has noted that appeals to countervailing norms can establish an ideational context for non-compliant acts. When states make legal appeals to countervailing norms, compliance acts prove much more difficult to effect. Belgrade, through appeals to the norm of state sovereignty, raised the domestic costs of compliance by de-legitimizing the ICTY. While the existence of Kocs' "legal structure" of international politics (1994: 535-556) remains to be demonstrated, long-term path dependent constraints can be attributed to state legal argumentation. In the case of non-compliance with ICTY orders, non-compliant states never conceded that they were in non-compliance with their imagined international legal obligations. Instead, two divergent legal rationalizations for non-compliance were articulated by Croatia and Serbia, which involved either the challenging of individual indictments or a challenging of the jurisdiction of the Tribunal itself. The former constituted an acceptance of the international criminal justice regime, while the latter constituted an appeal to the norm of Westphalian state sovereignty.

Even though Croatia proved susceptible to coercion during the 1990s, it was Zagreb's early acceptance of an international criminal tribunal regime that facilitated cooperation after Croatia's transition from authoritarianism to parliamentary democracy. Although the Croatian government proved reluctant to execute ICTY arrest and surrender orders, once Zagreb exhausted all legal avenues through which it could challenge the ICTY within the institution of the court, Croatian compliance was either forthcoming or Croatia fell back upon a claimed functional inability to effect an arrest. As in the case of Serbia, Croatia's interaction with the Tribunal was also framed in the context of considerable inter-state negotiation, first on the part of the US and later the EU, but coercion and inducements alone offer only a partial picture of Croatian cooperation with the ICTY. One negative effect of the bargaining process which took place during the 1990s between Zagreb and Washington was an internalization of an expectation for material rewards in return for fulfillment of legal obligations toward the Tribunal. Belgrade also increasingly perceived the presence of indicted war criminals as a bargaining asset. Both of the above suggest consequentialist approaches to human rights regime enforcement may undermine human rights norm internalization as compliance is no longer perceived as a legal obligation but rather a subject of inter-state negotiation.

It is revealing that the only state which was never found to be in non-compliance with ICTY obligations was Macedonia. Although the fact that Macedonia received only a single ICTY indictment must limit any conclusions drawn from the Macedonian case study, Macedonian compliance suggests domestic norms of appropriate action may serve to better explain compliance and non-compliance outcomes. After all, while coercion and inducements have often been the focus of rationalist research agendas, Freedman reminds us that the effectiveness of coercive threats remains dependent upon the constructed reality of those states which are the targets of coercion (2003: 36). This book has demonstrated that states were susceptible to endogenous ideational and material non-compliance pulls which served to reduce the effectiveness of exogenous material incentives or disincentives. Rather than focus solely on external coercion, it is the demand for justice within the very states to which Tribunal orders are addressed upon which ultimately the future success or failure of international criminal justice will depend. Thus, an understanding of why domestic civil society failed to mobilize in support of international criminal justice across the three case studies may serve to illuminate why causal pathways associated with the boomerang pattern and spiral effect were not observed in this book.

## Compliance under Diffuse Sovereignty or International Protectorates

Compliance literature, much like international law itself, remains to a large degree state-centric (Cassese 2005: 3). Despite the increasingly frequent deployment of multinational peace enforcement forces, which often assume *de facto* if not *de jure* sovereign authority over a given territory or state, the question of legal obligations to enforce international legal obligations upon local actors responsible for crimes against humanity or crimes of war has received little attention. As existing studies of compliance assume the state to be the subject of international legal obligations, the relationship between international judicial bodies and intergovernmental organizations has yet to coalesce. In the former Yugoslavia, international peacekeeping missions preferred to exercise the authority to arrest and transfer local officials wanted by the ICTY for serious violations of IHL, but denied a legal obligation to carry out such arrests. However, a state centric interpretation of Article 29, which permits intergovernmental organizations to deny a legal obligation to assist the Tribunal, runs counter to established ICTY case law.[21] Despite the fact Article 29 of the ICTY Statute appears to suggest states are the sole subjects of a legal obligation to cooperate with the Tribunal, Rule 59*bis* of

21 For example, criminal liability for command responsibility is inclusive of irregular or paramilitary forces operating in a territory under the functional control of a national military force.

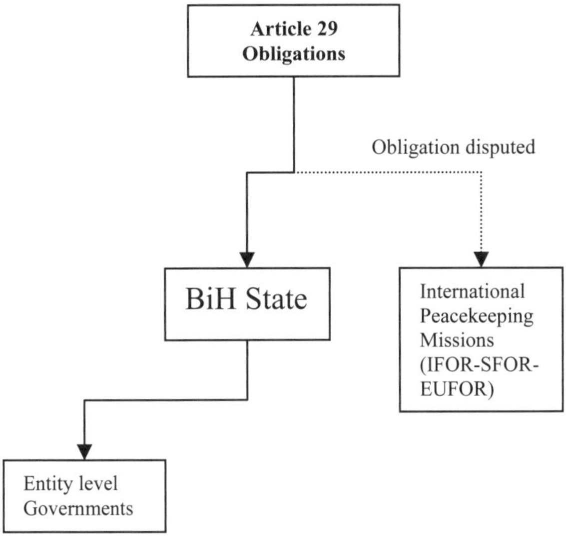


**Figure 7.4 Diffuse subjects of Article 29 obligations**

the ICTY's Rules of Procedure and Evidence makes references to an "appropriate authority or international body" (ICTY 2007: 49-50). Moreover in 2000, the ICTY Trial Chamber explicitly affirmed an obligation imposed upon intergovernmental organizations to comply with Tribunal orders (Decision on Motion for Judicial Assistance 2000).

Despite the Decision on Motion for Judicial Assistance to be provided by SFOR and Others in the *Prosecutor v. Simić et al.* case, non-cooperation on the part of multinational peacekeeping forces and civilian administrations proved a significant and persistent challenge to the Tribunal. Neither enforcement mechanism identified in Figure 7.3 nor in Figure 7.4 could be applied to exert pressure upon the multinational civilian and military missions in BiH and Kosovo, which both derived their mandates from the UNSC under Chapter VII of the UN Charter. Moreover, the primary contributing states for peacekeeping missions and civilian administrations in BiH and Kosovo were in many cases the very same states upon which the ICTY was dependent for voluntary contributions and seconded personnel. Instead, as has been demonstrated, the ICTY was almost entirely dependent upon shaming and persuasion as mechanisms to transform non-compliant behavior. But, before returning to the theoretical implications of Chapter 5 and 6, the variance in international legal identities between BiH and Kosovo requires us to first assess the implications of each of the case studies independently.

## *Bosnia-Herzegovina: Compliance under Diffuse Sovereignty*

In the case of BiH, the subject of ICTY legal obligations was diffused among international and local actors as BiH maintained its international legal personality as an independent UN member state while *de facto* sovereign control over the territory of BiH was ceded to the NATO-led peacekeeping mission and its civilian counterpart, the Office of the High Representative (OHR), in December 1995 (see Figure 7.5). Furthermore, two powerful entity-level governments were established through the 1995 Dayton Peace Agreement at the sub-state level, the Federation of Bosnia and Herzegovina and the *Republika Srpska*. The entities secured control over policing and judicial powers, thus leaving the control of law enforcement functions outside the control of state-level institutions.

Dayton bound the local parties to the peace agreement and Croatia, Bosnia-Herzegovina, and the Federal Republic of Yugoslavia were obligated to cooperate with the Tribunal. However, the non-recognition of Tribunal competencies on the part of the Bosnian Serb Republika Srpska went unchallenged by NATO and the OHR during 1996-1997. Additionally, NATO signaled a certain degree of ambivalence toward domestic war crimes trials through its support of the Rules of the Road agreement which prohibited local police forces from carrying out arrests of war crimes suspects without first having the indictment certified by the ICTY.[22] With regard to indictments transmitted from the ICTY, IFOR commander Admiral Leighton Smith appeared on Bosnian Serb television to reassure those under indictment that NATO forces would not carry out police functions.

However, in 1997 NATO reversed its position on policing duties, and NATO member states began to carry out arrest and transfer operations in support of the ICTY. During 1997 both the NATO led international peacekeeping mission, SFOR, and the international civilian administration led by the OHR also began to play a significantly more robust role in domestic Bosnian politics. At a time when the *Republika Srpska* was torn by an internal power struggle between Radovan Karadžić's anti-Dayton nationalists and Biljana Plavšić's relatively more moderate nationalists, the US and UK acted to strengthen Plavšić's moderates by undermining Karadžić's support base through targeted arrests of Karadžić supporters under ICTY indictment. Thus, it was no coincidence that in July 1997 NATO carried out its first arrest and transfer operation against an ICTY accused and the OHR was granted the Bonn powers which granted the OHR's High Representative the ability to remove local politicians for a number of offenses against the post-Dayton order including office for non-cooperation with the ICTY.

The July 1997 arrest and transfer of Milan Kovačević by UK peacekeeping forces in BiH marked the first time multinational forces operating under SFOR carried out an arrest of an individual under indictment by the ICTY. The fact that

---

22 As the ICTY's ability to review domestic war crimes indictments was inhibited by a lack of funding (see Chapter 5), the Rules of the Road effectively halted domestic war crimes proceedings during the 1990s.

Kovačević's arrest was subsequently followed by similar arrest operations carried out by US, Canadian and later French forces illustrates that there was a significant change in perception regarding the utility of carrying out arrest missions in support of the ICTY during the latter half of the 1990s. However, what was the causal phenomenon behind NATO's shift from a refusal to undertake policing missions to the pursuit of war crimes suspects? It appears that NATO's pursuit of war crimes suspects can be explained by either a "coincidence of interest" that emerged during the 1997 power struggle within the *Republika Srpska*, former ICTY Deputy Prosecutor Graham Blewitt's threat to publicly reveal NATO's obstruction of the pursuit of ICTY accused after NATO's initial refusal to accept sealed ICTY indictments, or the outcome of elections in the US (1996) and the UK (1997). While it is difficult to disentangle the extent to which the ICTY's threat of public shaming, the desire on the part of NATO to remove pro-Karadžić nationalists from RS political life or the 1997 change in UK government and Clinton's reelection as US president in 1996 brought about a transformation on the part of NATO governments in their willingness to engage in arrest operations in support of the ICTY, the fact that arrests and transfers continued beyond 1997 suggests that continued compliance goes beyond a "coincidence of interest" and demonstrates an acceptance of a responsibility to assist the ICTY, if not an obligation to do so. However, it is important to qualify the above observation by noting that NATO and later the EU never demonstrated a willingness to undertake high risk arrest and transfer missions against the former Bosnian Serb president Radovan Karadžić or the former head of the Bosnian Serb armed forces Ratko Mladić, who remained in Bosnia-Herzegovina until 2000. As former ICTY Chief Prosecutor Richard Goldstone noted, risk averseness on the part of international peacekeeping forces illustrates the gap between perceptions of international and domestic justice:

> On a national level, policemen are not infrequently obliged to arrest people who are armed and dangerous. Yet, it is inconceivable that an attorney general would call off the arrests because of the risks to the lives of the arresting officers (Scharf 1997: 225).

It is the above described risk aversion that perhaps explains why there remains considerable reluctance on the part of EUFOR to engage in high risk arrest operations or even accept a legal obligation to fulfill ICTY arrest and transfer requests. Thus, NATO and EUFOR's challenging of Article 29 obligations while also undertaking selective arrest and transfer operations suggests that rather than challenge the normative framework of international criminal justice, international peacekeeping forces seek to retain the flexibility to determine whether or not to undertake operations in support of international criminal tribunals. However, flexibility in executing arrest and surrender orders does contradict and undermine the assumed universally binding character of Tribunal orders.

*Kosovo: Compliance in an UN Protectorate*

In Kosovo, UNMIK and the NATO-led KFOR mission could not transpose their obligation to carry out Tribunal orders upon a state actor which lacked the capabilities or willingness to arrest and transfer accused persons to ICTY custody. At the time of Resolution 1244's drafting Security Council member states recognized that the legal subject of Tribunal obligations would have to be clarified given Kosovo's status as a province within the Republic of Serbia. Article 14 of Resolution 1244, therefore, went beyond Dayton's obligations, which were imposed exclusively upon the local parties to the 1995 peace agreement, and demanded cooperation with the ICTY on the part of the international security presence in Kosovo (Resolution 1244 1999: 4).[23] Having established an obligation to cooperate with the ICTY, it should be expected that UNMIK would demonstrate a greater degree of cooperation with the Tribunal than that which was observed in the previous case studies. After all, UNMIK itself was neither a state nor a party to the 1998-1999 conflict. Moreover, like the ICTY, UNMIK was a creation of the UNSC. Unfortunately, as has been demonstrated, UNMIK proved reluctant to assist the ICTY and in 2006 the ICTY reported UNMIK's non-cooperation to the UNSC (ICTY 2006: 666). In fact, as recently as December 2007, ICTY Chief Prosecutor claimed to be "stupefied" by the relationship between UNMIK officials and Ramush Haradinaj, who was indicted in 2005 by the ICTY for serious violations of IHL (Lee 2007).

Despite executing arrest and surrender orders,[24] UNMIK failed to assist the Tribunal in a wide range of functions from providing assistance to Tribunal personnel in Kosovo to providing adequate witness protection. Moreover, UNMIK also rejected any legal obligation to the ICTY under Article 29 of the Tribunal Statute. Paradoxically, while Resolution 1244 made reference to UNMIK obligations toward the ICTY, the very fact that UNMIK was an institution created under Chapter VII of the UN Charter meant that UNMIK enjoyed a horizontal legal relationship with the ICTY. This horizontality meant that the ICTY lacked any mechanism to legally challenge UNMIK non-cooperation. In fact, the only means by which non-cooperation on the part of UNMIK could be challenged would be by a UNSC revision of Resolution 1244 that would have explicitly stated UNMIK's relationship with the ICTY fell under Article 29 of the Tribunal Statute. It is important that UNMIK's contestation of Article 29 obligations not be dismissed as representative of a *sui generis* entity especially given the fact the proliferation of Chapter VII mandated UN peace enforcement operations

23 Interestingly, UNMIK argues its obligations toward the Tribunal stem exclusively from Resolution 1244's two vague references to the Tribunal and not from Article 29 of the Tribunal Statute which provides a detailed list of obligations.

24 Of course the two most high profile Kosovar indictees, Limaj and Haradinaj, were not arrested by UNMIK or KFOR. Limaj fled to Slovenia where he was subsequently arrested at the request of the ICTY while Haradinaj voluntarily surrendered to ICTY custody.

has occurred concurrent to the proliferation of international criminal tribunals. Instead, UNMIK's contestation of legal obligations imposed universally upon all UN member states should be seen as illustrative of the failure of IL or IR to grapple with the human rights obligations of non-traditional sovereign entities. As will be demonstrated below, the failure to incorporate non-traditional sovereign entities into studies of compliance with international law has severely limited the explanatory power of existing compliance theories.

### *Compliance, Diffuse Sovereignty and International Peacekeeping*

The rationalist neoliberal and neorealist theoretical framework must be almost entirely abandoned when explaining compliance on the part of non-traditional sovereign entities. Instead, the only available mechanism through which the ICTY could exert pressure upon NATO and UNMIK was through the public shaming of non-compliance acts and attempts at persuasion. With regard to the former, the ICTY's public Rule 61 hearings against Karadžić and Mladić and Graham Blewitt's threat to expose fraudulent behavior on the part of NATO illustrates the Tribunal's potential normative power over multinational peace enforcement missions. Additionally, when KFOR failed to apprehend Fatmir Limaj, Carla Del Ponte engaged in shaming when she publicly condemned UNMIK and KFOR. Del Ponte then requested Slovenia arrest and transfer Limaj to ICTY so as to prevent the accused's return to Kosovo. However, unlike in BiH, where the OHR, NATO and later EUFOR have acted to support the Tribunal, albeit while also failing to accept a legal obligation to do so or secure the custody of Radovan Karadžić, UNMIK has proved consistently unreceptive to ICTY requests for assistance. Yet, UNMIK does nonetheless attempt to portray itself as cooperating with the Tribunal, which does suggest UNMIK is sensitive to accusations of non-cooperation.

Meanwhile, attempts at persuasion, while including both a moral and legal dimension, primarily focused on attempts to demonstrate a convergence of interest between the ICTY and the NATO presence in BiH. As early as 1996 Richard Holbrooke suggested that the capture and transfer of individuals under ICTY indictment could have a transformative effect on the internal politics of the Bosnian Serb republic as more radical nationalist elements of the RS political community would be removed from the post-Dayton political process (1999: 339-342). The perception that ICTY indictees in the RS were a growing threat to the Dayton process could explain NATO's willingness to arrest and transfer Bosnian Serbs to Tribunal custody; however, it cannot explain NATO's arrest and transfer of former Bosnian Muslim combatants. Moreover, EUFOR has acted in support of BiH police forces in carrying out arrests of individuals under indictment by the Special War Crimes Court in Sarajevo, which suggests that, at least to a limited degree, there has been an internalization of the norm that international peacekeeping forces should act in support of efforts to prosecute individuals responsible for serious violations of IHL. However, unlike national judiciaries, which are prepared to undertake significant risks to secure custody of an accused, international peacekeeping forces remain unwilling to engage in high risk operations. Additionally, policing duties such as intelligence led activities required to locate an accused have not been undertaken by EUFOR, which instead depends upon other actors, such as the ICTY or local governments, informing EUFOR as to the whereabouts of an accused. The obligation to actively engage in the search for ICTY indictees is relevant given the fact Article 29 was interpreted as to require states to undertake aggressive intelligence led operations to locate persons under ICTY indictment. In the case of Croatia, the failure to actively search for Ante Gotovina was interpreted as a breach of Croatia's Article 29 obligations. Should non-traditional sovereign entities such as peacekeeping forces and civilian administration come under Article 29 obligations, the ICTY could demand a much greater level of assistance in efforts to locate and transfer war crimes suspects to Tribunal custody.

## Conclusions: Compliance Reconsidered

This book's exploration of compliance with ICTY orders has sought to introduce the question of compliance into international criminal justice literature, which has for the most part, either assumed compliance to be a function of legal obligation or has neglected the question of compliance altogether. Moreover, this book illustrated that compliance with international criminal tribunal orders cannot be assumed to be forthcoming or automatic. It was also demonstrated that the rationalist focus on material coercion or inducements offers only a partial picture of compliance. Goldsmith and Posner's focus on US military, diplomatic and financial power fails to capture the domestic legitimation processes behind compliance acts. Domestic norms of international justice can be both constituted and deconstructed by states, particularly when a justice constituency within domestic civil society is lacking. In the case of Croatia, Zagreb's affirmation of norms of international justice served to lead Croatia into a dialogue with the ICTY that occurred within the Tribunal's Appeals and Trial Chambers.

The lack of compliance on the part of multinational peacekeeping missions in the former Yugoslavia illustrates that compliance based research agendas must move beyond the state centric focus of IL. Rigid IR realist and neoliberal institutionalist conceptualizations of sovereignty and the state were also unable to either describe or explain the interaction between the ICTY and multinational missions in Bosnia-Herzegovina or Kosovo, nor can the realist and neoliberal focus on rational choice explain divergent compliance outcomes when states were faced with similar material incentives or disincentives. Instead, it has been demonstrated that state rationalizations of compliance acts and the identification of domestic justice constituencies, or the lack therefore, can illuminate ideational constraints to state compliance that can act to amplify or counteract the effectiveness of external material incentives or disincentives. The rationalization of compliance acts is particularly relevant when exploring compliance on the part of NATO in BiH and UNMIK in Kosovo given that neither accepted legal obligations to cooperate with the Tribunal under Article 29 of the Tribunal Statute. Therefore, the study of compliance would greatly benefit from integrating a focus on why states comply with a given law and how states rationalize compliance and non-compliance acts into existing rationalist research agendas that focus on interest and power.

With the coming into effect of the Statute of Rome in 2002 and the UNSC's referral of Sudan to the International Criminal Court through Resolution 1593 in 2005, states, post-conflict international civilian administrations, and military peacekeeping forces can expect to come into ever greater contact with the emerging infrastructure of international criminal justice. This book has explored compliance with ICTY orders in an effort to integrate understandings of compliance into international criminal justice scholarship. Although this book has been restricted in scope to the former Yugoslavia, it has been demonstrated that compliance with ICTY orders can only be understood through both material and ideational incentives.

# Appendices

## Appendix I: State Obligations under the Statute of the Tribunal (ICTY)

*Article 29*

1. States shall co-operate with the International Tribunal in the investigation and prosecution of persons accused of committing serious violations of international humanitarian law.

2. States shall comply without undue delay with any request for assistance or an order issued by the Trial Chamber, including, but not limited to:
    a. the identification and location of persons;
    b. the taking of testimony and the production of evidence;
    c. the service of documents;
    d. the arrest or detention of persons;
    e. the surrender or the transfer of the accused to the International Tribunal.

*Source*: *Statute of the Tribunal*, 1993.

## Appendix II: Croatia and the European Union

| | |
|---|---|
| January 15, 1992 | The European Community recognizes the Republic of Croatia as an independent state. |
| October 29, 2001 | Stability and Association Agreement signed between Croatia and the European Union. |
| February 21, 2003 | Croatia submits application for membership to the European Union. |
| April 1, 2004 | The European Parliament positively assesses Croatia's application for membership. |
| April 20, 2004 | The European Commission grants a positive avis to Croatia's application for membership. |
| June 18, 2004 | The European Council officially grants Croatia EU candidate status. |
| December 17, 2004 | The European Council recommends EU membership negotiations begin with Croatia in March 2005, commencement of negotiations linked to 'full Cooperation' with the ICTY. |
| February 1, 2005 | The Stability and Association Agreement takes effect following ratification by all EU member states. |
| March 16, 2005 | The European Union agrees upon a framework for membership negotiations; however, the commencement of membership negotiations is blocked by Croatia's failure to apprehend the fugitive general Ante Gotovina. |
| October 3, 2005 | Membership negotiations begin following Carla Del Ponte's certification of Croatia as being in full cooperation with the ICTY. |

## Appendix III: Serbia and the European Union

| | |
|---|---|
| May 3, 2006 | SAA negotiations cancelled as a result of Serbia's failure to arrest Ratko Mladić. |
| June 13, 2007 | SAA negotiations resume after the arrest of Zdravko Tolimir in the Bosnian Serb republic. |
| November 7, 2007 | SAA initialed ahead of the conclusion of Kosovo's final status negotiations. |
| April 29, 2008 | SAA and Interim Agreement on Trade and Trade-related issues signed on the eve of critical parliamentary elections held on May 11, in which the DS won the largest share of the vote. |

## Appendix IV: UNPREDEP Troop Contributing States

*States Contributing Troops to the UNPREDEP mission in Macedonia (as of February 1999)*

Argentina
Bangladesh
Belgium
Brazil
Canada
The Czech Republic
Denmark
Egypt
Finland
Ghana
Indonesia
Ireland
Jordan
Kenya
Nepal
New Zealand
Nigeria
Norway
Pakistan
Poland
Portugal
The Russian Federation
Sweden
Switzerland
Turkey
The Ukraine
The United States

*Source*: UNPREDEP.

## Appendix V: High Representatives of the OHR (1995-2009)

| | |
|---|---|
| **Carl Bildt** | December 1995-June 1997 |
| **Carlos Westendorp** | June 1997-July 1999 |
| **Wolfgang Petritsch** | August 1999-May 2002 |
| **Paddy Ashdown** | May 2002-January 2006 |
| **Christian Schwartz-Schilling** | February 2006-June 2007 |
| **Miroslav Lajcak** | July 2007-March 2009 |
| **Valentin Inzko** | March 2009-present |

## Appendix VI: Peace Implementation Council Membership

*PIC Members and Participants:*

*States:* Albania, Austria, Belgium, Bosnia and Herzegovina, Bulgaria, Canada, China (resigned in May 2000), Croatia, the Czech Republic, Denmark, Egypt, the Federal Republic of Yugoslavia, Finland, the Former Yugoslav Republic of Macedonia, France, Germany, Greece, Hungary, Ireland, Italy, Japan, Jordan, Luxembourg, Malaysia, Morocco, the Netherlands, Norway, Oman, Pakistan, Poland, Portugal, Romania, the Russian Federation, Saudi Arabia, the Slovak Republic, Slovenia, Spain, Sweden, Switzerland, Turkey, Ukraine, the United Kingdom, and the United States of America.

*Others:* The High Representative, the Brcko Arbitration Panel (*dissolved in 1999*), the Council of Europe, the European Bank for Reconstruction and Development (EBRD), the European Commission, the International Committee of the Red Cross (ICRC), the International Criminal Tribunal for the Former Yugoslavia (ICTY), the International Monetary Fund (IMF), the North Atlantic Treaty Organization (NATO), the Organization for Security and Cooperation in Europe (OSCE), the United Nations (UN), the UN High Commissioner for Human Rights (UNHCHR), the UN High Commissioner for Refugees (UNHCR), the UN Transitional Administration of Eastern Slavonia (UNTAES; *dissolved in 1998*), and the World Bank.

*PIC Observers* Australia, Central Bank of Bosnia and Herzegovina, European Investment Bank (EIB), Estonia, Holy See, Human Rights Ombudsperson in Bosnia and Herzegovina, Iceland, International Federation of Red Cross and Red Crescent Societies (IFRC), International Mediator for Bosnia and Herzegovina, International Organization for Migration (IOM), Latvia, Lithuania, New Zealand, Liechtenstein, South Africa, and the Special Coordinator of the Stability Pact for South Eastern Europe.

*PIC Steering Board* Canada, France, Germany, Italy, Japan, Russia, United Kingdom, United States, the Presidency of the European Union, the European Commission, and the Organization of the Islamic Conference (OIC), represented by Turkey.

*Source*: Office of the High Representative.

## Appendix VII: Responsibilities of the Provisional Institutions of Self-Government

- Economic and Fiscal Policy
- Fiscal and Budgetary Issues
- Administrative and Operation Customs Activities
- Domestic and Foreign Trade, Industry and Investments
- Education, Science and Technology
- Youth and Sport
- Culture
- Health
- Environmental Protection
- Labor and Social Welfare
- Family, Gender and Minors
- Transport, Post, Telecommunications and Information Technologies
- Public Administration Services
- Agriculture, Forestry and Rural Development
- Statistics
- Spatial Planning
- Tourism
- Good Governance, Human Rights and Equal Opportunities
- Non-Residential Affairs

*Source*: Constitutional Framework for Interim Self-Government 2001.

# References


Abbott, K.W. 1999. International Relations Theory, International Law, and Regime Governing Atrocities in Internal Conflicts. *The American Journal of International Law*, 93(2), 361-379.

Abramowitz, M. 2001. Witness Testimony. *U.S. Assistance to Serbia: Benchmarks for Certification*. Hearing before the Subcommittee on European Affairs of the Committee on Foreign Relations United States Senate, One Hundred and Seventh Congress, First Session, 6-13.

Aćimović, L. 1994. Pitanje kontinuiteta međunarodne ličnosti Jugoslavije i njenog članstva u Ujedinjenjim Nacijama. *Međunarodni Problemi*, XLVI(3), 413-424.

Ackermann, A. 1999. *Making Peace Prevail: Preventing Violent Conflict in Macedonia*. Syracuse: Syracuse University Press.

Ahtisaari, M. 2005. *Press Briefing by the UN Special Envoy Martti Ahtisaari and his Deputy Albert Rohan after their first visit to Kosovo, Press Briefings Unofficial Transcript*, United Nations Office of the Special Envoy of the Secretary General for the Future Status Process for Kosovo. [Online]. Available at: http://www.unosek.org/docref/fevrier/2005-11-23%20-%20Ahtisaari%20press%20briefing.pdf [accessed August 17, 2009].

Akhavan, P. 1998. Justice in The Hague, Peace in the Former Yugoslavia? A Commentary on the United Nations War Crimes Tribunal. *Human Rights Quarterly*, 20(4), 737-816.

Akhavan, P. 2001. Beyond Impunity: Can International Criminal Justice Prevent Future Atrocities? *The American Journal of International Law*, 95(1), 7-31.

Albright, M. 2003. *Madam Secretary: A Memoir*. London: Macmillan.

Allin, D.H. 2002. *NATO's Balkan Interventions*. Oxford: Oxford University Press.

Allison, E. 1998. News from the International War Crimes Tribunals. *American University Crimes of War Project*. [Online]. http://www.wcl.american.edu/hrbrief/v5i2/html/tri.htm [accessed August 13, 2009].

Arbour, L. 2004. The Crucial Years. *Journal of International Criminal Justice*, 2, 396-402.

Arslani, M. and Pavić, S. 2007. Haaški istražitelji nisu htjeli tražiti dokaze protiv Miloševića. *Jutarnji list*, September 11.

Ashdown, P. 2005. *Remarks by High Representative, Paddy Ashdown, at the Press Conference on the Removal of President Covic*. [Online]. http://www.ohr.int/ohr-dept/presso/pressb/default.asp?content_id=34399 [accessed July 5, 2007].

Axelrod, R. and Keohane, R.O. 1985. Achieving Cooperation under Anarchy: Strategies and Institutions. *World Politics*, 38(1), 226-254.

B92, 2006. *Del Ponte: Serbia's Painful Inability*. Belgrade: B92, October 30. [Online]. Available at: http://www.b92.net/eng/news/crimes-article.php?yyyy=2006&mm=10&dd=30&nav_id=37667 [accessed August 5, 2009].

B92, 2007a. *International Reactions to Election Results*. Belgrade: B92, January 22. [Online]. Available at: http://www.b92.net/eng/news/politics-article.php?yyyy=2007&mm=01&dd=22&nav_category=90&nav_id=39190/ [accessed August 6, 2009].

B92, 2007b. *Ljajic: Not much time left for Serbia to convince Hague*. Belgrade: B92, December 3. [Online]. Available at: http://www.b92.net/eng/news/comments.php?nav_id=45888 [accessed August 5, 2009].

Balkan Investigative Reporting Network, 2007. *Macedonia Marks Six Year Anniversary of Ohrid Peace Deal*, August 13. [Online]. Available at: http://www.birn.eu.com/en/98/15/3840 [accessed August 10, 2009].

Bang-Jensen, N. 2001. Witness Testimony. *U.S. Assistance to Serbia: Benchmarks for Certification*. Hearing before the Subcommittee on European Affairs of the Committee on Foreign Relations United States Senate, One Hundred and Seventh Congress, First Session, 15 March, 18-24.

Bass, G.J. 2002. *Stay the Hand of Vengeance: The Politics of War Crimes Tribunals*. Princeton, NJ: Princeton University Press.

Bass, W. 1998. The Triage of Dayton. *Foreign Affairs*, 77(5), 95-108.

Bassiouni, C.M. 1992. *Crimes Against Humanity in International Criminal Law*. London: Martinus Nijhoff Publishers.

Bassiouni, C.M. 2003a. *Introduction to International Criminal Law*. Ardsley, NY: Transnational Publishers Inc.

Bassiouni, C.M. 2003b. Justice and Peace: The Importance of Choosing Accountability over Realpolitik. *Case Western Reserve Journal of International Law*, 35(2), 191-204.

BBC News. 2003. *Kosovo Suspects Taken to The Hague*. [Online]. Available at: http://news.bbc.co.uk/1/hi/world/europe/2773773.stm [accessed August 14, 2009].

BBC News. 2004. *Trial of Kosovo Albanians Begins*. November 15. [Online]. Available at: http://news.bbc.co.uk/1/hi/world/europe/4012043.stm [accessed August 13, 2009].

Belgrade Center for Human Rights. 2005. *Public Opinion in Serbia: Opinions on the Domestic War Crimes Judiciary and The Hague Tribunal*. Belgrade: Belgrade Center for Human Rights.

Bergling, P. 2001. Judicial Reform under International Law: Notes from Bosnia and Herzegovina. *Nordic Journal of International Law*, 70, 489-511.

Bieber, F. 2003. The Serbian Opposition and Civil Society: Roots of the Delayed Transition in Serbia. *International Journal of Politics, Culture & Society*, 17(1), 73-90.

Blitz, B.K. 2006. New Beginning? Refugee Returns and Post-Conflict Integration in the former Yugoslavia, in *War and Change in the Balkans: Nationalism, Conflict and Cooperation*, edited by B.K. Blitz. Cambridge: Cambridge University Press, 239-266.

Boduszynski, M. 2001. *The Triumph of Agency? Leaders, Legacies, International Factors and Regime Change in Yugoslav Successor States*. Paper to the 97th Annual Meeting of the American Political Science Association, San Francisco, August 30-September 2.

Boduszynski, M. and Balalovska, K. 2004. Between a Rock and a Hard Place: Croatia, Macedonia and the Battle over Article 98. *Problems of Post-Communism*, 51(1), 18-30.

Bojičić-Dželilović, V. 2004. *Peace on whose Terms? War Veterans' Associations in Bosnia and Hercegovina, Spoilers of Peace Processes: Conflict Settlement and Devious Objectives*. New York: United Nations University Press.

Braddock, J. and Chatham, R. 2001. *Report of the Defense Science Board Task Force on Training Superiority and Training Surprise*. Washington DC: Office of the Undersecretary of Defense for Acquisition, Technology, and Logistics.

Brand, M.G. 2001. Institution-Building and Human Rights Protection in Kosovo in the Light of UNMIK Legislation. *Nordic Journal of International Law*, 70, 461-488.

Branković, S. 2002. The Yugoslav "Left" Parties: Continuities of Communist Tradition in the Milošević Era, in *The Communist Successor Parties of Central and Eastern Europe*, edited by A. Bozoki and J.T. Ishiyama. New York: M.E. Sharpe, 206-223.

Bridge, J.W. 1964. The Case for an International Court of Criminal Justice and the Formulation of International Criminal Law. *The International and Comparative Law Quarterly*, 13(4), 1255-1281.

Broomhall, B. 2003. *International Justice and the International Criminal Court*. Oxford: Oxford University Press.

Brown, P.M. 1941. International Criminal Justice. *The American Journal of International Law*, 35(1), 118-121.

Brunnbauer, U. 2002. The Implementation of the Ohrid Agreement: Ethnic Macedonian Resentments. *Journal on Ethnopolitics and Minority Issues in Europe*, 1, 1-24.

Brunnstrom, D. 2007. EU to Stop Short of Serbia War Crimes Concession. *Reuters*. [Online]. http://www.alertnet.org/thenews/newsdesk/L09248446.htm [accessed August 14, 2009].

Bulajić, R. 1997. Yugoslavia and European Union. *Review of International Affairs*, XLVIII(1052), 4-7.

Burley, A.M. 1992. Law among Liberal States: Liberal Internationalism and the Act of State Doctrine. *Columbia Law Review*, 92(8), 1907-1996.

Burns, N. 2002. *Burns Interview*, US Embassy Skopje. [Online]. Available at: http://skopje.usembassy.gov/burns_interview.html [accessed August 11, 2009].

Carlowitz, L. 2004. Crossing the Boundary from the International to the Domestic Legal Realm: UNMIK Lawmaking and Property Rights in Kosovo. *Global Governance*, 10, 307-331.

Carr, E.H. 1964. *The Twenty Years' Crisis, 1919-1939*. New York: Harper & Row Publishers Inc.

Cassese, A. 1994. *International Law in a Divided World*. Oxford: Clarendon.

Cassese, A. 1998. On the Current Trends Towards Criminal Prosecution and Punishment of Breaches of International Humanitarian Law. *European Journal of International Law*, 9(1), 2-17.

Cassese, A. 2005. *International Law*. Oxford: Oxford University Press.

Castle, S. 2002. NATO investigates claim French officer warned Karadzic with phone call. *The Independent*. March 5. [Online]. Available at: http://www.independent.co.uk/news/world/europe/nato-investigates-claim-french-officer-warned-karadzic-with-phone-call-660122.html [accessed August 14, 2009].

Chandler, D. 2005. Introduction: Peace without Politics? *International Peacekeeping*, 12(3), 307-321.

Chandler, D. 2006. State-Building in Bosnia: The Limits of "Informal Trusteeship." *International Journal of Peace Studies*, 11(1), 17-38.

Chartier, C. (ed.) 2006. *International Criminal Tribunal for the former Yugoslavia: 1994-2004, a Unique Decade*, 3rd edition. The Hague: Drukkerij Haasbeek.

Chayes, A. and Chayes, A. 1995. *The New Sovereignty: Compliance with International Regulatory Agreements*. Cambridge, MA: Harvard University Press.

Čičić, D. 1996. Svedoci na revers. *Nin*. March 22.

Clark, H. 2000. *Civil Resistance in Kosovo*. London: Pluto Press.

Clark, R.S. 1997. Nuremberg and Tokyo in Contemporary Perspective, in *The Law of War Crimes: National and International Approaches*, edited by T.L.H. McCormack and G.J. Simpson. London: Kluwer Law International.

Clark, W. 1998. Building a Lasting Peace in Bosnia and Herzegovina. *NATO Review*, 46, 19-22.

Clifford, L. 2007. Lajcak Gets Down to Business in Bosnia. *Institute for War and Peace Reporting*. [Online]. Available at: http://www.iwpr.net/?p=tri&s=f&o=337125&apc_state=henh [accessed: July 14, 2009].

CNN, 1997. *US Plans Loan Package to Bolster Plavsic*. [Online]. Available at: http://www.cnn.com/WORLD/9708/27/bosnia.aid/ [accessed August 13, 2009].

Cohen, L.J. 2002. *Serpent in the Bosom: The Rise and Fall of Slobodan Milošević*. Boulder, CO: Westview Press.

Colitti, M. 2005. The Experience of No Peace Without Justice, in *Civil Society, International Courts and Compliance Bodies*, edited by T. Treves, M. Frigessi di Rattalma, A. Tanzi, A. Fodella, C. Pitea and C. Ragni. The Hague: Asser Press, 107-112.

Cook, R. 2005. The Lesson I Learned from Milosevic: The Surrender of Kosovo's Prime Minister is an Act of Real Courage. *Guardian*. [Online] March 11.

Available at: http://www.guardian.co.uk/comment/story/0,,1435202,00.html [accessed: July 14, 2009].

Cooper, C. 2002. Macedonia Will Probe Killing of 7 Immigrants. *Wall Street Journal*, December 16. Available at: http://online.wsj.com/article/SB1039985885911028673.html?mod=googlewsj [accessed August 10, 2009].

Crawford, B. 1995. German Foreign Policy and European Political Cooperation: The Diplomatic Recognition of Croatia in 1991. *German Politics and Society*, 13(2), 1-34.

Croatian Government, 2003. *Germany Supports Croatia's Candidacy for Admission to the EU*. Croatian Government Bulletin. [Online]. Available at: http://www.vlada.hr/Bulletin/2003/january/cro-world.htm [accessed April 28, 2006].

Croatian Helsinki Committee, 2004. *Unprofessionalism, Misinformation and Intolerance in the Croatian Printed Media: 12 September – 31 December 2003*. Available at: http://www.hho.hr/otherstuff/reportNED.htm [accessed April 28, 2006].

Croatian Radio Television, 2000. *Pripadnici HVIDRE blokirali Mostar nakon uhicenja pripadnika HVO-a*. September 11. [Online]. Available at: http://vijesti.hrt.hr/arhiv/2000/09/11/index2.html [accessed August 13, 2009].

Crook, J.R. 2005. Contemporary Practice of the United States Relating to International Law. *American Journal of International Law*, 99(1), 253-254.

CSCE. 2003a. *Bringing Justice to Southeast Europe: Briefing of the Commission on Security and Cooperation in Europe*. Washington D.C: Commission on Security and Cooperation in Europe, May 15.

CSCE. 2003b. *Democracy, Rule of Law and Human Rights in Serbia*. Washington D.C: Commission on Security and Cooperation in Europe, June 3.

Danforth, L.M. 1993. Claims to Macedonian Identity: The Macedonian Question and the Breakup of Yugoslavia. *Anthropology Today*, 9(4), 3-10.

Dedushaj, N. 2007. *Between Public Diplomacy and Paradiplomacy: Establishing Kosova's Diplomatic Apparatus*. Paper to the International Conference: Foreign Ministries: Adaptation to a Changing World, Bangkok, Thailand, June 14-15.

Del Ponte, C. 2006. Investigation and Prosecution of Large-scale Crimes at the International Level: The Experience of the ICTY. *Journal of International Criminal Justice*, 4, 539-558.

Del Ponte, C. 2007a. *Address of Carla Del Ponte at the Policy Briefing, European Policy Centre, Brussels*. [Online]. Available at: http://www.un.org/icty/pressreal/2007/pr1172e-annex.htm [accessed January 18, 2008].

Del Ponte, C. 2007b. *Briefing by Carla Del Ponte, Prosecutor of the ICTY to the General Affairs and External Relations Council of the European Union*. [Online]. Available at: http://www.un.org/icty/pressreal/2007/pr1190e-annex.htm [accessed January 18, 2008].

Deluce, D. 2000/2001. Media Wars. *NATO Review*, 48, 16-21.

Demjaha, A. 2000. The Kosovo Conflict: A Perspective from the Inside, in *Kosovo and the Challenge of Humanitarian Intervention: Selective Indignation,*

*Collective Action, and International Citizenship*, edited by A. Schnabel and R. Thakur. New York: United Nations University Press.

Devic, A. 2006. Transnationalization of Civil Society in Kosovo: International and Local Limits of Peace and Multiculturalism. *Ethnopolitics*, 5(3), 257-273.

Dicker, R. and Leicht, L. 2008. Letter Commending Dutch Position on SAA with Serbia. *Human Rights Watch*. [Online]. Available at: http://hrw.org/english/docs/2008/02/12/nether18042.htm [accessed July 14, 2009].

Donnelly, J. 1986. International Human Rights: A Regime Analysis. *International Organization*, 40(3), 599-642.

Doubt, K. 1997. "We Had to Jump Over The Moral Bridge": Bosnia and the Pathetic Hegemony of Face-work, in *The Conceit of Innocence: Losing the Conscience of the West in the War against Bosnia*, edited by S.G. Mestrovic. College Station, TX: Texas A&M University Press, 120-141.

Dower, J.W. 1999. *Embracing Defeat: Japan in the Wake of World War II*. New York: W.W. Norton & Company Inc.

Edmunds, T. 2003. *Defence Reform in Croatia and Serbia-Montenegro*. Oxford: Oxford University Press.

Engelberg, S. 1996. U.N. Prosecutor Asks Serbs to Hand Over War-Crimes Suspect. *The New York Times*. [Online]. Available at: http://www.nytimes.com/1996/03/08/world/un-prosecutor-asks-serbs-to-hand-over-war-crimes-suspect.html [accessed August 20, 2009].

EUFOR, 2007a. EU Military Operations in Bosnia-Herzegovina. [Online]. Available at: http://www.euforbih.org/mission/mission.htm [accessed June 4, 2007].

EUFOR, 2007b. *EUFOR Role in Relation to Persons Indicted for War Crimes (PIFWICs)*. Unpublished document provided to author by EUFOR media spokesperson, 1 November 2007.

European Commission, 2005. *Croatia: 2005 Progress Report*. [Online]. Available at: http://ec.europa.eu/enlargement/archives/pdf/key_documents/2005/package/sec_1424_final_progress_report_hr_en.pdf [accessed August 17, 2009].

European Commission, 2007. *Enlargement: Financial Statistics 2000-2006*. [Online]. Available at: http://ec.europa.eu/enlargement/financial_assistance/cards/statistics2000-2006_en.htm#mac [accessed August 1, 2007].

European Commission Conflict Prevention and Crisis Management Unit, 2003. *Rapid Reaction Mechanism end of Programme Report: Former Yugoslav Republic of Macedonia*. [Online]. Available at: http://ec.europa.eu/external_relations/cfsp/cpcm/rrm/fyrom.pdf [accessed August 1, 2007].

European Commission Delegation to Bosnia and Herzegovina, 2007a. *The EU and BiH: The EC Delegation to BiH*. [Online]. Available at: http://www.europa.ba/?akcija=clanak&CID=7&jezik=2&LID=22 [accessed October 12, 2007].

European Commission Delegation to Bosnia and Herzegovina, 2007b. *The EU and BiH: The European Presence in BiH*. [Online]. Available at: http://www.europa.ba/?akcija=clanak&CID=9&jezik=2&LID=24 [accessed October 12, 2007].

European Commission Delegation to Bosnia and Herzegovina, 2007c. *The EU and BiH: The Main Objectives of Assistance*. [Online]. Available at: http://www.europa.ba/?akcija=clanak&CID=8&jezik=2&LID=23 [accessed October 12, 2007].

European Commission Delegation to Bosnia and Herzegovina, 2007d. *EU Assistance to BiH: Administrative Capacity Building*. [Online]. Available at: http://www.europa.ba/?akcija=clanak&CID=18&jezik=2&LID=38 [accessed August 13, 2009].

European Council, 2003. *Thessaloniki Agenda for the Western Balkans*, June 16.

European Council, 2004. *Presidency Conclusions*. December 16/17. [Online]. Available at: http://www.consilium.europa.eu/ueDocs/cms_Data/docs/pressData/en/ec/83201.pdf [accessed August 17, 2009].

European Council, 2005a. *Press Release: 2641st Council Meeting*. General Affairs and External Relations. [Online]. Available at: http://ec.europa.eu/external_relations/gac/date/2005/02_210205_er.pdf [accessed August 17, 2009].

European Council 2005b. *Press Release, 2678th Council Meeting*. General Affairs and External Relations. [Online]. Available at: http://www.consilium.europa.eu/ueDocs/cms_Data/docs/pressData/en/gena/86442.pdf [accessed August 17, 2009].

European Council, 2006. *Council Decision of 30 January 2006 on the principles, priorities and conditions contained in the European Partnership with Serbia and Montenegro including Kosovo as defined by the United Nations Security Council Resolution 1244 of 10 June 1999 and repealing Decision 2004/520/EC*, 2006/56/EC, January 30. [Online]. Available at: http://eur-lex.europa.eu/smartapi/cgi/sga_doc?smartapi!celexplus!prod!CELEXnumdoc&numdoc=306D0056&lg=en [accessed August 17, 2009].

European Council Secretariat, 2007. *EU Council Secretariat Factsheet: EU Special Representatives (EUSRs)*. [Online]. Available at: http://www.eusrbih.org/gen-info/?cid=283,1,1 [accessed August 13, 2009].

Fatić, A. 2002. Međunarodni krivični tribunal za bivšu Jugoslaviju u savremonoj diplomatiji. *Međunarodni Problemi*, LIV(1-2), 73-98.

Ferencz, B.B. 1980. *An International Criminal Court a Step Toward World Peace: A Documentary, History and Analysis*, volume II. Portland, OR: Oceana Publishers.

Figa-Talamanca, N. 1996. The Role of NATO in the Peace Agreement for Bosnia-Herzegovina. *European Journal of International Law*, 7(2), 164-175.

Finnemore, M. 1996. *National Interests in International Society*. Ithaca, NY: Cornell University Press.

Finnemore, M. and Sikkink, K. 1998. International Norm Dynamics and Political Change. *International Organization*, 52(4), 887-917.

Fisher, R. 1961. Bringing Law to Bear on Governments. *Harvard Law Review*, 74(6), 1130-1140.

Fisher, R. 1981. *Improving Compliance with International Law*. Charlottesville, VA: University of Virginia Press.

Fisher, S. 2003. Contentious Politics in Croatia: The War Veterans Movement, in *Uncivil Society? Contentious Politics in Post-Communist Europe*. London: Routledge, 74-92.

Fontaine, Y.J. 1997/1998. Strategic Logistics for Intervention Forces. *Parameters*, 42-59.

Foreign and Commonwealth Office, 2003. *Foreign & Commonwealth Office Annual Human Rights Report*, London.

Franck, T.M. 1990. *The Power of Legitimacy Among Nations*. Oxford: Oxford University Press.

Franck, T.M. 1998. Legitimacy and the International System. *The American Journal of International Law*, 82(4), 705-759.

Freedman, L. 2003. Strategic Coercion, in *Strategic Coercion: Concepts and Cases*, edited by L. Freedman. Oxford: Oxford University Press, 15-36.

Freedom House, 2005. *Freedom of the Press – Croatia 2005*. [Online]. Available at: http://www.freedomhouse.org/template.cfm?page=16&year=2005&country6720 [accessed April 28, 2006].

Garms, U. and Peschke, K. 2006. War Crimes Prosecution in Bosnia and Herzegovina (1992-2002): An Analysis through the Jurisprudence of the Human Rights Chamber. *Journal of International Criminal Justice*, 4, 128-282.

Glassborow, K. and Eichstaedt, P. 2008. Ugandan Rebels to Appeal ICC Warrants. Institute for War and Peace Reporting. [Online]. Available at: http://www.iwpr.net/?p=acr&s=f&o=343316&apc_state=henpacr [accessed July 14, 2009].

Goldsmith, J.L. and Posner, E.A. 2005. *The Limits of International Law*. Oxford: Oxford University Press.

Gordy, E. 1999. *The Culture of Power in Serbia: Nationalism and the Destruction of Alternatives*. University Park, PA: Pennsylvania State University Press.

Government of the Republic of Croatia, 2005. *Sanader za ORF: Gotovina mora u Haag*. [Online]. Available at: http://www.vlada.hr/hr/aktualne_teme_i_projekti/aktualne_teme/hrvatska_i_haag/sanader_za_orf_gotovina_mora_u_haag [accessed August 13, 2009].

Gow, J. 1997. *The Triumph of the Lack of Will: International Diplomacy and the Yugoslav War*. London: Hurst & Company.

Gow, J. 2006. The ICTY, War Crimes Enforcement and Dayton: The Ghost in the Machine. *Ethnopolitics*, 5(1), 49-65.

Granić, M. 2005. *Vanjski poslovi: iza kulisa politike*. Algoritam: Zagreb.

Grčić, M. (ed.) 1997. *Tko je tko u NDH*. Zagreb: Minerva.

Green, L.C. 1993. *The Contemporary Law of Armed Conflict*. Manchester: Manchester University Press.

Grieco, J.M. 1988. Anarchy and the Limits of Cooperation: A Realist Critique of the Newest Liberal Institutionalism. *International Organization*, 42, 485-507.

Grodeland, A.B. 2006. Public Perceptions of Non-Governmental Organizations in Serbia, Bosnia-Hercegovina and Macedonia. *Communist and Post-Communist Studies*, 39(3), 221-246.

Gruevski, N. 2004. Macedonia on the Way to NATO and the EU. VMRO-DPMNE. [Online]. Available at: http://www.vmro-dpmne.org.mk/english/Vesti/vest.asp?id=123 [accessed August 1, 2007].

Gruevski, N. 2007. Nikola Gruevski: We Have Introduced New Standards in the Political History of Macedonia. VMRO-DPMNE. [Online]. Available at: http://www.vmro-dpmne.org.mk/english/Vesti/vest.asp?id=149 [accessed August 1, 2007].

Gurowitz, A. 1999. Mobilizing International Norms: Domestic Actors, Immigrants and the Japanese State. *World Politics*, 51(3), 413-445.

Gutman, R. and Barry, J. 2001. What did the CIA know? *Newsweek*, 30.

Guzman, A.T. 2002. A Compliance-Based Theory of International Law. *California Law Review*, 90, 1823-1887.

Guzman, A.T. 2008. *How International Law Works: A Rational Choice Theory*. Oxford: Oxford University Press.

Hafner-Burton, E.M. and Tsutsui, K. 2007. Justice Lost! The Failure of International Human Rights Law to Matter Where Needed Most. *Journal of Peace Research*, 44(4), 407-425.

Hagan, J. 2003. *Justice in the Balkans: Prosecuting War Crimes in The Hague Tribunal*. Chicago: University of Chicago Press.

Haraszti, M. 2007. State of Freedom of the Media in Bosnia and Herzegovina: The Public Service Broadcasting. Sarajevo: OSCE.

Hartmann, F. 2007. *Paix et Châtiment: Les Guerres Secrètes de la Politique et de la Justice Internationales*. Paris: Flammarion.

Hayden, R.M. 2002. Constitutional Nationalism in the Formerly Yugoslav Republics. *Slavic Review*, 51(4), 654-673.

Hazan, P. 2004. *Justice in a Time of War: The True Story behind the International Criminal Tribunal for the former Yugoslavia*, translated by J.T. Snyder. College Station, TX: Texas A&M University Press.

Hebrang, A. 2005. Sanader voli fritule, a ja štrukle: to je jedina razlika između nas. *Nacional*, December 27, 20.

Hedl, D. 2002. *Croatia Faces Sanctions Over Bobetko*. Institute for War and Peace Reporting. [Online]. Available at: http://www.iwpr.net/index.php?apc_state=hen&s=o&o=p=bcr&l=EN&s=f&o=249710 [accessed August 13, 2009].

Hehir, A. 2006. Autonomous Province Building: Identification Theory and the Failure of UNMIK. *International Peacekeeping*, 13(2), 200-213.

Helfer, L.R. and Slaughter, A.M. 1997. Toward a Theory of Effective Supranational Adjudication. *Yale Law Journal*, 107(2), 273-391.

Henkin, L. 1968. *How Nations Behave: Law and Foreign Policy*. London: Pall Mall Press.

Henkin, L. 1979. *How Nations Behave: Law and Foreign Policy*, second edition. New York: Columbia University Press.

Herring, E. 2001. From Rambouillet to the Kosovo Accords: NATO's War against Serbia and its Aftermath, in *The Kosovo Tragedy: The Human Rights Dimensions*, edited by K. Booth. London: Frank Cass, 225-245.

Holbrooke, R. 1999. *To End a War*. New York: Random House Inc.

Holliday, M. 2005. *Serbia and the ICTY: Paying the Price*. Transitions Online. [Online]. Available at: http://www.ceeol.com/aspx/getdocument.aspx?logid=5&id=C3291DB3-B3C4-4443-8105-27590F02183D [accessed August 13, 2009].

Hopkinson, B. 2006. The International Administration of Kosovo since 1999. in *War and Change in the Balkans: Nationalism, Conflict and Cooperation*, edited by B.K. Blitz. Cambridge: Cambridge University Press, 169-176.

Hosmer, S.T. 2001. *The Conflict over Kosovo: Why Milosevic Decided to Settle When He Did*. Santa Monica, CA: RAND Monographs.

Humanitarian Law Center, 2007. *State of Human Rights Defenders in Serbia*. September 19. [Online]. Available at: http://www.hlc-rdc.org/PravdaIReforma/POLOZAJ-ZASTITNIKA-LJUDSKIH-PRAVA-U-SRBIJI/820.sr.html [accessed September 16, 2006].

Human Rights Watch, 2001. Crimes Against Civilians: Abuses by Macedonian Forces in Ljuboten, August 10-12 2001. [Online]. Available at: http://www.hrw.org/legacy/reports/2001/macedonia/ [accessed August 10, 2009].

Human Rights Watch, 2004. *Failure to Protect*: *Anti-Minority Violence in Kosovo*. Available at: http://www.hrw.org/reports/2004/kosovo0704/6.htm [accessed August 17, 2009].

Hurd, I. 2007. *After Anarchy: Legitimacy and Power in the United Nations Security Council*. Princeton, NJ: Princeton University Press.

ICTY, 1996. *Erdemovic and Kremenovic – update 1 – Prosecutor seeks deferral of Erdemovic case; Kremenovic to be remanded back to the FRY*. Press Release. [Online]. Available at: http://www.icty.org/sid/7358 [accessed August 20, 2009].

ICTY, 2001. *Weekly Press Briefing 21 February 2001*. [Online]. Available at: http://www.un.org/icty/briefing/PB210201.htm [accessed August 19, 2009].

ICTY, 2005. *International Criminal Tribunal for the Former Yugoslavia: Amended Statute of the International Tribunal*. [Online]. Available at: http://www.un.org/icty/legaldoc-e/index.htm [accessed December 5, 2005].

ICTY, 2007. *Rules Procedure and Evidence*. IT/32/Rev.40. The Hague: International Criminal Tribunal for the Prosecution of Persons Responsible for Serious Violations of International Humanitarian Law Committed in the Territory of the Former Yugoslavia since 1991, July 12.

ICTY Press Release, 2002. *The Former Yugoslav Republic of Macedonia Requested to Defer Five Cases to the Competence of the International Tribunal*. October 7. [Online]. Available at: http://www.icty.org/sid/8069 [accessed August 7, 2009].

Institute of Social Sciences, 2004. *Stavovi građana o međunarodnoj zajednici i odnosima Srbije i Crne Gore krajem 2004. godine*. On file with author.

International Crisis Group, 1997. *Dayton Two Years On: A Review of Progress Implementing the Dayton Peace Accords in Bosnia*. [Online]. Available at:

http://www.crisisgroup.org/home/index.cfm/index.cfm?l=1&id=1574 [accessed August 14, 2009].

International Crisis Group, 2000. *War Criminals in Bosnia's Republika Srpska: Who Are the People in Your Neighbourhood?* [Online]. Available at: http://www.crisisgroup.org/home/index.cfm?l=1&id=1518 [accessed August 13, 2009].

International Crisis Group, 2001a. *Macedonia: The Last Chance for Peace*. Europe Report No. 113. June 20. Available at: http://www.crisisgroup.org/home/index.cfm?id=1692&l=1 [accessed August 7, 2009].

International Crisis Group, 2001b. *The Wages of Sin: Confronting Bosnia's Republika Srpska*. [Online]. Available at: http://www.crisisgroup.org/home/index.cfm?id=1478&l=6 [accessed August 13, 2009].

International Crisis Group, 2005. *Kosovo after Haradinaj*. Available at: http://www.crisisgroup.org/home/index.cfm?id=3474 [accessed August 17, 2009].

Jackson, M. 2007. *Soldier: The Autobiography*. London: Bantham Press.

Janjević, M. 1999. The Euro and Yugoslavia. *Review of International Affairs*, L(1076), 4-8.

Jeffrey, A. 2006. Building State Capacity in Post-Conflict Bosnia and Herzegovina: The Case of the Brčko District. *Political Geography*, 25, 203-227.

Josipović, I. 2005. Implementation of the International Criminal Law in the National Legal System and the Liability for War Crimes: Example of the Republic of Croatia, in *Responsibility for War Crimes: Croatian Perspective – Selected Issues*, edited by I. Josipović. Zagreb: Faculty of Law, 185-234.

Jovanović, Ž. 1999-2000. Cooperation between Yugoslavia and Russia. *Review of International Affairs*, L-LI(1087-1088), 26-31.

Jovanovski, V. 2001. *The Crimes of Ljuboten*. Institute for War and Peace Reporting. [Online]. Available at: http://iwpr.net/?p=bcr&s=f&o=156355&apc_state=henibcr2001 [accessed August 6, 2009].

Jovanovski, V. 2002. *Macedonia: Tribunal Probes Ljuboten Massacres*. Institute for War and Peace Reporting. [Online]. Available at: http://iwpr.net/?p=tri&s=f&o=166337&apc_state=henitri2002 [accessed August 6, 2009].

Jutarnji List, 2002. Kostović: Nitko se još nije ispričao za zločin na Bleiburgu' *Jutarnji list*, May 15, 2.

Jutarnji List, 2003. Prijetnje Mesiću i Račanu: 'Što prije doručkujte s drugom Đinđićem. *Jutarnji list*, March 27, 3.

Kasapović, M. 2002. Demokratska tranzicija i političke institucije u Hrvatskoj, in *Hrvatska politologija*, edited by R. Knežević and S. Ravlić. Zagreb: Fakultet politički znanosti, 285-300.

Kaufman, J.P. 2004. The Politics of Negotiation: A Comparative Study of Dayton and Rambouillet', in *Sovereignty and the Global Community: The Quest for Order in the International System*, edited by H.M. Hansel. Aldershot: Ashgate, 125-150.

Keck, M.E. and Sikkink, K. 1998. *Activists beyond Borders: Advocacy Networks in International Politics*. Ithaca, NY: Cornell University Press.

Keohane, R.O. 1984. *After Hegemony: Cooperation and Discord in the World Political Economy*. Princeton, NJ: Princeton University Press.

Keohane, R.O. 1986. Reciprocity in International Relations. *International Organization*, 40(1), 1-27.

Keohane, R.O. 1988. International Institutions: Two Approaches. *International Studies Quarterly*, 32, 379-396.

Keohane, R.O. and Martin, L. 1995. The Promise of Institutionalist Theory. *International Security*, 20, 39-51.

Keohane, R.O. and Nye, J.S. 2001. *Power and Interdependence*, Third Edition. New York: Longman.

Kerr, R. 2004. *The International Criminal Tribunal for the Former Yugoslavia: An Exercise in Law, Politics and Diplomacy*. Oxford: Oxford University Press.

Kerr, R. 2005. The Road from Dayton to Brussels? The International Criminal Tribunal for the Former Yugoslavia and the Politics of War Crimes in Bosnia. *European Security*, 14(3), 319-337.

Kivimäki, T.A. 1994. National Diplomacy for Human Rights: A Study of US Exercise of Power in Indonesia, 1974-1979. *Human Rights Quarterly*, 16(2), 415-431.

Klotz, A. 1995. Norms Reconstituting Interests: Global Racial Equality and U.S. Sanctions against South Africa. *International Organization*, 49(3), 451-478.

Kočić, A. 2007. Gotovinu odao mobitel njegove spruge Dunje, *24 Sata*, July 4. Available at: http://www.24sata.hr/index.php?cmd=show_clanak&tekst_id=22458 [accessed August 7, 2009].

Kocs, S.A. 1994. Explaining the Strategic Behavior of States: International Law as System Structure. *International Studies Quarterly*, 38(4), 535-556.

Kola, P. 2003. *The Search for Greater Albania*. London: Hurst & Company.

Kosovar Institute for Policy Research and Development, 2005. *A Changing Society, A Changing Civil Society: Kosovo's NGO Sector after the War*. Pristina: KIPRED.

Kostovicova, D. and Bechev, D. 2004. *Kosovo: The Successes and Failures of International Civil and Military Involvement*. Oxford: Centre for the Study of Global Governance.

Krasner, S.D. (ed.) 1983, *International Regimes*. Ithaca, NY: Cornell University Press.

Krasner, S.D. 1995/1996. Compromising Westphalia. *International Security*, 20(3), 115-151.

Krasner, S.D. 1999. *Sovereignty: Organized Hypocrisy*. Princeton, NJ: Princeton University.

Krasner, S.D. 2001. Abiding Sovereignty. *International Political Science Review*, 22(3), 229-251.

Krasner, S.D. 2004. Sharing Sovereignty: New Institutions for Collapsed and Failing States. *International Security*, 29(2), 85-120.

Kratochwil, F. 1984. The Force of Prescriptions. *International Organization*, 38(4), 685-708.

Kratochwil, F. 1989. *Rules, Norms, and Decisions: On the Conditions of Practical Legal Reasoning in International Relations and Domestic Affairs*. Cambridge: Cambridge University Press.

Kreća, M. 1994. A Few Remarks about the Continuity of the FR Yugoslavia and its Membership in the United Nations. *Međunarodni Problemi*, XLVI(3), 399-412.

Lalić, D. 2002. Domovinski rat i mir, *Nacional*, 22 October: 20.

Lambeth, B.S. 2001. *NATO's Air War for Kosovo: A Strategic and Operational Assessment*. Santa Monica, CA: RAND Monographs.

Lamont, C. 2004. A New Croatian Right: Nationalist Political Parties and Contemporary Croatian Politics. *Balkanistica*, 17, 45-66.

Lamont, C. 2008a. Bargaining for Justice: The Domestic and International Politics of Croatian State Compliance with Article 29(d) and (e) Obligations, in *Global Affairs in a Turbulent World*, edited by Y.A. Stivachtis. Athens: ATINER, 129-142.

Lamont, C. 2008b. Explaining the Regeneration of the Croatian Democratic Union in Post-Presidential Authoritarian Croatia: Elites, Legacies and Party Organization. *Balkanistica*, 21, 57-86.

Lamont, C. 2009. Negotiating Compliance: Sanader's Croatia and the International Criminal Tribunal for the former Yugoslavia. *Transitional Justice Institute Research Paper No. 09-07*. [Online]. Available at: http://papers.ssrn.com/sol3/papers.cfm?abstract_id=1425511 [accessed August 19, 2009].

Lazić, D. 1999. *Yugoslav Foreign Policy – the Need for Fundamental Change*. Belgrade: Center for Strategic Studies.

Lee, M.R. 2007. At UN, Del Ponte "Stupified" by UNMIK's Support for Haradinaj, Dodges UN's Srebrenica Role. Inner City Press. [Online]. Available at: http://www.innercitypress.com/ictykosovo121007.html [accessed August 11, 2009].

Libal, M. 1997. *Limits of Persuasion: Germany and the Yugoslav Crisis, 1991-1992*. London: Praeger.

Lobjakas, A. 2008. Serbia: So Close, Yet So Far for Belgrade's EU Dreams. *Radio Free Europe – Radio Liberty*. [Online]. Available at: http://www.rferl.org/content/Article/1109549.html [accessed August 20, 2009].

Lopandić, B. 2004. Gotovina mora u Haag, a kako će doći tamo stvar je generala i hrvatska vlada. *Vjesnik*, 1.

Lukić, S. 2001. Kakav stav HSLS-a na izjasnjavanju o povjerenju Vladi? *Glas Amerike*.

Lutz, E.L. and Sikkink, K. 2000. International Human Rights Law and Practice in Latin America. *International Organization*, 54(3), 633-659.

MacDonald, D.B. 2002. *Balkan Holocausts? Serbian and Croatian victim-centred Propaganda and the War in Yugoslavia*. Manchester: Manchester University Press.

MacDonald, N. 2009. Missing Military File Could Hit Croatia Accession. *The Financial Times*. [Online]. Available at: http://www.ft.com/cms/s/0/34b402dc-f25c-11dd-9678-0000779fd2ac.html?nclick_check=1 [accessed March 31, 2009].

MacDonald, N. and Dombey, D. 2007. Serbia to Resume EU Talks after War Crimes Arrest. *Financial Times*, 2 June. [Online]. Available at: http://www.ft.com/cms/s/a669af0a-10a7-11dc-96d3-000b5df10621.html [accessed August 13, 2009].

Makfax, 2006. Gruevski Pledges for Close Cooperation with the ICTY. [Online]. Available at: http://www.makfax.com.mk/look/agencija/article.tpl?IdLanguage=1&IdPublication=2&NrArticle=36478&NrIssue=139&NrSection=10 [accessed September 1, 2007].

Malešević, S. 2002. *Ideology, Legitimacy and the New State: Yugoslavia, Serbia and Croatia*. London: Frank Cass.

Maleski, D. 2003. Macedonia at a Crossroads. *New Balkan Politics – Journal of Politics*, 6. [Online]. Available at: http://newbalkanpolitics.org.mk/OldSite/Issue_6/denko.macedonia.eng.asp [accessed August 10, 2009].

Maogoto, J.N. 2004. *War Crimes and Realpolitik: International Justice from World War I to the 21st Century*. London: Lynne Rienner Publishers Inc.

March, J.G. and Olsen, J.P. 1998. The Institutional Dynamics of International Political Orders. *International Organization*, 52(4), 943-969.

Massari, M. 2005. Do All Roads Lead to Brussels? Analysis of the Different Trajectories of Croatia, Serbia-Montenegro and Bosnia-Herzegovina. *Cambridge Review of International Affairs*, 18(2), 259-273.

Matheson, M.J. 2001. United Nations Governance of Post-Conflict Societies. *The American Journal of International Law*, 95(1), 76-85.

May, L. 2005. *Crimes Against Humanity: A Normative Account*. Cambridge: Cambridge University Press.

McCormack, T.L.H. 1997. From Sun Tzu to the Sixth Committee: The Evolution of an International Criminal Law Regime, in *The Law of War Crimes: National and International Approaches*, edited by T.L.H. McCormack and G.J. Simpson. London: Kluwer Law International.

McCoubrey, H. 1990, *International Humanitarian Law: The Regulation of Armed Conflicts*. Worcester: Dartmouth Publishing Company Limited.

McGeary, J. 1999, *Why He Blinked*. Time. [Online]. Available at: http://www.time.com/time/magazine/article/0,9171,991203-4,00.html [accessed August 13, 2009].

Mearsheimer, J.J. 1994-1995. The False Promise of International Institutions. *International Security*, 19(3), 5-49.

Mearsheimer, J.J. 2001. *The Tragedy of Great Power Politics*. New York: W. W. Norton & Company.

Meron, T. 1998. *War Crimes Law Comes of Age: Essays*. Oxford: Clarendon.

Mertus, J. 2004. Improving International Peacebuilding Efforts: The Example of Human Rights Culture in Kosovo. *Global Governance*, 10, 333-351.

Meštrović, S. 1997. Introduction, in *The Conceit of Innocence*, edited by S. Meštrović. College Station, TX: Texas A&M University Press.

Milošević, S. 1990. *Closing Statement to the First Congress of the Socialist Party of Serbia*. Belgrade: Socialist Party of Serbia. On file with author.

Moravcsik, A. 1995. Explaining International Human Rights Regimes: Liberal Theory and Western Europe. *European Journal of International Relations*, 1(2), 157-189.

Morgenthau, H.J. 1978. *Politics among Nations: The Struggle for Power and Peace*, Fifth edition. New York: Alfred A. Knopf.

National Public Radio, 1999. *Serbia Must Hand over Milošević to Remain in Community of Nations says Albright*. [Online]. Available at: http://www.npr.org/about/press/990528.albright.html [accessed September 16, 2006].

Neier, A. 1998. *War Crimes: Brutality, Genocide, Terror, and the Struggle for Justice*. New York: Random House.

Nettelfield, L.J. 2006. *Courting Democracy: The Hague Tribunal's Impact in Bosnia-Herzegovina*. Unpublished thesis. Columbia University.

Nosov, A. (ed.) 2005. *Journalists Can do It*. Belgrade: Youth Initiative for Human Rights.

Nurković, E. and Golčevski, N. 2009. *Sa suđenja Florans Artman*. Humanitarian Law Center. [Online]. Available at: http://www.hlc-rdc.org/uploads/editor/Sudjenje%20F%20Artman(2).pdf [accessed August 18, 2009].

Obradović, K. 1994. Obligation of States to Cooperate with the International Criminal Tribunal. *Međunarodni Problemi*, XLVI(1), 23-38.

Office of European Integration, 1999. *Government of the Republic of Croatia Action Plan for European Integration*. Zagreb: Office of European Integration.

Ordanovski, S. 2004. Lions & Tigers: The Militarisation of the Macedonian Right. *Conflict Studies Research Centre Balkan Series*, 04/15. [Online]. Available at: http://www.da.mod.uk/colleges/arag/document-listings/balkan/csrc_mpf-2004-07-22/04%2815%29-Chap2-JP.pdf/?searchterm= [accessed August 7, 2009].

OSCE, 2002a. *Background Report: The ICTY and General Janko Bobetko*. Zagreb: OSCE.

OSCE, 2002b. *Status Report No. 11*. Zagreb: OSCE.

OSCE, 2005. *War Crimes Trials before the Domestic Courts of Bosnia and Herzegovina: Progress and Obstacles*. [Online]. Available at: http://www.oscebih.org/documents/1407-eng.pdf [accessed August 13, 2009].

Owen, D. 1993. The Future of the Balkans: an Interview with David Owen. *Foreign Affairs*, 72(2), 9.

Palariat, M. 2001. The Economic Consequences of Slobodan Milošević. *Europe-Asia Studies*, 53(6), 903-920.

Pavić, S. 2004. Vlada će pomoći Blaškićevoj obitelji. *Slobodna Dalmacija*. [Online]. Available at: http://arhiv.slobodnadalmacija.hr/20040805/novosti01.asp [accessed August 18, 2009].

Pavlaković, V. 2005. Serbia Transformed? Political Dynamics in the Milošević Era and After, in *Serbia since 1989: Politics and Society under Milošević and*

*After*, edited by Ramet, S.P. and Pavlaković, V. Seattle, WA: University of Washington Press, 13-53.

Peci, L. 2007. *Kosovo's Foreign Policy: Strategic Factors, Objectives and Challenges*. Pristina: KIPRED.

Pelser, W. 2005. *Will ICC Prosecutions Threaten Ugandan Peace Process?* Institute for War and Peace Reporting. [Online]. Available at: http://www.iwpr.net/?p=acr&s=f&o=257727&apc_state=henpacr [accessed January 17, 2006.

Perry, D.M. 1997. The Republic of Macedonia: Finding its Way, in *Politics, Power, and the Struggle for Democracy in South-East Europe*, edited by K. Dawisha and B. Parrott. Cambridge: Cambridge University Press, 226-284.

Peskin, V. 2008. *International Justice in Rwanda and the Balkans: Virtual Trials and the Struggle for State Cooperation*. Cambridge: Cambridge University Press.

Peskin, V. and Boduszyński, M. 2003. International Politics and Domestic Politics: Post-Tuđman Croatia and the International Criminal Tribunal for the Former Yugoslavia. *Europe-Asia Studies*, 55(7), 1117-1142.

Petković, R. 1992. The Non-Aligned in Jakarta. *Review of International Affairs*, XLIII(1007-1008), 7-8, 29.

Petruševa, A. 2005a, *Macedonians Rail against 'Biased' Boskoski Indictment*. Institute for War and Peace Reporting. [Online]. Available at: http://iwpr.net/?p=bcr&s=f&o=241971&apc_state=henibcr2005 [accessed August 10, 2009].

Petruševa, A. 2005b, *Rise and Fall of Macedonia's Nationalist Showman*. Institute for War and Peace Reporting. [Online]. Available at: http://iwpr.net/?p=tri&s=f&o=235641&apc_state=henitri2005 [accessed 10 August, 2009].

Pettifer, J. 1992. The New Macedonian Question. *International Affairs*, 68(3), 475-485.

Pettifer, J. 2006. Macedonian Elections 2006: Ohrid Accords Survive. *Conflict Studies Research Centre Balkan Series*, 06/35. [Online]. Available at: http://www.da.mod.uk/colleges/arag/document-listings/balkan/06(35)JP.pdf/view [accessed August 7, 2009].

Pevehouse, J.C. and Goldstein, J.S. 1999. Serbian Compliance or Defiance in Kosovo? Statistical Analysis and Real Time Predictions. *Journal of Conflict Resolution*, 43(4), 538-546.

Posner, E. and Yoo, J.C. 2005. Judicial Independence in International Tribunals. *California Law Review*, 93(1), 1-74.

Poulton, H. 2000. *Who are the Macedonians?* London: Hurst & Co.

Power, S. 2000. Mute Justice, *The New Republic*, April 17-24, 20-24.

Presidential Documents: Executive Order 13304 of May 28, 2003. *Federal Register*, 68(103), 32315-32317.

*Program of the Socialist Party of Serbia*, 1992. Belgrade: Socialist Party of Serbia. On file with author.

*Program of the Serbian Radical Party*, 2001. Belgrade: Serbian Radical Party. On file with author.

Program of VMRO-DPMNE for Rebirth 2006-2010: Rebirth in 100 Steps, 2006. Skopje: VMRO-DPMNE. On file with author.

Putnam, R.D. 1988. Diplomacy and Domestic Politics: The Logic of Two-Level Games. *International Organization*, 42(3), 427-460.

Ramet, S. 2005. Under the Holy Lime Tree: The Inculcation of Neurotic and Psychotic Syndromes as a Serbian Wartime Strategy, 1986-95, in *Serbia since 1989: Politics and Society under Milošević and After*, edited by S.P. Ramet and V. Pavlaković. Seattle, WA: University of Washington Press, 125-142.

Republic of Macedonia Ministry of Defense, 2007a. *International Cooperation*. [Online]. Available at: http://www.morm.gov.mk: 8080/morm/en/nato/nato_pfp/international_cooperation.htm [accessed August 7, 2009].

Republic of Macedonia Ministry of Defense, 2007b. *Republic of Macedonia Partnership for Peace*. [Online]. Available at: http://www.morm.gov.mk: 8080/morm/en/nato/nato_pfp/RM_and_the_PfP.html [accessed August 7, 2009].

Reus-Smit, C. 2004. The Politics of International Law, in *The Politics of International Law*, edited by C. Reus-Smit. Cambridge: Cambridge University Press, 14-44.

Risse, T. 2001. "Let's Argue!" Communicative Action in World Politics, *International Organization*, 54(1), 1-39.

Risse, T. and Sikkink, K. 1999. The Socialization of International Human Rights Norms into Domestic Practices: Introduction, in *The Power of Human Rights: International Norms and Domestic Change*, edited by T. Risse, S.C. Ropp and K. Sikkink. Cambridge: Cambridge University Press, 1-38.

Risteska, M. 2007. *The Macedonian Accession to the European Union*. Institute for European Policy. [Online]. http://www.europeum.org/doc/pdf/860.pdf [accessed August 11, 2009].

Rossos, A. 2006. The Disintegration of Yugoslavia, Macedonia's Independence and Stability in the Balkans, in *War and Change in the Balkans: Nationalism, Conflict and Cooperation*, edited by B.K. Blitz. Cambridge: Cambridge University Press, 110-117.

Rudolph, C. 2001. Constructing an Atrocities Regime: The Politics of War Crimes Tribunals. *International Organization*, 55(3), 655-691.

*Russia Today*, 2009. Mladic: One Man's War Criminal, Another Man's Hero. [Online]. Available at: http://www.russiatoday.com/Top_News/2009-03-12/Mladic__one_man_s_war_criminal__another_man_s_hero.html [accessed August 27, 2009].

Sadović, M. 2007. *Was Tolimir Arrest Staged?* Institute for War and Peace Reporting Tribunal Update. [Online]. Available at: http://iwpr.net/?p=tri&s=f&o=336214&apc_state=henitri200706 [accessed August 13, 2009].

Sagrak, D. 1995. *Zagreb 1941-1945*. Zagreb: Tiskara Puljko.

Salihbegović, A. and Trkanjec, Ž. 2002. NATO prozvao RH zbog korupcije, nacionalizma, Srba, Pirana i Bobetka. *Jutarnji list*, November 19, 3.

Sanader, I. 2001. Boljitak Hrvatske i obrana nacionalnih i državnih interesa, in *HDZ za Hrvatsku, u novom vremenu pred novim izazovima: Izbor iz govora održanih između dva Sabora Hrvatske demokratske zajednice*, edited by I. Sanader. Zagreb: HDZ, 118-127.

Saxon, D. 2005. Exploring Justice: Perceptions of the ICTY Among the Serbian, Croatian, and Muslim Communities in the Former Yugoslavia. *Journal of Human Rights*, 4, 559-572.

Scharf, M.P. 1997. *Balkan Justice: The Story Behind the First International War Crimes Trial Since Nuremberg*. Durham, NC: Carolina Academic Press.

Schear, J.A. 1996. Bosnia's Post-Dayton Traumas. *Foreign Policy*, 104, 86-101.

Scheffer, D. 2003. Arresting War Criminals: Mission Creep or Mission Impossible? *Case Western Reserve Journal of International Law*, 35(2), 319-323.

Schwarzenberger, G. 1941. *Power Politics: An Introduction to the Study of International Relations and Post-War Planning*. London: Jonathan Cape.

Sekelj, L. 2000. Parties and Elections: The Federal Republic of Yugoslavia, Change without Transformation, *Europe-Asia Studies*, 52(1), 57-76.

Serbian Government, 2003. *Albanian Terrorism and Organized Crime in Kosovo*. Belgrade: Serbian Government. [Online]. Available at: http://www.media.srbija.sr.gov.yu/medeng/documents/albanian_terrorism_crime1.pdf [accessed August 5, 2009].

Serbian Government, 2005. *Return of Krajina Serbs and Respect for Human Rights Must be Secured. Belgrade*: Serbian Government. [Online]. Available at: http://www.srbija.sr.gov.yu/vesti/vest.php?id=14831&q=Krajina [accessed September 16, 2006].

Šešelj, V. 2006. *Srpski narod i novi svetski poredak*. [Online]. http://www.antiglobalizam.com/?lang=lat&str=nsp [accessed September 19, 2006].

Shannon, V.P. 2000. Norms Are What States Make of Them: The Political Psychology of Norm Violation. *International Studies Quarterly*, 44(2), 293-316.

Sharp, J.M.O. 1997/1998. Dayton Report Card. *International Security*, 22(3), 101-137.

Sikkink, K. 1993, Human Rights, Principled Issue Networks and Sovereignty in Latin America, *International Organization*, 47(3), 411-441.

Sikkink, K. and Walling, C.B. 2005, *Errors about Trials: The Political Reality of the Justice Cascade and Its Impact*. Paper presented to the Annual Meeting of the APSA, Washington DC.

Silber, L. 1996. The "Hero" of Dayton: Slobodan Milosevic and the Politics of War and Peace, *World Policy Journal*, 13(1), 63-64.

Šimonović, I. 1998. *Agenda Item 41: The Situation in Bosnia and Herzegovina, United Nations General Assembly 53rd Session*, New York. Foreign Ministry of the Republic of Croatia.

Simpson, G. 2007. *Law, War and Crime: War Crimes Trials and the Reinvention of International Law*. Cambridge: Polity Press.

Skjold Lexau, S. 2004. *Bosnia and Herzegovina: Advisor to the Political Department of the Office of the High Representative 2003-2004*. Olso: NORDEM.

Slaughter, A.M., Tulumello, A.S, and Wood, S. 1998. International Law and International Relations Theory: A New Generation of Interdisciplinary Scholarship, *The American Journal of International Law*, 92(3), 367-397.

*Specially Designated Nationals List*, 2007. Washington DC: Office of Foreign Assets Control, United States Department of Treasury. [Online]. Available at: http://www.ustreas.gov/offices/enforcement/ofac/sdn/t11sdn.pdf [accessed August 17, 2009].

*Statement Delivered by the Croatian Delegation to the 6th Committee during the 56th Session of the General Assembly under Agenda Item "International Criminal Court"*. [Online]. Available at: http://www.iccnow.org/documents/Croatia6thComm56GA01.pdf [accessed August 17, 2009].

Steinbaum, J. 2005. *Engel Statement on Indictment of Haradinaj*. Office of Representative Eliot L. Engel, Washington DC.

Tagliabue, J. 1991. Conflict in Yugoslavia: Yugoslavia's Army Issues Ultimatum to Rebel Republic. *New York Times*, June 30, 1.

Thorpe, N. 2005. *MI6 and the Croatian General*. BBC News. [Online]. Available at: http://news.bbc.co.uk/1/hi/programmes/from_our_own_correspondent/4497385.stm [accessed August 13, 2009].

Tribunal Update, 1998. *Furundzija Trial: Accounts Of Sexual Violence*, Institute for War and Peace Reporting. [Online]. Available at: http://www.iwpr.net/index.php?apc_state=hen&s=o&o=p=tri&l=EN&s=f&o=180499 [accessed August 13, 2009].

UNDP, 2004. *Human Development Report Kosovo 2004 The Rise of the Citizen: Challenges and Choices*. Pristina: United Nations Development Program.

United Nations, 2006. *Kosovo envoy tells Security Council delay of status proposal raised tension*. Department of Public Information News and Media Division. [Online]. Available at: http://www.un.org/News/Press/docs/2006/sc8900.doc.htm [accessed August 14, 2009].

United Nations Security Council, 1993a. *United Nations Security Council Resolution 808*, S/RES/808, February 22.

United Nations Security Council, 1993b. *United Nations Security Council Resolution 827*, S/RES/827, May 25.

United Nations Security Council, 1999. *United Nations Security Council Resolution 1244*, S/RES/1244, June 10.

United Nations Security Council, 2003. *United Nations Security Council Resolution 1503*, S/RES/1503, August 28.

UNMIK, 2000. *UNMIK-JIAS Fact Sheet*. [Online]. Available at: http://www.unmikonline.org/1styear/jias.htm [accessed August 17, 2009].

UNMIK, 2003. *Local Media*. UNMIK Division of Public Information and Media Monitoring. [Online]. Available at: http://www.unmikonline.org/press/lmm03.htm [accessed August 14, 2009].

UNMIK, 2005. *Local Media*. UNMIK Division of Public Information and Media Monitoring. [Online]. Available at: http://www.unmikonline.org/dpi/localmed.nsf/f0300?OpenForm [accessed August 14, 2009].

UNMIK, 2007. *Kosovo Standards Process: 2003-2007*. Pristina: UNMIK.
UNMIK Press Office, 2005. *RSG's Statement on the Prime Minister's Resignation*.
US Department of State, 1995. *The Road to Dayton: US Diplomacy and the Bosnia Peace Process*. Washington DC: United States Department of State.
Vasović, A. 2007. *Serbia May Trade Mladić for Concessions on Kovoso*. Balkan Investigative Reporting Network. [Online]. Available at: http://www.birn.eu.com/en/88/10/3354/ [accessed August 17, 2009].
Vinjamuri, L. and Snyder, J. 2004. Advocacy and Scholarhsip in the Study of International War Crime Tribunals and Transitional Justice. *Annual Review of Political Science*, 345-362
Vjesnik, 1999. Hrvatska treba ubrzati i okončati postupak protiv Tute? August 30, 1.
Vladisavljević, N. 2002. Nationalism, Social Movement Theory and the Grass Roots Movements of Kosovo Serbs, 1985-1988. *Europe-Asia Studies*, 54(5), 771-790.
Vogel, T.K. 2006. In Bosnia, War by Other Means. *Wall Street Journal*, September 29. [Online]. Available at: http://online.wsj.com/article/SB115948744688477415.html?mod=opinion_main_europe_asia [accessed August 14, 2009].
Vukasović, V. 1994. Sukobi u bivšoj Jugoslaviji i međunarodno krivično i humanitarno pravo. *Međunarodni Problemi*, XLVI(1), 9-22.
Walker, R. 2008. EU Ministers Hail Radovan Karadzic Arrest. *Guardian*. [Online]. Available at: http://www.guardian.co.uk/world/2008/jul/22/radovankaradzic.serbia2?gusrc%3Drss%26feed%3Dworldnews [accessed August 20, 2009].
Waltz, K.N. 1979. *Theory of International Politics*. New York: McGraw-Hill.
Waltz, K.N. 2000. Structural Realism after the Cold War. *International Security*, 25(1), 5-41.
Wendt, A. 1992. Anarchy is what States Make of it: The Social Construction of Power Politics. *International Organization*, 46(2), 391-425.
Wendt, A. 1995. Constructing International Politics. *International Security*, 20(1), 71-81.
Wendt, A. 1999. *Social Theory of International Politics*. Cambridge: Cambridge University Press.
Western, J. 2004. U.S. Policy and Human Rights in Bosnia: The Transformation of Strategic Interests, in *Implementing U.S. Human Rights Policy: Agendas, Policies, and Praticies*, edited by D. Liang-Fenton. Washington DC: United States Institute for Peace, 217-244.
Williams, P.R. and Scharf, M.P. 2002. *Peace with Justice? War Crimes and Accountability in the former Yugoslavia*. Lanham, MD: Rowman & Littlefield Publishers, Inc.
Williams, P.R. and Taft, P. 2003. The Role of Justice in the Former Yugoslavia: Antidote or Placebo for Coercive Appeasement? *Case Western Reserve Journal of International Law*, 35, 219-255.

Williams, P.R. and Waller, K.M. 2002. Coercive Appeasement: The Flawed International Response to the Serbian Rogue Regime. *New England Law Review*, 36, 825-889.

Wood, N. 2006. Trial Reveals How Serbian Fugitive Hid. *The New York Times*. [Online]. Available at: http://www.nytimes.com/2006/12/26/world/europe/26serbia.html [accessed August 20, 2009].

Yannis, A. 2004. The UN as Government in Kosovo. *Global Governance*, 10, 67-81.

Zakošek, N. 2002. *Politički sustav Hrvatske*. Zagreb: Fakultet političkih znanosti.

Zhou, H.R. 2006. The Enforcement of Arrest Warrants by International Forces: From the ICTY to the ICC. *Journal of International Criminal Justice*, 4(2), 202-218.

## ICTY Annual Reports

*Report of the International Criminal Tribunal for the Prosecution of Persons Responsible for Serious Violations of International Humanitarian Law Committed in the Territory of the Former Yugoslavia since 1991*, 1994. A/49/342-S/1994/1007, August 29.

*Report of the International Criminal Tribunal for the Prosecution of Persons Responsible for Serious Violations of International Humanitarian Law Committed in the Territory of the Former Yugoslavia since 1991*, 1995. A/50/365-S/1995/728, August 23.

*Report of the International Criminal Tribunal for the Prosecution of Persons Responsible for Serious Violations of International Humanitarian Law Committed in the Territory of the Former Yugoslavia since 1991*, 1996. A/51/292-S/1996/665, August 16.

*Report of the International Criminal Tribunal for the Prosecution of Persons Responsible for Serious Violations of International Humanitarian Law Committed in the Territory of the Former Yugoslavia since 1991*, 1997. A/52/375-S/1997/729, September 18.

*Report of the International Criminal Tribunal for the Prosecution of Persons Responsible for Serious Violations of International Humanitarian Law Committed in the Territory of the Former Yugoslavia since 1991*, 1998. A/53/219-S/1998/737, August 10.

*Report of the International Criminal Tribunal for the Prosecution of Persons Responsible for Serious Violations of International Humanitarian Law Committed in the Territory of the Former Yugoslavia since 1991*, 1999. A/45/187-S/1999/846, August 25.

*Report of the International Criminal Tribunal for the Prosecution of Persons Responsible for Serious Violations of International Humanitarian Law*

*Committed in the Territory of the Former Yugoslavia since 1991*, 2000. A/55/273-S/2000/777, August 7.

*Report of the International Criminal Tribunal for the Prosecution of Persons Responsible for Serious Violations of International Humanitarian Law Committed in the Territory of the Former Yugoslavia since 1991*, 2001. A/56/352-S/2001/865, September, 17.

*Report of the International Criminal Tribunal for the Prosecution of Persons Responsible for Serious Violations of International Humanitarian Law Committed in the Territory of the Former Yugoslavia since 1991*, 2002. A/57/379-S/2002/985, September 4.

*Report of the International Criminal Tribunal for the Prosecution of Persons Responsible for Serious Violations of International Humanitarian Law Committed in the Territory of the Former Yugoslavia since 1991*, 2003. A/58/297-S/2003/829, August 20.

*Report of the International Criminal Tribunal for the Prosecution of Persons Responsible for Serious Violations of International Humanitarian Law Committed in the Territory of the Former Yugoslavia since 1991*, 2004. A/59/215-S/2004/627, August 13.

*Report of the International Criminal Tribunal for the Prosecution of Persons Responsible for Serious Violations of International Humanitarian Law Committed in the Territory of the Former Yugoslavia since 1991*, 2005. A/60/267-S/2005/532, August 15.

*Report of the International Criminal Tribunal for the Prosecution of Persons Responsible for Serious Violations of International Humanitarian Law Committed in the Territory of the Former Yugoslavia since 1991*, 2006. A/61/271-S/2006/666, August 21.

*Report of the International Criminal Tribunal for the Prosecution of Persons Responsible for Serious Violations of International Humanitarian Law Committed in the Territory of the Former Yugoslavia since 1991*, 2007. A/62/172-S/2007/469, August 1.

*Report of the International Criminal Tribunal for the Prosecution of Persons Responsible for Serious Violations of International Humanitarian Law Committed in the Territory of the Former Yugoslavia since 1991*, 2008. A/63/210-S/2008/515, August 4.

## ICTY Cases, Decisions and Indictments

*Bosnia-Herzegovina v. Serbia and Montenegro*: Judgment of the 26 February 2007, Application of the Genocide Convention on the Prevention and Punishment of the Crime of Genocide. International Court of Justice, The Hague, February 26, 2007.

Decision on Challenge by Croatia to Decision and Orders of Confirming Judge, *The Prosecutor v. Janko Bobetko*, The International Criminal Tribunal for the former Yugoslavia, The Hague, November 29, 2002.

Decision on Defence Motion for Access to EUMM Archives, *The Prosecutor v. Enver Hadzihasanovic and Amir Kubura*, The International Criminal Tribunal for the former Yugoslavia, The Hague, December 15, 2003.

Decision on Motion for Judicial Assistance to be Provided by SFOR and Others, *The Prosecutor v. Blagoje Šimić et al.*, The International Criminal Tribunal for the former Yugoslavia, The Hague, October 18, 2000.

Order for the Production of Documents by the European Community Monitoring Mission and Its Member States, *The Prosecutor v. Dario Kordić and Mario Čerkez, Ex Parte: Partly Confidential*. The International Criminal Tribunal for the Former Yugoslavia, The Hague, August 4, 2000.

Order in Relation to the Prosecution's Application for an Order Pursuant to Rule 54bis, *Prosecutor v. Ante Gotovina, Ivan Čermak and Mladen Markač*, The International Criminal Tribunal for the former Yugoslavia, September 16, 2008.

Prosecution's Response Opposing Gotovina's Request for Provisional Release, *The Prosecutor v. Ante Gotovina, Ivan Čermak and Mladan Markač*. The International Criminal Tribunal for the former Yugoslavia, The Hague, August 22, 2007.

The Judgment on the Request of the Republic of Croatia for Review of the Decision of Trial Chamber II of July 18, 1997, *The Prosecutor v. Tihomir Blaškić*. International Criminal Tribunal for the former Yugoslaiva, The Hague, October 29, 1997.

*The Proscutor v. Rahim Ademi and Mirko Norac: Consolidated Indictment*. International Criminal Tribunal for the former Yugoslavia, The Hague, July 30, 2004.

*The Prosecutor v. Vidoje Blagojević and Dragan Jokić: Amended Joinder Indictment*. International Criminal Tribunal for the former Yugoslavia, The Hague, May 26, 2003.

*The Prosecutor v. Janko Bobetko*. International Criminal Tribunal for the former Yugoslavia, The Hague, September 17, 2002.

*The Prosecutor v. Ljube Boškoski and Johan Tarčulovski: Amended Indictment*. International Criminal Tribunal for the former Yugoslavia, The Hague, November 2, 2005.

*The Prosecutor v. Ante Gotovina: Initial Indictment*. International Criminal Tribunal for the former Yugoslavia, The Hague, 8 June 2001.

*The Prosecutor v. Ante Gotovina, Ivan Čermak and Mladen Markač: Joinder Indictment Modified by Order Pursuant to Rule 73bis D to Reduce the Indictment*. International Criminal Tribunal for the former Yugoslavia, The Hague, February 21, 2007.

*The Prosecutor v. Slobodan Milošević, Milan Milutinović, Nikola Sainović, Dragoljub Ojdanić and Vlatko Stojiljković*. International Criminal Tribunal for the former Yugoslavia, The Hague, May 24, 1999.

*The Prosecutor v. Slobodan Milošević*(a). International Criminal Tribunal for the former Yugoslavia, The Hague, October 8, 2001.

*The Prosecutor v. Slobodan Milošević*(b). International Criminal Tribunal for the former Yugoslavia, The Hague, November 22, 2001.

## Other Documents

*Constitutional Framework for Interim Self-Government*, Regulation No. 2001/9. UNMIK. May 15, 2001.

*Dayton Peace Agreement* [General Framework Agreement for Peace in Bosnia and Herzegovina], 1995. [Online]. Available at: http://www.oscebih.org/overview/gfap/eng/home.asp [accessed March 17, 2007].

*Declaration on Cooperation with the International Criminal Tribunal in The Hague*. Croatian Parliament, April 14, 2000. On file with author.

*Foreign Operations, Export Financing and Related Programs Appropriations Act 2006*. Section 563. Public Law 109-102. November 14, 2005: 2224-2225.

*Istanbul Summit Communiqué*, 2004. Issued by the Heads of State and Government Participating in the Meeting of the North Atlantic Council, June 28.

*Memorandum of the Government of Yugoslavia on the Crime of Genocide in Croatia, and the Vandalizing of the Memorial in Jasenovac, Government of Yugoslavia*, 1992. Belgrade: Government of the Federal Republic of Yugoslavia.

*Ohrid Framework Agreement*, August 13, 2001.

*Republic of Serbia Census*, 1991. Belgrade: Statistical Office of the Republic.

# Index